Praise for Carnivorous Nights

"A top-drawer journey into the natural history of Tasmania from two Brooklyn-based nature writers . . . neatly and wonderfully sews together natural science and travel yarn." —*Kirkus Reviews* (starred review)

"The quixotic quest at the heart of *Carnivorous Nights* is more than just endearing and engrossing, it's inspiring." —Jonathan Safran Foer, author of *Everything Is Illuminated* and *Extremely Loud and Incredibly Close*

"Beautifully observed, excitingly reported, [and] laugh-out-loud funny . . . This book will surely become a classic of wildlife adventure and travel writing." —Marie Winn, author of *Red-Tails in Love: A Wildlife Drama in Central Park*

"A detailed nature guide and a humorous and engaging adventure story." —*Science News*

"Engaging, witty . . . [with] stunning drawings of the wildlife . . . From Mittelbach and Crewdson's descriptions, it's hard not to become enamored of the tiger . . . and the cavalcade of human characters is just as compelling." —*Plenty* magazine

"A stuffed tiger sends three New Yorkers to the ends of the earth—where they encounter devils, charnel houses and eco-madness. The Devil's Isle will never be the same again. This is taxidermy's greatest tough-love story." —Tim Flannery, author of *A Gap in Nature: Discovering the World's Extinct Animals*

"Sit down in a comfortable chair and get totally absorbed, as I did, with companions every bit as charming and more informative than André (as in *My Dinner with*)." —Jeffrey Moussaieff Masson, author of *Dogs Never Lie About Love* and *When Elephants Weep: The Emotional Lives of Animals*

carnivorous nights

ᴠɪʟʟᴀʀᴅ Ⓥ ɴᴇᴡ ʏᴏʀᴋ

CARNIVOROUS NIGHTS

On the Trail of the Tasmanian Tiger

MARGARET MITTELBACH

and

MICHAEL CREWDSON

Artwork by
ALEXIS ROCKMAN

2006 Villard Books Trade Paperback Edition

Originally published in hardcover in the United States by Villard Books, an
imprint of The Random House Publishing Group, a division of Random House,
Inc., in 2005.

Library of Congress Cataloging-in-Publication Data
Mittelbach, Margaret.
    Carnivorous nights: on the trail of the Tasmanian tiger/Margaret Mittelbach
and Michael Crewdson; artwork by Alexis Rockman.
        p. cm.
    Includes bibliographical references.
    ISBN 0-8129-6769-0
    1. Thylacine—Australia—Tasmania. 2. Natural history—Australia—
Tasmania. 3. Tasmania. I. Crewdson, Michael. II. Title.
    QL737.M336M58 2005
    508.946—dc22   2004059553

www.villard.com

Printed in the United States of America

9 8 7 6 5 4 3 2 1

Text design by Simon M. Sullivan

Dedicated to

Charemaine and Quinn Li
—M.C.

Jon Carlo, Molly, and Danilo
—M.M.

my father, Raphael Russell Rockman
—A.R.

contents

List of Illustrations

Artist's Conception of Tasmania.

CARNIVOROUS NIGHTS

1. a peculiar animal

A few years ago we began visiting a stuffed and mounted animal skin with something akin to amorous fervor. We didn't tell our friends about this secret relationship. We feared they would think it was unhealthy to be infatuated with a dead animal.

The object of our obsession resided at the American Museum of Natural History in Manhattan. Best known for its towering dinosaur skeletons and beautiful but creepy dioramas of gorillas and stuffed birds, the museum also housed a library where we did research. On the way there, we would walk through the perpetual twilight of the museum's halls, passing meteorite fragments, African carvings, and a life-sized herd of motionless pachyderms.

When exactly we first saw this magnificent animal is lost in the recesses of memory, but we remember being instantly captivated by its exotic form. We marveled at its still limbs, at its head posed coyly downward, at its glorious Seussian stripes. It was a taxidermy of a Tasmanian tiger inside a rectangular glass case, and it was positioned in such a lifelike manner, its mouth curved in a friendly canine smile, that we found ourselves feeling affection for it as if it were a long-lost pet. It had fifteen dark brown stripes across the back of its ginger-colored coat, which is why it was called a tiger, but the stripes were where that resemblance ended. Its body was shaped more like a wolf's or wild dog's.

Discreetly tucked between the "Birds of the World" dioramas and a man-jaguar monster carved in jade, the tiger did not seem to be a very popular exhibit. Despite our own fascination, there was never a crowd around it. Many visitors walked by without giving it a glance. Admittedly, the tiger was not the museum's newest attraction. In fact, it was an antique. A fading label said the animal from which it was fashioned died in 1919.

As the months passed, our attentions became more pointed. We spent our lunch breaks in front of the tiger, admiring its doggish head and wicket-shaped grin. We became so enamored that we began daydreaming about it while we were supposed to be reading about the mating behavior of horseshoe crabs in the library. Sometimes we imagined our tiger stalking through a generic jungle habitat in search of unknown prey, its bold stripes rippling through a scrim of green. We often wondered if Tasmania was as unlikely and exotic as the tiger itself.

Finally, we decided to do a background check on the specimen. The museum, in addition to its main library, had avenues of research normally off-limits to the public. But as nature writers we could always talk our way behind the scenes. We made an appointment to visit the museum's mammal library, and when we walked in, it felt like we had traveled back in time or at least walked onto the set of a period film. There were heavy wooden railings, black wrought iron shelves, tiled glass walkways, and an old dumbwaiter. Near the door, cabinets filled with yellowing ledger books chronicled the mammalogy department's acquisitions, starting in 1885. Each numbered entry, written in the feathery black ink of a fountain pen, listed the specimen's scientific name, where it was collected, the name of the collector, and when the specimen was received.

We started to go through the entries, and it was daunting. There were thousands of them. Not being 100 percent familiar with the arcana of scientific nomenclature, we had to rely on fading memories of Greek and Latin studied years ago. For example, Volume 5 of the mammal catalogue listed no. 32732 as the skull of *Loxodonta africana,* an African elephant shot by Theodore Roosevelt "East of Meru Boma, just north of Kenia." No. 27901 was the skull of *Rangifer pearyi,* a type of caribou, collected in the "Arctic Regions" by Commodore Robert E. Peary. No. 35185 was the skeleton of another *Loxodonta africana,* this one a circus elephant, donated by Barnum & Bailey. No. 35180 was the carcass of *Canis familiaris,* a domestic dog (actually a French poodle) collected at 62½ East 125th Street in Manhattan and donated by a Dr. Blackburne. And finally there was *our* specimen. No. 35866 was the body of *Thylacinus cyno-cephalus*, donated by the Bronx Zoo in 1919.

We learned that the scientific name *Thylacinus cynocephalus* meant "pouched animal with a dog head." And the name thylacine (THY-luh-scene) was used almost as commonly as Tasmanian tiger. We also discovered that the animal was a marsupial, with a pouch like a kangaroo or a possum, and not closely related to tigers, wolves, dogs, or any of the familiar species it somewhat resembled. The museum's thylacine had been caught in the wild on the island of Tasmania, brought to New York on a creaking ship, and displayed at the Bronx Zoo for two years. When it died, its body was sent over to the Museum of Natural History to be preserved.

Taxidermy has always been a strange art. From old letters in the library's files, we gathered that the zoo frequently provided the museum with specimens of exotic animals. The zoo's first director, William Temple Hornaday, had a strong interest in taxidermy, and the curator of the museum's mammal department, J. A. Allen, had provided him with arsenic to help preserve the bodies, pelts, and skins. In this case, the tiger's skin had been skillfully stitched to a wire-and-clay model and the result was an almost flawless simulacrum of a Tasmanian tiger.

Out of a collection of more than 32 million specimens, the Tasmanian tiger is designated one of the museum's fifty most treasured items. Why? Because there are remarkably few specimens. The Tasmanian tiger is presumed to be extinct. That makes specimen no. 35866 rarer than a star sapphire, rarer than a Rembrandt.

The fact that our beloved tiger had a tragic past increased our interest. This rare species had lived in Tasmania for thousands of years and been the island's top predator. But when the British colonized the island in the early nineteenth century, what had been an ark, floating serenely in southern seas, became a deathtrap. The tiger was considered a threat to the colonists' livestock and they began hunting it down. A bounty was paid to anyone who brought in a dead tiger—and by the early part of the twentieth century, the Tasmanian tiger's population began to hang in the balance.

On September 7, 1936, at a small zoo in Hobart, Tasmania's capital, a thylacine (the last one in captivity anywhere in the world) passed away in the middle of the night. It's believed that it died of exposure. Numerous searches were launched to replace it. Traps were set. But no more tigers, live or dead, were captured. The Hobart zoo's thylacine became the proverbial "last tiger." For the next fifty years, the searches continued, but no tangible evidence of the tiger was uncovered. In 1986, the thylacine was declared extinct by international standards. But this announcement did not fully penetrate on the island.

In Tasmania people continued to look for the tiger. What's more people *saw* it. Multiple sightings of the thylacine are still reported each year. It's seen chasing a wallaby, crossing a road, running along the island's shore. These sightings raise a glimmer of hope that the species survives. How bright that glimmer was we didn't know. The thrill of such a sighting swept over us. We imagined being in Tasmania and seeing a tiger gripping a dead kangaroo in its mouth, racing past our flickering campfire deep in the bush. We knew it was a long shot. But the tiger seemed to be calling our names.

Nearly seventy years after the last confirmed thylacine died, we stood in front of specimen no. 35866 at the Museum of Natural History. The taxidermy was so exquisite it seemed frozen in time. Sometimes we fantasized our tiger might be reanimated, that it might bust out of its glass case and trot down the museum's halls, its smiling mouth gleaming with rows of sharp teeth as it bade adieu to the dusty old animals that complacently accepted their fates. Maybe it would bite a tourist on its way out the door.

Then one day we went to visit and the tiger wasn't there. Its glass case was empty. A wave of panic swept over us. We asked around, but no one knew where it had gone. Finally, a clerk in the library told us she thought the thylacine had been moved to a temporary exhibit on genomics. *Genomics?* What was it doing there?

After navigating the museum's long hallways and winding stairwells, we found it. The exhibit, called "The Genomics Revolution," was jarring, filled with lights flashing the letters A, T, C, and G, the primary components of DNA. Miniature video screens surrounded a huge DNA model. The thylacine was hard to see and crammed in the very back. A card explained why the thylacine had been moved. Halfway across the world in an Australian lab, scientists were initiating a project to clone the Tasmanian tiger. Their goal was to bring this vanished species back to life. A specimen pickled in alcohol more than one hundred years ago was said to have enough intact DNA to make it possible. Seeing our tiger friend in this new light gave us a chill. The thylacine was teetering unsteadily between the categories of "presumed extinct" and "soon-to-be-alive." We didn't know what to make of it. Apparently, we weren't the only ones obsessed with this animal. We were overcome with a sudden urge to meet the people who believed the tiger was still lurking in its old island haunts, the scientists who planned to resurrect it, and the pundits who cast it into the oblivion of extinction. Maybe they could help us sort it all out.

We had recently written a book about New York City's wildlife. Coyotes in the Bronx. Bald eagles flying over Central Park. Cockroaches in the kitchen sink. It was time, we decided, to explore something more exotic. Our friend Alexis Rockman, an artist with a similar fixation on nature, certainly thought so. He had been pestering us to go on a trip, some kind of working adventure, for years. We would write. He would paint. "Enough with the rats and pigeons," he said. "Let's blow this town."

Alexis was the one person who knew about our relationship with the thylacine. His mother was an archaeologist who had worked at the natural history museum when he was a kid, and its hallways—filled with fossils, habitat dioramas, and dead animals—had been his childhood playground. He knew every inch of the place. As a result, he shared our fascination with the thylacine, though not to the same obsessive degree.

We found Alexis at his basement studio in Tribeca. He was adding tiny species of tropical butterflies to a five-foot-by-seven-foot scene of a South American rain forest. We took a seat on his couch and studied the vines and weird, sinister blooms.

What we would find hanging in Alexis's studio was always a surprise. One week it might be a giant picture of a tree of life gone haywire. Another time it might be a self-portrait of Alexis, his own body lying dead and decomposing in a jungle. Or maybe raccoons having sex with roosters. His paintings were imbued with dark and disturbing images from the natural world—of species, extinction, evolution, and coming disaster. They pictured lurid landscapes filled with real and imaginary creatures.

The crammed bookshelves in his studio reflected these interests. Beside coffee-table books on artists such as Winslow Homer and Martin Johnson Heade, titles included the *Golden Guide to Spiders and Their*

Kin, Dangerous Animals, and *Dearest Pet: On Bestiality.* He had his own small collection of taxidermy—as well as a well-loved (living) pet cat—and on his desk he kept a dried-out bat in a jar.

"We've just been to the museum," we told him.

"Have you been indulging your thylacine fetish again?" He flicked a dot of red onto the wings of the butterfly he was painting. "That taxidermy's so fucking beautiful—and incredibly sad."

"So you think it's extinct?"

"Of course."

"You probably wouldn't want to go to Tasmania then."

He didn't answer right away. Instead, he cleaned off his palette and put his brushes in turpentine. Then he stretched out on the floor of his studio with his shorts hiked up and took a drag on a joint. Though we were eager for him to say yes, we were anxious about what that might mean. Our eyes followed the thin column of smoke emanating from his mouth as we tried to picture what Alexis would be like as a traveling companion. On the one hand, he was superconfident, talented, and successful. Just over six feet tall, he had lanky, model good looks and magazines such as *Vogue* and *Elle* were nearly as likely to print a photo of him as they were one of his paintings. He was also athletic. He played highly competitive basketball and might have played college ball if Manhattan's School of Visual Arts had fielded a team. Over the years, he had produced hundreds of paintings—oils, watercolors—that had sold through his Chelsea art gallery for millions of dollars. On the other hand, he oozed vibes of self-doubt, and his moods were unpredictable. He was a New York neurotic with a twist: George Costanza in the body of Narcissus. Nothing was ever enough. If he had a solo show at a gallery, he wanted a traveling museum retrospective that focused on his entire career. He was a workaholic, simultaneously driven and racked by anxiety, and at one time had smoked two and a half packs of Camel filters a day to calm himself down. Lately, he had switched from cigarettes to marijuana, and this self-prescribed after-hours hit of pot really seemed to do the trick, bringing his jittery brand of ambition down to the level of the average superachiever.

"Tasmania," he said slowly. "I don't know . . . I have to prepare for a big show in London next year."

We had brought over our laptop and clicked on a forty-second black-

and-white film of the Tasmanian tiger taken in 1933. Filmed at the Hobart zoo, the footage had a creepy air of unreality. The tiger—the last one confirmed to be alive—paced back and forth in its cage, showing off rangy, muscular legs and zebralike stripes. After a few seconds, it yawned, revealing a set of razor-sharp teeth, and extended its jaws almost impossibly wide. For a moment, it looked like a crocodile. Then it flopped down and lifted its big head like a dog.

"Holy shit," Alexis said. "I would have killed to see that."

Alexis pulled down a beat-up old atlas and opened it to a page showing a map of Australasia—New Guinea, Australia, New Zealand, Indonesia, and Malaysia. Tasmania was a little triangle floating near the bottom, about 150 miles south of the Australian mainland. A dotted line ran through the blue ink of the Indian Ocean. It arced through the Malay Archipelago and cut a swath between the islands of Bali and Lombok, between Borneo and Sulawesi. It was marked "Wallace's Line."

Alexis traced the line with the tips of his fingers. "This is what makes it interesting," he said.

Alfred Russel Wallace was a naturalist, a contemporary of Darwin's, who in 1856 had traveled from Bali to Lombok—a space of just fifteen watery miles—and been in for the surprise of his life. It was as if he had passed through a veil into another world. Species were more different between those two islands than they were across oceans. While Wallace primarily focused on birds in his study of the region, the most obvious difference to us was that the mammals on the other side of Wallace's Line had pouches. Australasia was filled with odd creatures such as kangaroos and koalas. And Tasmania was home to some of the strangest of all the region's animals. Many species that had died out or were barely hanging on elsewhere survived on the island: the Tasmanian devil, the spotted-tailed quoll, the long-nosed potoroo. The idea that Tasmania could still be a haven for the thylacine was tantalizing.

"So do you want to go to Tasmania?" we asked again.

"Sure, as long as I can paint some fucked-up critters." Then he added, "And I'll have to be able to get some pot."

Our decision to go to Tasmania was made in the spring—the Northern Hemisphere spring. Since we wanted to go to Tasmania in the summer, we would have to wait for our winter—December, January, February. That gave us plenty of time to think about the tiger.

What was the likelihood that the thylacine survived, we wondered? It depended upon who we talked to and what we read.

Most scientists were fairly emphatic that the tiger's time had passed. But occasionally studies came out suggesting the tiger might have eluded searchers. Tasmania's rugged, mountainous terrain and highly varied habitats would serve to protect an animal like the thylacine. About one third of Tasmania's land was protected in national parks. If it still existed, there were places for the thylacine to hide and game for it to hunt.

On the survival side were people who had devoted their lives to finding the thylacine. They searched areas where there had been credible sightings, looking for evidence such as tracks and animal scat. We knew that the Museum of Natural History in New York had received packages of carnivore feces from Down Under, with requests that the scats be analyzed for possible thylacine DNA. In the survival camp, there were also cryptozoologists. They were a curious group. The word "cryptozoology" means the study of hidden animals. And it applies to the search for the Loch Ness Monster and Bigfoot, as well as to the discovery of real species. Cryptozoology claimed such animals as the African okapi, the pygmy hippo, the Vu Quang ox of Vietnam, even the giant panda and mountain gorilla as successes—all creatures whose existence had been scoffed at until they were discovered in the twentieth century. Cryptozoologists had taken the thylacine into their stable of real and imagined creatures, refusing to believe in its extinction.

We also researched Tasmania itself. Our almanac said it was 26,383 square miles (about the size of Ireland or West Virginia). Its population was 472,610. Beyond that our knowledge of Tasmania was appallingly limited. For one thing, we were happy to find out that English was spoken on the island. And not only that but it was part of Australia. When we talked to Tasmanians on the phone, we discovered they had a softened, lilting version of the famous Aussie twang.

In addition we researched the other animals that lived in Tasmania. Though the tiger might be gone or hiding, these creatures were equally odd and amazing, and we planned to see as many as possible. We also determined to visit the Australian mainland. The thylacine had a history there—and possibly a future if the cloning experts had any success. We purchased plane tickets for Sydney, Australia's oldest and largest city, and arranged for ferry passage to Tasmania.

As for the Tasmanian wilderness, we weren't sure how deep into the bush our investigations would take us. Were there any dangerous animals we needed to worry about? Our research turned up three species of venomous snakes, several vicious stinging ants, and two species of bloodsucking land leeches. *Land leeches?*

Unlike North American leeches, which have the decency to remain in water, Tasmania's leeches lurked in the forest—on plants and shrubs—waiting for a warm snack to wander by. We read about people covered in hundreds of land leeches gorging on their blood. Land leeches became a focal point of our anxieties. We imagined thousands of tiny bloodsucking periscopes twisting in the trees waiting to sense our heat. We read about leech socks, which were essentially pantyhose, and considered the possibility of having to wear black nylons as we traveled through the Tasmanian wilds.

We went with Alexis to a discount camping store in New Jersey to get supplies. New hiking boots. Water sandals. Backpacks. Flashlights. Polartec pullovers. Waterproof notepads. Australian electrical outlet converters. Socks with "wicking" properties. Lightweight aluminized emergency blankets. Water purification tablets. Afterward, we felt even less prepared than when we had arrived. The store didn't sell leech repellent.

About a month before the trip, we visited Alexis in his studio again. This time he stopped painting and sat down right next to us.

"I have something to tell you guys."

He's backing out at the last minute!

"My wife and I are getting separated."

"Oh, that's terrible. We're so sorry."

There was a pause for sad feelings to sink in.

Then he said, "Do you mind if I bring a friend on the trip? She would just come for the beginning part on the mainland."

"Uh—" The friend in question, Dorothy Spears, was a beautiful and wealthy art journalist—also recently separated—who had a penchant for wearing skintight leopard-print pants. Usually she vacationed in Majorca, the Greek islands, and the Hamptons.

We asked Alexis if she had ever encountered anything like a land leech. "Other than me?" he said. "Not that I know of."

In the remaining time before we left, we contacted all sorts of tiger experts via phone and e-mail, setting up future appointments and getting the lowdown on what to expect. One person we talked with was Nick Mooney, an officer with the Tasmanian Parks and Wildlife Service who had been involved in official searches for the tiger for twenty years. When we reached him, he was out somewhere in the Tasmanian bush and his cell phone kept cutting out. Although Nick couldn't deny the possibility of the tiger's survival, he didn't think it very likely. That said, the thylacine was terribly important to Tasmanian culture. The tiger was Tasmania's bald eagle, its grizzly bear, and timber wolf, all rolled into one. If we dreamed about the thylacine, we could only imagine the dreams Tasmanians had. Later, Nick e-mailed us with a list of people to meet on the island.

As the day of our departure approached, we put everything in order. We assembled our research materials: field guides, articles, accounts of the island written by early explorers and naturalists. Alexis put together a case full of paintbrushes, drawing paper, and chemical solutions for mixing his own pigments. Because we were traveling on separate flights, we agreed to rendezvous with Alexis and Dorothy in Sydney. That was where we would begin our search for traces of the tiger.

Shortly before we left, Alexis informed us another friend of his might be joining us in Tasmania. This time, we prayed it would be someone useful—an entomologist or DNA expert.

"He's a world traveler," Alexis said. "He just likes exotic adventures."

"How well do you know him?"

"I met him about a month ago at a dinner party."

We were starting to lose control of this tiger.

When we arrived in Sydney we dropped our bags at a hotel in the business district and set off on our first expedition—to the State Library of New South Wales. We spent many hours there, looking at old documents and folios, trying to get to know our quarry—its habits and history. In Sydney, we would be looking at the thylacine's distant past and possible future. But in Tasmania, who knew? We had only a week before leaving for the island and wanted to be prepared for anything. In one old account at the library, it was claimed that if you grabbed the thylacine by its stiff tail, it wouldn't be able to turn around and bite you. Another old bushie wrote that the tiger could be tied up, but never tamed. We wondered if this information would ever come in handy.

Taking a break from our research, we sat with Alexis and Dorothy at the city's Royal Botanic Gardens, having tea with scones and observing a bird. A big white ibis with a thin, curving beak flapped up onto a café table, gobbled up some crumbs, and then dipped the tip of its foot-long beak into a pot of clotted cream. Suddenly a woman shrieked. "Oh, shooo! Shoooooo!" The ibis flapped down to the ground and began strolling along on stiltlike gray legs. A few seconds later, it sidled up alongside another table and began probing the interior of another patron's pocketbook with its cream-smeared beak.

Alexis was delighted by the bird's bad behavior. "That bird needs handcuffs," he said. We hadn't even gotten as far as Tasmania and the wildlife was already bizarre.

Exotic ibises wandered Sydney's streets like pigeons, cadging freebies and putting their beaks where they didn't belong. But they were just the beginning of the city's strange animals. The night before, we had been standing outside an oyster bar in Kings Cross—Sydney's version of Times Square—and a huge creature had flown toward us, circled, and then landed with a thump in a small street tree. It hung there like a gremlin, its leathery wings folded, and chattered spookily. For a moment, we were petrified. Was this some sort of supernatural being? When we mustered the courage to look at it more closely, we realized it was a flying fox. A megabat.

At the Royal Botanic Gardens, we had a chance to observe these big bats as intently as we liked. The gardens were home to a roosting colony of about five thousand gray-headed flying foxes. Walking along the greenery-lined pathways, we followed the sounds of screeching and squawking until we stood before a grove of palm trees laden with what looked like giant pods twisting in the hot breeze. Hanging upside down by their claws, the flying foxes were the size of cats. Though most were sleeping, a few were unusually active, using hooklike fingers on the edges of their wings to climb like monkeys from branch to branch. Through binoculars we could see their gray-furred, intelligent-looking faces and a ruff of red

fur around their necks. Beneath the trees, the walkways were coated with
a yellowish slime—bat scat—that threw off a sweet decaying scent.

Dorothy and Alexis walked arm in arm down a path bursting with
tropical blooms beneath the bat camp, seemingly blissfully unaware of the
perils both above and below. They were a strange pair. Alexis had been
wearing the same gray shorts and Timberland T-shirt for forty-eight

hours whereas Dorothy was decked out for a romantic vacation and had
made several wardrobe changes each day. At present, she was wearing a
low-cut strawberry print sundress, open-toed sandals, and Gucci sunglasses.

"Watch out for the bat guano," we yelled.

"It's not guano," Alexis said. "Bat guano is produced by insect-eating
bats." These bats ate fruit.

"Well, watch out for the *shit*." He was steering Dorothy perilously
close to a section of the path occasionally hit by a rain of yellow goo.
"Eeew," said Dorothy, looking down at the bat slime, which was chunky
with fig seeds. "Yuck."

We had only been in Sydney for a few days and Alexis had already invited Dorothy to extend her stay for a week and come to Tasmania with us. We were concerned she wasn't properly prepared and wondered if in addition to sliplike dresses and strappy shoes, she had brought any bush gear. Long pants, hiking boots, sweatshirts, that sort of thing?

Dorothy seemed blithely unconcerned. "You guys are so funny," she said when we asked if she had packed any sneakers or walking shoes. Her plan was to buy whatever she needed along the way.

We went back to watching the bats. They chattered and quarreled and muscled each other for roosting positions. Occasionally, one would circle down from the bright sky and hit a branch hard, causing it to bend low with its weight.

"This could only be better if we were high," said Alexis. He cleared his throat. "Any news on my pot?" This was the third time he had asked in an hour.

In between scheduling and finalizing appointments, we had attempted to make his pot connection several times. Through the grapevine, we learned of a dealer, a muscle-bound woman whose street name suggested a high-octane fuel. She would be easy to recognize we were told because she had a shaved head and tattoos. She was supposed to be at a particular bar at a particular time. But she kept not showing up. That night, we began to get desperate. Alexis's complaining was driving us crazy. Then as if we were being rewarded for paying homage to the bat gods, the muscle-bound dealer came through. We rushed over to the ritzy hotel where Alexis and Dorothy were staying and found them lounging on the deck by a saltwater pool. Alexis opened the bag, fingered the aromatic plant matter, and pulled out a pinch. "Oh yeah, baby," he said, taking a whiff. Then he pushed the pot into a small, one-hit pipe with his index finger, flicked his lighter, and took a long drag. He looked relieved and then surprised. "This is strong shit," he coughed. Sydney was coming through—at least for Alexis. But we were still jonesing. Our urge for even a tiny taste of the tiger was yet to be satisfied.

A few days later, a man named Les Bursill was, with difficulty, navigating a boat we had rented. It was a houseboat, really just a raft on pontoons, with a 30 horsepower engine in the back. "This thing drives like a steamed pudding," he informed us.

As soon as we had left the dock, Alexis and Dorothy disappeared onto the boat's roof deck, stripped down to their bathing suits, and lay out in the sun. We had rented the boat out of Cronulla, a surf town on the southern edge of the Sydney suburbs, and were entering Port Hacking, an enormous bay with multiple arms and inlets. Million-dollar homes were built into the sandstone cliffs that rose up on either side.

As we plied down the main waterway, we were accompanied by other party boats, heading out for a day of fishing, swimming, and picnicking. But our destination was different. "It's something few people on this earth have seen," said Les.

He spread out a map next to the wheel and indicated the southern section of Port Hacking. "That's Royal National Park," he said. It was the second oldest national park in the world after Yellowstone, and it was filled with aboriginal artifacts, including ancient rock paintings. The native people who had lived in Port Hacking had vanished within a few years of British settlement in the early nineteenth century. The area around us was an aboriginal ghost town.

Les, a heavyset man with a graying beard and mustache, was an expert on the park's aboriginal rock art, and he was part-aboriginal himself—though he had not discovered this fact until he was in his late thirties. When his grandmother died, he found some photographs that suggested his family—ostensibly white and European—had an aboriginal heritage. "I traced my lineage back to a man named Dr. Ellis. He was a full-blooded aboriginal and a kaditcha man, a medicine man or witch doctor you might call it. His daughter, Susan Ellis, married my great-grandfather—he was a convict who'd been transported to Australia from England for stealing linen. So I'm one of just a few people who can trace their ancestry back to the original inhabitants of this region, the Tharawal people."

That was saying something. "The last Tharawal people in this area were wiped out by disease by 1835, 1840. It's very sad," said Les. "You'll find a drawing of a kangaroo that's half finished as if someone has put down their pen and never come back."

In 1985 while he was working on his master's degree in anthropology, Les was asked to do a complete survey of aboriginal rock art in Royal. When he and his team began their research, fewer than forty rock art sites had been documented. By the time they were finished, they had found more than one thousand. And there was one in particular that he wanted us to see: an aboriginal drawing of a thylacine.

Although there is aboriginal rock art all over Australia, rock art depicting thylacines is rare. When the first aboriginals arrived in Australia about sixty thousand years ago, the thylacine was one of the fiercest predators on the continent. Over fifty millennia, aboriginals and thylacines lived together, and the thylacines were woven into aboriginal dreamtime stories and artwork. But then five thousand years ago, the dingo—a breed of domestic dog—was introduced to Australia (probably by Southeast Asian seafarers). Scientists believe that as the dingoes went wild, they killed off the thylacines in the same way that wolves will kill off coyotes in their territory to get rid of the competition. About three thousand years ago, thylacines disappeared from the mainland. They survived on the island of Tasmania only because dingoes never crossed the water.

When the mainland thylacines died out, so did the rock art. Now the only reminders of the mainland thylacines are fossilized bones, dehydrated body parts preserved in outback deserts, and a handful of ancient paintings.

Les said his discovery of a thylacine drawing in the environs of Australia's largest city had been slightly controversial in archaeological circles. "There's actually some debate about whether it *is* a tiger," he said. "The jury's about 60–40 in my favor. Some people think it's a kangaroo with stripes."

Les turned off the main channel, and we headed into a branch of the estuary known as the Southwest Arm that reached into the national park. The arm was lousy with sandbars, and at one point we ran aground. Les put the engine in reverse and it made a disturbing grinding noise. As the pudding chugged on, the hillside homes receded. Sea eagles circled in the distance. Pied cormorants, seagulls, and pelicans flew by. Climbing up the walls of pale gray sandstone were thin silver-barked, gray-barked, and red-barked eucalyptus trees, topped with tufts of brilliant green leaves. There were also native fruit trees: figs, wombat berry, and yellow-berried tuckeroo. Les estimated one hundred aboriginal people had lived in this bay. There were signs of aboriginal habitation everywhere: shell middens, fire pits, engravings of dolphins and whales, paintings of fish drawn in yellow ocher, drawings of flying foxes hanging upside down in charcoal.

Les pointed out an ancient midden, an aboriginal rubbish heap of oyster and mussel shells that now formed part of the shoreline. "Some of these middens are dated to have been in use for six thousand years." Les coaxed the boat into shallow water. It scraped against the rocky shoreline with a ripping sound and Les cut the engine. "I want to show you something up here. It's just a quick detour."

Sun-doped, Alexis and Dorothy staggered down the stairs and followed Les out of the boat. We hopped out, too, and scrambled up a short, nearly vertical trail, pulling ourselves along by grabbing on to the roots of eucalyptus trees. White shells crunched beneath our feet. Les led us to a narrow sandstone ledge surmounted by an overhang of dark rock.

"What do you see?" he said.

We peered at the rock. There was nothing there. It looked like any other outcrop, rough and streaked with age.

"Give it a minute," Les said. "It's like an optical illusion."

Then, like a photo in a developing bath, four black hands slowly emerged from the rock face. "Hand stencils," Les explained. They were made by Tharawal people who lived here hundreds of years ago. Each was framed by a ragged halo of white.

"That's intense," said Dorothy. "It's like they're reaching out and grabbing us."

Alexis studied the pigments, black and white on gray rock. "How did they make these?" he asked.

"It's sprayed on," Les said. "They filled their mouth with water and chewed-up charcoal, and sprayed the rock in a series of short bursts. That created a black background. Then they would fill their mouths with white clay to make a white pigment, place their hand against the rock, and spray around it." He pantomimed spitting out pigment with his hand flush against the rock.

Les wasn't sure what the hand stencils meant—or if they had a meaning. Archaeologists have found similar stencils in radically different parts of the world: Africa, Europe, the Americas. The question was, were they signatures (an ancient "Kilroy was here")? Messages? Les thought the positioning of the fingers might be some sort of signaling, or bush code. "In some instances, there's such a lot of effort that's gone into the preparation of the surface and then the way the fingers are splayed. I think there are meanings we don't understand." Hand stencils could also have a spiritual significance. Some archaeologists theorize the rocks used for hand stenciling served as doors to the spirit world. By covering a hand with dark pigment, it seemed to dissolve into and behind the rock, reaching into a realm beyond.

We returned to the boat and continued down the arm of the bay. The water was becoming extremely shallow, shifting in color from electric blue to muddy green. "The tide's going out," Les said. To reach the thylacine, he was going to anchor at an uncharted bay that locals called Tiger Shark Hole. "It's not exactly navigable," he added.

"Are there really tiger sharks in the water?" we asked. Suddenly running aground didn't seem like such a big deal.

"Well, I used to put my boat in there, and I would swim and fish. I was telling an old-timer about it—and he said that back in the old days they used to fish for shark there because they loved that deep hole. They used to hang the sharks up from the gum trees, cut their throats, and let the blood run into the pool. Of course that would act as a lure . . . I never swum there again."

Les saw our eyes popping and told us not to worry. There had only been one serious shark attack in Port Hacking's history. "In 1927, a young boy dived off a boat and was eaten amongst his friends. By the time they got him ashore, he'd lost an arm and a leg and a large lump out of his side. He died on the way to the hospital." The attack had inspired a Sydney balladeer to write a verse about it:

The day was fine, the water clear,
And as smooth as a pond;
But the surfers never thought of
What danger lurked beyond.
It was a shark, some twelve feet long
And in shallow water,
His eyes were bulging from his head,
Anxious for the slaughter.

Water/slaughter. We had to admit it was a good rhyme. By the time we reached Tiger Shark Hole, the little engine had begun to complain and spew smoke fitfully. "I'm just going to try and get us anchored here," Les said. The shallow green water was full of jumping fish. We scanned the surface for fins.

The tide was so low that the exposed part of the sandstone shore was covered with clumps of live oysters. Les jumped out of the boat, pried one loose with his pocketknife, and ate it raw. "This is gorgeous real estate," he said surveying the scene. "There was so much game here." Les delighted in the idea of living off the land. "When I was a kid, my family would do that for a month every year." And when he was working on the rock art survey in Royal, he had spent months camping out beneath the stars, hiking to his heart's content, paddling a canoe, and dining on fish.

We all walked along the rocky shore, stepping over fallen eucalyptus branches. Though Dorothy was wearing a sarong, she seemed to maneuver over the obstacles with ease. Les turned up a wisp of a path—it was wide enough for a dunnart (the marsupial version of a mouse) to pass through easily—and we climbed two hundred feet up the cliffside through tangy-smelling eucalyptus and red-barked Angophora trees. Near the top, we reached a long sandstone shelf paralleling the ridgeline. It gave us a bird's-eye view of the flat, blue-green waters below. Across the inlet, a mangrove swamp shimmered in the light.

We followed Les along a sandy track covered with broken shells. The yellowish gray cliffside curled over our heads.

"Talk about *Picnic at Hanging Rock*," said Alexis.

For a natural area, it seemed strangely barren. "Where are all the animals?" we asked.

Les pointed out tracks in the sand, impressions of little claws and long feet. "Wallaby," he said. "They're active at night."

We walked beneath the hanging cliff for about a quarter of a mile. Then Les stopped and gestured toward the underside of the shelter. The rock was stained pink, brown, and white, and it was covered in dark, swirling lines. "This is it," he said.

At first we couldn't see anything. But then the dark lines seemed to shift and reassemble themselves. They formed a picture of three animals: a menagerie à trois.

We could make out a python with a thick, coiled body, its head pointed upward, its tongue in mid-flick. There was a kangaroo that had a long muzzle and short, pointed ears. It was looking to the right with an almost arrogant expression on its face. The third animal was Les's tiger—*was it a tiger?* It had a big, doggy head with triangular ears (one facing forward and one back), a skinny neck, two stumpy front legs, and dark stripes across its elongated body. It appeared to be speared through by the tail of the haughty kangaroo.

The drawings were made using charcoal. Les showed us a large oval of ash on the ground. It was an ancient fire pit, one of three in this rock shelter, and it was thousands of years old. Les thought two, maybe three aboriginal families had spent their evenings at this spot regularly. "These fire mounds were used for cooking large animals. They would have dragged a kangaroo up here and covered it over." Then he added, "Pythons have a lot of meat on them, too." We began to wonder if the rock art was actually an ancient menu.

The python was probably a diamond python, a species that grows to about six feet and still lives in Royal National Park (it eats bats, other small mammals, birds, and lizards). The wallaby was probably the brushtail rock wallaby, now an endangered species. All, including the thylacine, were nocturnal.

We began to look for something besides the stripes that might indicate this drawing was a tiger, rather than a crosshatched kangaroo. Its eye was a deep black almond, which gave it a slightly savage appearance. Very thylacine-y. Then again, from different angles, the animal looked more like a kangaroo than a tiger.

Then we saw something. It could have been just a fold in the rock, but there it was, a charcoal line, the tiger's mouth. We had spent too much time at the museum looking at the tiger to miss it. Tasmanian tigers have a wicket-shaped grin. The line of their mouths extends far back into their heads toward the ears and turns up at the corners—a feature that allows them to open their mouths in an unusually wide gape. When we saw that crafty grin beaming out at us across the millennia, we knew we would join the 60 percent crowd.

"It looks like I have another convert," Les said.

We looked at the charcoal lines marking the sandstone. What made this thylacine drawing all the more remarkable was that it survived when so many aboriginal drawings had been lost.

At one time, Les explained, every inch of this rock shelter would have been covered with paintings. In fact, in the background behind the python-wallaby-thylacine were the faded or partial beginnings of many other drawings—the un-filled-in outline of a disembodied head, a featureless kangaroo in mid-leap.

These three charcoal drawings had survived because they were protected from the fading rays of the sun and covered with a clear skin of silica that had leached out of the rock face and formed a protective sheath.

"The wonderful thing about this drawing is that it's no longer on the surface of the rock. It's *in* the rock. It's probably preserved forever now."

"How old is this drawing?" we asked.

Les borrowed one of our notebooks and drew three kangaroo heads. On one, he drew two stick ears—just two lines. On another he drew triangular ears, and on the last one he drew rounded ears. Stick ears were used on the oldest Tharawal drawings: 4,500 to 8,500 years old. Triangle ears dated from 3,500 to 4,500 years ago. Rounded ears were the most recent, disappearing only with European occupation less than two hundred years ago.

He circled the kangaroo with the triangular ears. "That's what we're looking at, and I reckon it's about four thousand years old." The date fit. Thylacines were still living on the mainland then.

"Why did aboriginal people draw the thylacine?"

"Oh, there could have been lots of reasons," Les said. Sometimes animals were drawn to tell a story or they could be totem animals, drawn to call on their spirits. In rock shelters like this one where families gathered for warmth and shelter at night, the rock art is often diary-like. "It's sort of *Days of Our Lives*," Les continued. "They're keeping a record. 'I saw a thylacine today.' That would be a remarkable occurrence, I think, even for an aboriginal person. They're such a cunning and secretive animal. When you saw one, it was an event." We imagined a thylacine passing unseen in the night and the drawings of the animals moving and dancing in the light of the flickering fire pits.

It was tragic that the thylacine was extinct on the mainland. But had it completely vanished from the earth? We asked Les what he thought. Les said he believed the thylacine survived in Tasmania. "They say there are no dingoes in this park, but I've seen them," he said. "Tasmania's a big place with many untouched wild areas. The thylacine is out there. It has to be."

As we were talking, Alexis had begun collecting chunks of charcoal left over from a recent bushfire and bits of yellow ocher. He planned to use them as drawing materials. He hadn't said much while we were looking at the ancient animal triptych, though he had photographed it with his digital camera and made a quick sketch.

"Do you think it's a thylacine?" we asked.

"Maybe," Alexis said. "But it could be a rabbit for all I know." Then he looked admiringly at the work of these long-vanished artists. "I know one thing. I hope my shit's still around in four thousand years."

By the time we got back to the boat, it was nearly beached. With some difficulty, Les extricated the pudding from Tiger Shark Hole and anchored in the main part of the Southwest Arm. In the distance, we saw the tiny figures of water-skiers, swimmers, and numerous pleasure craft. Alexis and Dorothy decided to go for a dip and leapt into the green water. We advised them to watch out for tiger sharks, but they paid no attention.

Les pulled out a cold can of Victoria Bitter and popped the top. "Nothing I like better than a day on the water, good conversation, and a good beer," he said. Then he began telling us about his day job. It turned out studying rock art was a sideline for him these days. He worked with the New South Wales Department of Corrective Services, counseling prisoners and parolees with drug, alcohol, mental health, and violence problems. Some of his work was profoundly gratifying, helping people get straight, putting their lives back together. But in the criminal justice system, he also encountered some hard nuts—murderers, serial killers.

"Working in the jails, we have a saying: Yes, I'm paranoid. But am I paranoid enough?" Alexis and Dorothy climbed out of the water and retreated to their sunny perch on the roof.

Drug addiction, Les continued, really exacerbated the problems of felons. Surprisingly, he said the most problematic drug he had to deal with was marijuana. It caused tremendous social problems. "In my experience it's worse than heroin," he said. "It affects brain function."

"Really?" we said.

We excused ourselves and went onto the roof of the boat. Dorothy, in a gingham bikini and with her Gucci sunglasses propped on her head, was giving Alexis a shoulder rub. He took his pot pipe out. Clearly, he had been eavesdropping. "Tell Les I'm killing my last brain cell," he said, flicking his lighter.

3. the once and future tiger

A few nights after our visit to the ancient portrait gallery, we sat on benches in Sydney's Hyde Park beneath the thick, tropical leaves of Moreton Bay figs. Flying foxes were jostling for position in the trees. Once in a while, one of them would take off, its four-foot-long, leathery wings silhouetted against the city's skyscrapers. It was odd. Animals the size of cats were flying through the evening air and the city's residents barely seemed to notice.

Across the street at the venerable Australian Museum, something else strange was going on. Cloning scientists were trying to bring the Tasmanian tiger back from the dead. We had made an appointment with the cloning team and been casing the museum for days beforehand, visiting exhibits on ancient Australian megafauna, purchasing tiger souvenirs in the gift shop (most notably a bronze tiger tiepin)—and hanging out in the park with the megabats.

The cloning project had received an enormous amount of press in Australia. Our favorite headline had been, "Get a Life, Scientists Tell Extinct Tiger." Most of the articles were accompanied by a photo of a specimen from the museum's collection: a perfectly preserved thylacine pup, eyes closed and floating in a jar of alcohol.

Sitting in the park, we reflected on the similarities between the flying foxes and the thylacine. Just as the thylacine had been in the nineteenth century, flying foxes were regarded as pests and, despite their abundance in Sydney, were actually rare. In many areas of Australia the bats' forest homes had been chopped down, and they had turned to eating fruit crops. As a result, farmers started killing the creatures, and in 2001 the gray-headed flying foxes wound up being listed as a threatened species. The difference was that, while rare, the megabats were still around, managing to survive in this busy, human-created environment, flying past church steeples and landing in street trees. The thylacine hadn't been so lucky. Protection efforts came too late. Now human beings—the same creatures that had hounded thylacines to the vanishing point—felt they had no recourse but to try and jump-start this species' flatlining heart.

As we watched the flying foxes, we began to wonder, What *is* life anyway? We remembered a scene from the 1931 movie *Frankenstein*. Dr. Frankenstein cranks open the ceiling above his lab, revealing a thunderstorm. As electric current surges through a V-shaped Tesla coil, the electricity reanimates slabs of graveyard flesh that Dr. Frankenstein's stitched together, and he screams, "*IT'S ALIVE. IT'S ALI-I-IVE!*"

That was cinematic science fiction. Dead humans can't be brought back to life—at least not yet. What the Australian Museum's scientists were proposing was that species could be. The implication? Extinction may not be as final as it sounds.

On the morning of our appointment, Alexis accompanied us to the

Australian Museum—Dorothy was spending the A.M. buying souvenirs—and we were ushered into the museum's Evolutionary Biology Unit. If we had imagined it would be outfitted like a mad scientist's lab, nothing could have been further from reality. It was a long room with cubicles, paper-piled desks, computer terminals, a coffeepot, and a small conference table. The unit's lead scientist, Don Colgan, was also distinctly un-Frankensteinian. His hair was not electroshocked but smooth, brown, and neatly parted. He didn't rant. In fact, at times, he was such a low talker, it was difficult to hear him.

Don introduced us to his colleague Karen Firestone, an expert on ancient DNA and marsupial carnivores. We all sat down at the conference table, and they offered us cups of tea.

We had looked up Don's curriculum vitae on the Internet. Typically, geneticists working at natural history museums were primarily concerned with taxa. How are species related? How did they evolve? When did one species branch off to form another? Much of Don's own work had to do with invertebrates—aquatic snails, spiders, shellfish—and how they fit into the tree of life. Ultimately, the work was historical: he used genetics to explain how species became the way they are. How had he gotten involved with this radically futuristic project?

It all started, he said, with another work of science fiction, *Jurassic Park*. In the book and subsequent movie, dinosaurs were brought back to life, using ancient dinosaur DNA extracted from amber fossils. After reading the book and seeing the movie, people started wondering if the Tasmanian tiger could be brought back in the same way, using DNA extracted from specimens at the Australian Museum. Don said no. Not possible. The question kept coming up and he kept saying no, *really*, it can't be done. In fact, it got to the point that he felt the need to write a detailed letter to his museum's director, the well-known paleontologist Mike Archer, explaining why cloning a tiger wouldn't work.

"The director took that as unequivocal support for the idea," Don said. "Since then it's generated its own momentum. The animal is in the national psyche."

Karen, an American in her thirties, had been hired specifically for the tiger project. "Before, I was working with dried skins to look at the population and conservation genetics of living carnivorous marsupials," she said. "It just seemed like a natural progression to work on a bigger, deader animal."

The cloning project was premised on the notion that the Australian Museum had this wonderfully intact antique specimen of a tiger pup preserved whole. The plan was that they would extract DNA strands from the pup's soft tissue—its heart, its liver—and reassemble those strands to re-create the tiger's entire genome. Once the tiger's DNA had been copied, catalogued, and sequenced, they would create a thylacine DNA molecule in the lab. From that DNA molecule, this one-of-a-kind striped carnivore could be reborn.

It was mind-boggling, thrilling, and slightly disturbing. And given the pace of biotechnology—the mapping of the human genome, gene therapy—it seemed well within the realm of possibility. "So, within twenty years or so, will cloning extinct species be routine?" we asked. We imagined a zoo of once extinct animals: dodos, passenger pigeons, woolly mammoths.

Don looked at us as if we were the mad scientists. "We have to mitigate the enthusiasm with the reality of what we're doing," he said gently.

DNA is not life, he reminded us. It's a blueprint for life, meaning that it tells a life, an organism, what species it will be, what it will look like, how it will grow. Sometimes it tells an organism how to behave or what its disposition will be. Because DNA is itself inanimate and made up of chemicals, an organism's DNA can survive well after death, sometimes for thousands of years.

Retrieving thylacine DNA was the cloning team's first task. Because the tiger pup was so old, dating from the mid-nineteenth century, it was preserved in ethyl alcohol (ethanol) rather than formalin as more recent specimens would be. (Formalin, a preservative that came into vogue around the same time the pup was pickled, destroys DNA; ethanol doesn't.) The scientists took samples from the tiger pup—from its organs, muscle, and bone marrow—and then extracted hundreds of thousands of DNA strands. In the media, the extraction was hailed as a triumph. Later, upon analysis, however, the DNA was found to be contaminated. It was a bit awkward. The pickled tiger pup had figured prominently in the press as the key to bringing the thylacine back to life—and the museum had already announced that the extraction had been successful. But what could they do? They were scientists, not sideshow barkers. They began to look at other tiger specimens in the collection. The museum owned thylacine pelts, organs, bones. Ultimately, the cloning team extracted DNA from a thylacine femur and molar. It was good—in thousands of fragments—but they could work with it.

The next step was making sure they had all the correct bits and pieces of the tiger's DNA. They still needed to figure out how many chromosomes the tiger had and what was in them. Later, they would reassemble the DNA, like the pieces of a jigsaw puzzle. Karen led us over to her computer terminal. It was awash with graphs and symbols, documenting the tiger's life code.

When—*if*—they were able to re-create the tiger's entire genome (which in itself would be an incredible scientific achievement, Don pointed out), they would be ready for the ultimate stage of the project: cloning a tiger.

"Of course, having just one wouldn't do any good," Karen said. "We'd have to make at least two hundred tigers." Then she and Don began to laugh. Even in the heart of the cloning project it seemed like science fiction.

"There's really a lot of pressure," said Don, still laughing and wiping tears from his eyes. The chances of success—of creating just one thylacine— were 5 to 8 percent in twenty years.

But, he added, the odds could get better. Technology was improving all the time. Since the discovery of the structure of DNA in 1953, scientists have learned to dissect, copy, map, manipulate, and even change the code of life. Through genetic modification, they've created insect-resistant breeds of corn. Tomatoes that have extended shelf lives. They have bioengineered cows to produce "farmaceuticals," including potential treatments for blood clots, anemia, hemophilia, and emphysema. They have put bioluminescent jellyfish DNA into white rabbits to make them glow under ultraviolet light—and they have even introduced spider DNA into goats, causing them to produce copious amounts of super-strong silk webbing in their milk.

Cloning, or bringing to life the twin of an individual, has also become a reality. The first mammal clone, Dolly the Sheep, was created in 1996 from a single cell nucleus taken from the udder of an adult sheep. Recently, clones of the first endangered species were created by implanting their DNA into the eggs of related animals.

The first such trans-species birth was in 2001 when a cloned guar—an extremely rare species of wild ox that lives in Southeast Asia—was brought to term inside a cow named Bessie. This experiment was followed up in 2003 when a cloned Javanese banteng, a rare species of wild cattle, was born on an Iowa farm. The banteng's "mother" was a beef cow. In China, scientists are currently working to produce embryonic clones of giant pandas that could be "mothered" by black bears.

This is how the tiger clone would be created. If cloning scientists are able to reconstitute the thylacine's genome, they will need to pick a species to be the tiger's surrogate mother, an Eve for a new race of thylacines. This animal will have to be as closely related to the tiger as possible—which presents a bit of a problem.

"The thylacine was the sole remaining representative of its family," Don said. As a species, the Tasmanian tiger diverged from its closest cousin 25 million years ago. Of the sixty or so species of living marsupial carnivores—all of which are potential candidates—none look very much like the tiger. These species include such creatures as the dusky antechinus, a mouse-sized marsupial with a giant-sized sex life (its copulation is described as "violent" and the males all die of stress-related disease within three weeks of mating); the spotted-tailed quoll, a forest predator that looks like a cross between a cat and a weasel; and the Tasmanian devil, a black-furred scavenger with powerful, bone-crunching jaws.

"I think it would come down to the devil really," said Karen. "The devil is the largest of the carnivorous marsupials."

Although only one third the size of the thylacine, the Tasmanian devil is a fierce beast. And like the thylacine and all marsupials, the devil gives birth to tiny incompletely developed young, which it suckles in a protective pouch.

To create this devil of a tiger, the cloning scientists would take an unfertilized egg from a female Tasmanian devil, remove all the devil DNA from inside, and then micro-inject the tiger's DNA into the egg. Then they would zap the egg with an electrical pulse. The egg and DNA would fuse, and cell division would begin. Shortly thereafter, they would implant the resulting microscopic embryo into the devil's womb and a few weeks later a tiny tiger would be born.

Alexis, who had been quiet up to this point, suddenly perked up. "So are you saying the tiger would be part devil?" he asked. His eyes gleamed as if he were picturing what a thyla-devil would look like.

Don laughed, three short barks.

In fact, he said, they would have to drive the devil out. A tiny portion of the devil's genome would get into the tiger clone. "It would be less than a millionth devil," Don said. "We would have to disable the mitochondria if we wanted it to be entirely thylacine."

Karen was less concerned about the bedeviled eggs. "It might just be that they can survive with devil mitochondria," she said.

When it came to the question of what would happen to the tiger after its birth, they were stumped. Hand it off to the vet? Marsupials aren't like placentals. The birth occurs when the young are blind, hairless, and in a state of very early development. These underdeveloped infants have to crawl on their own power to the safety of their mother's pouch, where they develop further over many months. How would a cloned tiger make it to the devil's pouch? Could it drink devil milk? Would pet food companies have to develop a baby tiger formula?

"I don't know. Perhaps it might be safer if they were attached and suckling," Karen said hesitantly. Then again, there was the possibility that the devil stepmom might eat it. Some carnivorous marsupials, she pointed out, can give birth to supernumerary young. "They give birth to many more than they can actually carry. But I don't know of a documented case where carnivorous marsupials have cannibalized their own pouch young."

"I think it would be fed with droppers," Don added.

Then there was the problem of the young tiger's health. Clones were difficult to bring to term and not always healthy. Dolly (one of twenty-seven implantations that survived) had actually been rather sickly. It was suggested she suffered from premature aging. The cloned guar had died two days after its birth from dysentery. And the second cloned banteng suffered from large-offspring syndrome, weighing eighty pounds at birth (twice the normal size), and was euthanized. Don thought some of the kinks from these early cloning attempts would be worked out by the time the thylacine was cloned. "That was the first experiment," he said of Dolly. "Fifteen years down the track, I imagine there will be a success rate of at least one in two. It will become much more routine." Still, it was possible things wouldn't work right immediately. What they were doing was much more difficult than borrowing DNA from a living animal like a sheep. They were making the tiger's DNA, reconstructing it from tiny fragments in their lab.

Ultimately, their goal was to create a living animal that was genetically close enough to have interbred with a thylacine from the nineteenth or early twentieth century. But their creation would be synthetic, its DNA a best-guess reconstruction. Like a cubic zirconia, the thylacine clone would not be quite the real thing. For example, it might be born missing its stripes. If they chose to or needed to, however, they could manipulate the DNA, tweak it, make little changes to fix any problems.

That was a sobering thought—and one that went way beyond natural selection. It began to remind us of some of Alexis's paintings. In one piece called *The Farm*, which imagined the future of biotechnology, he had painted brick-shaped watermelon, a cow with a rectangular body and eight udders, and a chicken with six wings. Would a future thylacine ever be "fixed" along those lines? It had already been suggested that the tiger clones be made bigger and fiercer so that they could be released on the Australian mainland and compete with dingoes. Would cloning scientists create a super-thylacine, immune to disease and with bulletproof skin? What about making them smaller and more docile? Then they could be sold in a late-twenty-first-century pet shop. They could probably even be made to glow in the dark.

We suspected Don would have been horrified if he could have heard our stream-of-consciousness, horror-movie-driven thoughts. His goals were conservation, preservation, and of course knowledge. Still, he recognized the cloning project had a metaphysical dimension.

Even if his team got the DNA perfectly right (no tweaking, no manipulation, a perfect twin), the question remained: Is DNA what truly makes a species or an individual animal?

"It depends on what a thylacine is, doesn't it?" Don said. "Is the essence of that animal its genetic component, or does it include its behavior and so forth?" Maybe thylacines were passing down information from generation to generation, along with their genes, over tens of thousands of years. Maybe hunting techniques and vocalizations were learned, not innate. Assuming the thylacine clone had a place to live, how would it know what to do?

And what about a place to live? The obvious choice would be to release the tiger clones into protected habitat in Tasmania. David Brower, the longtime director of the Sierra Club, once said, "Wild species are 2 percent flesh and bone and 98 percent place." Outside its true habitat, the thylacine clone would be nothing but a glorified lab rat. Don agreed. "We want to use this project to reinforce the importance of conserving habitat in Australia. Whatever we'll spend in the lab, we'll need to spend ten times that on habitat protection. We've spoken to the parks and wildlife people in Tasmania, who inform us that there *is* a lot of suitable habitat down there."

There was just one small problem with that idea. At present, Tasmania does not permit the use of genetically modified crops, let alone the release of genetically modified animals.

Don was undaunted. "There's also habitat that would be suitable in other areas of the country," he said. In other words, reintroducing the thylacine onto the Australian mainland was a possibility.

"Near Sydney?"

"Well, the Blue Mountains would be fine."

"Maybe they could move in with the flying foxes in the botanical gardens," Alexis chimed in. Alexis was more comfortable with blurring boundaries than most people. In one of his paintings, *Rat Evolution,* an everyday rat was transformed over a series of three mutations into a freakish species of the future, a furless, kangaroo-like beast with armor-plated hindquarters and six-inch-long incisors. Perhaps the Evolutionary Biology Unit would want to look into making those superpowered dingo-fighting tigers after all.

We only had one more question: "Do you think there's any possibility that the tiger isn't extinct?"

Karen laughed. "Some people still swear they see them."

Don took it more seriously.

"I'm presuming it's extinct," he said carefully.

"What about the people who believe the tiger's still out there?"

He paused. "Let's hope it is."

We knew he didn't believe it for a second. But it was a happy thought. If nothing else, it would make his job a whole lot easier.

4. THE EXTINCTION CABINET

Before we met Don Colgan, we had been pondering the nature of life. Now we were wondering, what exactly was death? Such thoughts were driven sharply to the surface as Don led us through the museum's osteology exhibit. In it were scores of articulated skeletons, their bones blanched white. The sinuous vertebrae of a python were poised to strike, a furless fur seal hung from the ceiling suspended by wires, and a swan posed with its featherless wings outstretched. Beneath a sampler that read "Home Sweet Home," a human skeleton sat in a rocking chair powered by an invisible motor.

Next to the scrawny remains of a rat darting into a mouse hole, a hidden door led to the museum's basement collections. We walked down a steep staircase and into a hallway, passing a metal cart crammed with jars containing pickled bats and taxidermies of an echidna and mountain brushtail possum. The whole area smelled funereal, a combination of mothballs, alcohol, and formaldehyde used to preserve the old specimens. In front of a stiff mounted wombat, Don passed us off to Sandy Ingleby, the Australian Museum's curator of mammals. She was the custodian of the dead objects that contained the tiger's life code.

"Cute wombat," Alexis said, pointing at the taxidermy.

Sandy laughed and flicked her flaming red hair. We noticed she lacked the semi-embalmed look of other specimen curators we had met. As she took us past the rows of mint green metal cabinets that held her lifeless charges, we caught a few of the labels: kangaroos, sugar gliders, quolls. All together, Sandy said, there were 41,300 specimens in the Australian Museum's mammal collection. Next to a tall, padlocked cabinet set slightly apart from the rest, we saw a photograph of a Tasmanian tiger with three half-grown pups backed into the corner of a wooden enclosure. With their wide eyes, they looked both wary and vulnerable. The photograph was taken in 1924.

"I call this my exhibit of extinct mammal specimens," Sandy said, unlocking the cabinet. Inside, sliding trays were jammed with pelts, skulls, taxidermy, and boxes and jars containing body parts—each neatly numbered and labeled. Sandy reeled off some of the names of the dead: the Tasmanian tiger, the Toolache wallaby, the desert bandicoot, the broad-faced potoroo, the lesser bilby, the Darling Downs hopping mouse.

Though nearly two dozen animals were represented, half the space was devoted to the remains of the thylacine, totaling fifty-seven items. Sandy pulled out a tray and showed us the flattened, tanned pelt of a tiger. Its head was wolflike, the triangular ears crumpled with age, its eyeless sockets staring up at us. To say these objects were rare was an understatement. "They're not making any more of these," Sandy pointed out. "At least not that we know of."

The fur of the tiger pelt was ginger-colored (a mixture of brown, wheat, and gold). Broad chocolate brown stripes cut across the back, tapering to a point on the lower flanks. Each stripe was different, like a ragged brushstroke.

"Can we touch it?"

"Go ahead."

We ran our fingers lightly down the stripes. The fur felt rough, slightly bristly. We wondered if it had felt softer in life.

Sandy lifted up a female specimen and pointed out the pouch on its pale belly. It was a scooplike indentation just beneath the tail. "The thylacine pouch is round and rearward-facing, because it's an animal on all fours," she said. Unlike a kangaroo, whose pouch opens forward and up, the thylacine pouch faced backward, so that mother tigers could run through the bush without injuring their pups. Inside the pouch, Sandy showed us that one of the dead thylacine's four teats was enlarged. The animal had been suckling a pup when it was killed.

Wearing white cotton gloves, Sandy assembled a still life of tiger remains on a long table, laying out two skulls, an articulated skeleton, a tiger brain in a jar of yellow-green liquid, and a skin.

For some people, being around preserved body parts, bones, and pickled organs might be uncomfortable. Not Alexis. He was like Norman Bates at a taxidermy blowout sale, rearranging the body bits and pieces, posing them for photographs. He fingered the heavy, elongated skulls, opening and closing the jaws to re-create the tiger's famous 120-degree gape. Their inch-long, inward-curving fangs were backed up by rows of knife-sharp teeth.

Sandy didn't seem to think there was anything strange about Alexis's fascination. She pulled out a taxidermy of a tiger—a skin mounted on a frame, with glass eyes inserted into the head. It wasn't very good. The tiger looked like it had died of a hangover—it was bug-eyed, cringing, and posed unnaturally in mid-crouch. A patch of hair below the neck had come off. We could never have fallen in love with this sad creature.

"What a hack job," said Alexis.

Sandy agreed. "The mounting is of pretty low quality. It's fairly Eurocentric, very placental mammal rather than marsupial."

"Looks like it's part mongoose," Alexis added.

When Alexis had finished probing and critiquing the tiger remains, Sandy led us back to the extinction cabinet. None of the other animals in-

side were as well-known as the thylacine, but each had its own long history and expiration date.

- The Eastern hare wallaby was a small kangaroo with a face like a rabbit
  and reputedly could jump over a horse—last confirmed sighting 1890.

- The Toolache was a plump, four-foot-tall wallaby with a black stripe on
  its muzzle—last seen 1937.

- The crescent nailtail wallaby was a golden brown hopper with enormous ears—last seen early 1960s.

- The broad-faced potoroo was a tiny hunchbacked kangaroo that dined
  primarily on truffles—last seen 1875.

- The lesser bilby was a needle-nosed burrower, with rabbit ears and a
  bottlebrush tail—last confirmed sighting 1931.

- The pig-footed bandicoot was a small, plump creature with a narrow
  snout, long skinny legs, and delicate hooflike feet—last confirmed
  sighting 1907.

Most of these extinct animals had never been photographed. Their
likenesses survived only in artists' watercolors. This cabinet contained all
that was left of them—and sometimes all that remained was a skull. If the
cloning of extinct species ever became a reality, there would be plenty to
rectify.

Ever since Europeans arrived in Australia, mammals have been disappearing at an astonishing rate. "Australia has the unfortunate distinction
of being the continent in which the most mammal species have become
extinct over the last two hundred years," said Sandy. Nearly half of all the
modern-day mammal extinctions worldwide have been from Australia—
totaling nineteen species.

What caused all these extinctions? Sandy said certain factors came into
play repeatedly in Australia. For starters, Europeans didn't arrive on the
continent alone. They brought pets and other hangers-on with them and
introduced them into the wild. The fox, rabbit, and cat arrived with
British settlers in the nineteenth century, and all have made trouble for
native creatures—eating them, taking over their habitats, and out-

competing them for food. The settlers also disastrously altered the habitats of native animals, chopping down forests, planting nonnative crops, using up precious water resources, and suppressing fires that aboriginal people set to maintain grassy areas and increase game.

The thylacine's story was a little bit different. By the time Europeans arrived in Australia, thylacines survived only in Tasmania. In this last oasis, there was only one reason the tiger began to vanish. Sandy pointed to a ragged hole in the top of a taxidermy specimen's head. "I suspect that's a bullet hole," she said. "They probably caught the animal in a trap and then shot it at close range."

Most of Australia's mammal extinctions had resulted from "collateral damage." They had not been intentional, but the result of poor land use and a thoughtless grab for resources. But thylacines were purposely exterminated. From a twenty-first-century perspective, it was hard to believe people had been so foolish, so wasteful, so disregarding of the thylacine's biological uniqueness, its beauty. It was also hard to accept that such an ancient species could be snuffed out so quickly. Wasn't it possible thylacines had resources the hunters knew nothing about: places to hide, strategies of cunning and avoidance? It was these niggling doubts that kept the tiger's status unresolved. So many people believed—or hoped—it would still be found one day that it was trapped in a state of limbo. We conjured up an image of the thylacine ferrying forever between life and death in the River Styx, but never quite reaching either shore.

We asked Sandy why she thought the extinction of the thylacine was so hard to accept.

"It's such a tragic story," she said. "And it's so recent, isn't it?"

Was there any chance that a few Tasmanian tigers had eluded the traps and guns—that the moment of extinction had not yet arrived? Sandy said that a few Australian animals had, in fact, made it back across the River Styx. After disappearing in 1909, Leadbeater's possum was rediscovered in 1961. It lived in communal nests with up to eight possums and remained extremely rare, living in a small area of old-growth forest in Eastern Victoria. The Central rock rat, a desert species with a fat carroty tail that weighed only a few ounces, had been missing for twenty-five years when it was rediscovered in 1996. A few isolated populations clung to survival on a forty-eight-mile strip of land in Australia's Northern Territory. In 1989, the mahogany glider, a big brown-eyed possum with a black stripe that runs from the tip of its nose to the end of its tail and which sails through the air on a parachute-like gliding membrane, was rediscovered after an absence of more than a hundred years. It was immediately declared an endangered species.

Could this happen with the thylacine, too? Would it be found inhabiting an isolated pocket in Tasmania's hard-to-reach backcountry? Sandy didn't think so. For every rediscovered animal in the cabinet—for every one that had received a pardon—there were five that had vanished, most likely irrevocably. Plus, she said, the few Australian animals that had been rediscovered were all on the small side. "Something as large as the tiger would be hard to miss," she said.

For big animals like the Tasmanian tiger, the River Styx is wider, deeper, choppier—easier to get lost in. As far as the Australian Museum was concerned, cloning was the only hope for the tiger. And if Don and Karen were successful, future searches for the thylacine would be rendered a moot point.

Sandy said the specimen that had inspired the cloning project—the rare intact pouch pup—was kept in an area even more secure than the extinction cabinet. She led us back down the hallway and stopped in front of a steel metal door. Behind it was a room-sized safe. Two people were required to open it: One museum official had the safe's combination and another had the key. "I think it was originally built to protect the gem collection," said Sandy.

For insurance purposes, the pickled pouch pup was valued at $1.5 million. And the staff couldn't be too careful with an object as rare as this one. In fact, there had been a rash of thefts at the museum in previous years. They had been inside jobs, too, with hundreds of specimens going missing, including an entire stuffed gorilla.

Given the security procedures involved in opening the safe, we were surprised when they finally opened the door. We had expected a high-tech facility with a subzero refrigerator and elaborate temperature controls. It looked more like a large broom closet. And the paint was peeling.

Alexis frowned. "Where do they keep the pouch pup?"

"It's in a bucket."

After a moment of rummaging, Sandy pulled out a white janitor's pail and put it on top of an antique safe that looked like it had come off the set of a Wild West movie. The bucket was heavily padded with foam rubber.

"This is the type of specimen jar they used during the 1800s and early 1900s," she said, lifting out an eighteen-inch-high glass container filled with fluid. When we saw what was inside, we forgot about the peeling paint.

Immersed in liquid and curled up as if resting in its mother's pouch was the body of a Tasmanian tiger pup. The fur was palest gold, with brown whispers of stripes across the back and flanks. Its eyes were closed as if sleeping, and its right paw was tucked under its chin. We could see tiny sharp claws emerging from the paws and delicate whiskers floating in front of the muzzle. The tail was curved around the feet, and tiny, triangular ears lay against its blocky, outsized head. Spreading across the length of its short snout was a familiar grin. A white card taped to the jar read: "♀Juvenile. Coll. Masters, 1866 from Tasmania." It had been floating in alcohol for nearly 140 years.

If the pouch pup's digs weren't as posh as they might be, Sandy said we should have seen how it was stored before. For decades, the pouch pup was kept in the museum's "spirit house," hidden among jars of kangaroo kidneys, monkeys, fetuses, and the brains of whales, all preserved in ethanol. "It wasn't even locked up. The spirit house was actually open from the street at one stage, so you could just walk right in there." When Sandy took over the mammal collection in 1996, she helped move the marinated tiger pup inside the museum, down to the basement, and under lock and key.

We looked at the white card attached to the jar again. "What does 'Coll. Masters' mean?"

"George Masters was employed as the museum's collector. He went to Tasmania in the 1800s and captured wildlife and sent it back to the museum." She said there were no details about how Masters acquired the pup. Almost certainly it had been captured and killed along with its mother.

We turned the jar halfway around and saw that the pup's belly had been slit open. "What's that?"

"Masters probably did that in the field when he collected it. If you put a whole animal like that into spirit, the spirit will only penetrate the outer surface and the internal organs will rot. So he slit it open to let the preservative go in."

When this thylacine was first born it was less than an inch long—undeveloped, weak, defenseless. At that tiny size, it had to crawl across its mother's belly, clinging to her fur, and find its way into her backward-facing pouch. There, the pup would have lived attached to a teat, until it was old enough to be left alone in a den while the mother went hunting. The pouch pup preserved in the bottle was probably at that stage, still reliant on its mother, but big enough to leave the pouch.

"We estimate it's three months old," said Sandy. But no one could say for sure. Thylacines had never been bred in captivity. No scientific observations of thylacines were ever made in the wild. Everything that was surmised about their development was based on studies of other distantly related marsupial carnivores.

We thought back to the thylacine skin Sandy had shown us in the cabinet of extinct mammals. One teat in the pouch had been enlarged. Had that thylacine been feeding this pup? Sandy had wondered about that, too. Unfortunately, she said, the museum's old collection records did not include that information. Family relationships among specimens had not been documented.

We studied the pup and felt almost voyeuristic, putting our noses right up to the side of the glass. The fur was so thin and wispy, the pup looked almost naked. To all appearances, it was still as vulnerable as it had been when it was taken from its mother's pouch. We could see why it had been the inspiration for so much scientific longing.

We didn't know if the Australian Museum would ever succeed with cloning the tiger—or even if it was a good idea. All we knew was that we were head over heels again for the tiger.

After nearly twenty minutes inside the safe, we were starting to feel woozy from the fumes emanating from the flask and the temperature had risen uncomfortably. "Do you mind if we get some fresh air?" we asked Sandy.

Alexis gave the pouch pup a parting look as Sandy put it back in its bucket. "Hey," he said. "Here's something that will fulfill your fantasies. What if its eyes suddenly popped open?"

We quickly came up with a movie title: *The Reawakening of Baby Thylanstein*. But then we thought better of it.

"Let it sleep," we said. Maybe it was dreaming of Tasmania.

5. CROSSING the strait

We had two major biogeographical boundaries to traverse to reach Tasmania. The first one—Wallace's Line—had been crossed a week before on board a plane on our way to Sydney. The second—the Bass Strait—was yet to be breached.

Separating Tasmania from the Australian continent, the Bass Strait is a formidable barrier. One hundred fifty miles wide, it roils and churns unpredictably. Countless craft lay at its bottom, and it had claimed the lives of thousands of sailors. It's possible to fly across the strait and avoid the notoriously treacherous waters, but we wanted to savor the experience of crossing into a new world. The Bass Strait ferry, the *Spirit of Tasmania*, left every night (weather permitting) from Melbourne on the mainland's southern tip. We caught a short flight south and that night rendezvoused with Alexis and Dorothy at a Thai restaurant in Melbourne's South Yarra district. We had to be at the ferry at 8:00 P.M.

Just as we were diving into spring rolls, a stranger walked up to the table. He was boyish-looking, with light brown hair and a crooked smile. Suddenly, he threw his arms around our shoulders and gave us a squeeze.

"Hey, team!" He had an American accent.

Who was this guy?

Alexis jumped up immediately and shook his hand. It was Alexis's friend from New York, the one he had said "might" be coming.

The newcomer sat down, bit into a spring roll, and introduced himself. His name was Chris Vroom. He was thrilled about the idea of going to Tasmania. And we rapidly absorbed his life story. As a Wall Street analyst, he had made a killing during the Internet boom and at age thirty-seven was already semiretired. Since Chris didn't have to work, he indulged his two passions, travel and art. He traveled whenever he got the urge and recently had been to Antarctica and the Himalayas. As for his other interest, he had immersed himself in New York's contemporary art scene, becoming a serious collector and using his own money to start a nonprofit organization that gave grants to promising young artists. One of his prize possessions was a sculpture constructed entirely from police officers' batons. Chris and Dorothy hit it off immediately and began talking about galleries, who was on the board of what museum, and who had sneaked off with whom at the last Venice Biennale.

We broke in. "So what made you decide to take a trip to Tasmania?"

"Alexis invited me," he responded enthusiastically.

Oh. Right. This was rapidly evolving from "might" be joining us to full-fledged expedition member. We continued our inquiry. "What was the thing that intrigued you most about the idea?" We were still hoping to uncover a latent scientific background, a degree in biology or an unrequited passion for meat-eating marsupials. Even an interest in Bigfoot would do.

But it was Tasmania's scenery and adventure sports that had caught Chris's attention. He had read about the island's glorious beaches, great swimming, and incredible surfing—and he mentioned seaplanes and scuba diving. It sounded exciting. Too bad we wouldn't be doing any of that stuff.

"We're pretty much focusing the trip around the tiger," we said. "Its natural and cultural history, its iconography, the possible veracity of eyewitness reports."

We were trying to make our plans sound as boring as possible, but

Chris's face betrayed a hint of alarm. "There are tigers in Tasmania?" he said. Apparently Alexis had failed to brief him on the thylacine aspect of our trip.

"Don't worry," Alexis shouted across a plate of pad thai. "They're extinct—probably."

For the next hour, Chris and Dorothy returned to their discussion about art. The tiger receded into the background.

When it was time to head off for the ferry, Chris explained he hadn't been able to book a cabin and was flying into Devonport, the Tasmanian city where the ferry docked. He would meet us there the following morning.

"So, what's the agenda?" he said. "Can I have a copy of the itinerary?"

"Uh—" *Itinerary*? "Well, the day after tomorrow we're going to see devils . . . hopefully."

This time Dorothy looked at us strangely. Then she said, "Those are animals, right?"

Twenty minutes later we were at Melbourne's Station Pier, entering the ferry's cavernous bowels. Hundreds of cars were creeping on board and stacks of pet-filled cages were being rolled off to an unseen kennel area. Because of Tasmania's island status—and freedom from many of the exotic species that plagued the mainland—restrictions on bringing in plants, animals, even certain types of food were taken very seriously. We joined a line of passengers waiting to have their luggage checked. Every bag was opened, poked, and occasionally thoroughly searched. According to a pamphlet we had been given, the inspectors were primarily looking for fresh fruit and illegal animals, such as foxes and pythons. But Alexis looked nervous.

"Did you bring the P-O-T with you?" we whispered loudly.

"Shhhhhhh . . . I was afraid to bring it on the plane from Sydney. But I got some more here. It's way down in the stuff sack of my sleeping bag."

When it was Alexis's turn to have his bag searched, he suddenly became oversolicitous and hyper. "Do you want me to open that for you? No problem. I can undo that strap. Do you need me to unzip anything? How about this? This? No, thank *you*."

When we heaved our bags forward, however, the inspector gave us a piercing look. We had been selected for extreme searching. She carefully opened each compartment and removed our things: clothes, underwear. Then she pulled out a stack of books we were carrying and stared at the title on top. We hoped it was something like *The Future Eaters,* an irreproachable ecological history of Australasia. But when we glanced down, we saw it was *Cryptozoology A to Z: The Encyclopedia of Loch Monsters, Sasquatch, Chupacabras, and Other Authentic Mysteries of Nature.*

"Okaaay, then," she said, rapidly shoving our stuff back inside our bags. "You have a nice *trip.*" We followed Alexis and Dorothy onto the upper decks.

Ahhhh, it felt good to be on board. Behind us were the glass skyscrapers of Melbourne. In front of us open water. Our adventure was about to begin. We passed a ship's officer wearing a blue blazer with brass buttons. "Do you think this will be a smooth crossing?" we asked. The *Spirit of Tasmania* was designed to handle waves as high as twenty-five feet. It had recently replaced a high-speed, wave-smashing catamaran that—though reducing the ferry trip from fourteen hours to six—had been decommissioned after earning itself the nickname "Vomit Comet."

The officer looked at us blankly. "The waves should only be up to thirty meters tonight," he said. *Mother of Poseidon!* We started to do the math. Thirty meters was three times bigger than the Banzai Pipeline. It was *Perfect Storm* size. The officer watched our faces turn a pale shade of green. *Wait a second . . .* Then he added with the faintest suggestion of a smile, "No worries. This should be an easy night." We gulped down some Dramamine anyway.

As the *Spirit* pulled away from the dock, we stood by the railing and watched the lights of the city fade away. The sheltering arms of Port Phillip, Melbourne's harbor, stretched out for miles. It felt like we were traveling over smooth, smoky glass. If this was the badass Bass Strait, we could handle it. Of course, it wasn't. The moment the ferry passed beyond the harbor's reach, the *Spirit* began to pitch and we felt the strait's force yanking at our innards. It seemed to be sending us a message: "Don't underestimate my power, landlubbers."

The Bass Strait has been described as "rough," "capricious," and "dangerous." It's shallow and easily disturbed—nowhere more than 230 feet deep—so when waves come rolling in from either side, they grow in height and sometimes break like surf against a beach. From the west, the wind comes from the Roaring 40s, a raging circum-global system that barrels across the open ocean and reaches screaming speed when it funnels into the Bass Strait.

By the standards of the strait, we were in for a calm night. Still, when we looked down at the tossing waters lit up by the lights of the ferry, the waves looked ominous. One misstep on the slippery deck and we would be swept away, like cigarette butts down a storm drain.

To get a different perspective, we climbed up three flights of narrow metal stairs and felt the sucking pull of shifting gravity as the boat knocked us from side to side. On the top deck, the force of the wind made it hard to walk and whipped our hair into Medusan up-dos. High Plexiglas barriers ringed the perimeter. When we looked out, it was too dark to see the tempestuous chop below. And all we could hear was the howling wind. The only other people who had ventured this high were two drinking buddies, leaning into seats fastened to the deck.

Despite the Bass Strait's ferocity, we knew many animals negotiated its turbulent waters. Seals and sharks. Little blue penguins, albatrosses, and other birds that nested on the strait's many islands.

Alexis peered down toward the dark water and yelled above the wind. "You know, twelve thousand years ago, we could have taken this journey by foot," he said.

We imagined a sped-up version of geological events dating back 250 million years. At the start of the film, all the world's continents are joined together in one big mass called Pangea. Then Pangea splits in two. The great southern continent—Gondwanaland—is created. And slowly Gondwanaland begins stretching like taffy. First Africa breaks away, then South America. Now, just Antarctica and Australia are left jammed together—and Tasmania is the sticking point. Finally after much straining and pulling, Antarctica drifts off, leaving Australia and Tasmania still connected. Millions of years pass, and a series of Ice Ages begin. Australia and Tasmania remain fitfully connected by a land bridge. Aboriginal people, tigers, wallabies, and other animals travel back and forth.

Then about twelve thousand years ago, the last Ice Age ends and glaciers begin to melt. The seas rise, flooding the shallow valley between Tasmania and Melbourne and forming the Bass Strait. Tasmania is turned into an island. Nothing goes in and nothing goes out, unless it has wings or fins, for thousands of years. For the tigers, that separation turns out to be a good thing. On the mainland the tigers die out, but they live on in Tasmania—the furthest outpost beyond Wallace's Line. The film ends.

In those years during which the island was completely isolated, the only people who encountered the Tasmanian tiger or even knew it existed were the aboriginals who lived there. Geographers have calculated that about four thousand people and four thousand thylacines lived in Tasmania at any given time. This delicate balance was maintained for a remarkable ten thousand years. Along with the thylacines the island sheltered other curious animals: Tasmanian devils, unusual kangaroos, flightless birds, spiky anteaters. The Bass Strait was like a moat and Tasmania was an impregnable citadel.

In 1642 the citadel's walls were breached when the Dutch explorer Abel Tasman was commissioned to map Terra Australis Incognita (the Unknown Southland) and came across Tasmania instead. After landing, he and his crew reported seeing smoke from the fires of the aboriginals, enormous towering trees, and animal tracks on the ground "not unlike the paws of a tiger." Tasman christened the island Van Diemen's Land after his patron, Anthony van Diemen, the governor-general of the Dutch East India Company—and Van Diemen's Land was the name in use until 1856 when the island was renamed for Tasman himself.

After Tasman's departure, Van Diemen's Land was not called on again for more than a hundred years. But in the 1770s there were a rash of short visits. Captain Marion du Fresne stopped in on behalf of France in 1772, Commander Tobias Furneaux investigated for England in 1773 (as part of the expedition of Captain James Cook), and Captain Cook himself dropped by in 1777.

In 1770 Cook had claimed the Australian mainland for England, and this visit ultimately resulted in the Sydney area's being settled as a prison colony for British convicts in 1788. A few years later, when French explorers and scientists aboard the ships *Géographe* and *Naturaliste* began surveying the area around Van Diemen's Land, the British decided it was time to stake another claim. In 1803 they set up a second convict settlement on the southeast coast of Van Diemen's Land. From 1803 to 1853, about seventy thousand prisoners were transported from England and Ireland, and the island quickly earned a reputation as a cruel "convict hell." If the condemned weren't doing hard labor under threat of the lash in prisons such as Port Arthur and Macquarie Harbour, they were "assigned" to work for private landowners. As one convict ballad from the early nineteenth century warned:

The first day that we landed upon that fatal shore,
The planters they came round us full twenty score or more,
They rank'd us up like horses, and sold us out of hand,
They yok'd us unto ploughs, my boys, to plough Van Dieman's land.

The cottages that we live in were built of clod and clay,
And rotten straw for bedding, & we dare not say nay,
Our cots were fenc'd with fire, we slumber when we can,
To drive away wolves and tigers upon Van Dieman's land.

Wolves *and* tigers? The confusion was understandable. Van Diemen's Land was a strange place—unknown, unfamiliar, and filled with bewildering plants and animals. When the colonists spotted their first thylacine, they weren't sure if it was a wolf, a tiger, or *what* it was. In 1805 William Paterson, one of the island's first lieutenant governors, reported that an "animal of a truly singular and nouvel description" and "of the carnivorous and voracious tribe" was killed by dogs on the island's north coast. At the outset, the colonists couldn't agree what name to give this unfamiliar beast. Paterson thought it looked like a hyena or a "low wolf dog," and for many years it was variously dubbed hyena, hyena opossum, zebra opossum, dog-headed opossum, zebra wolf, panther, tyger, tiger wolf, striped wolf, and Tasmanian dingo. Sightings were rare in the colony's first years, and in 1810 the explorer John Oxley wrote that the tiger "flies at the approach of Man, and has not been known to do any Mischief." This status as a benign new animal didn't last long, however. The first reported killing of a sheep by a thylacine was in 1817. From that moment on, thylacines had a price on their heads.

We headed back down the metal stairs, experiencing an increasing sense of vertigo. The ship was designed to focus passengers inward. The size of a cruise ship, it had once plied the Adriatic Sea. Its built-in stabilizers and size insulated it from the roughness of the strait. And when we were inside—out of the wind—we barely noticed we were on the water. There was a bar, a restaurant, a tiny dance floor, a sitting area with TV monitors showing the Australian Open and the movie *Police Academy,* and a room filled with slot machines called the Admiral's Gaming Lounge.

When we visited the onboard gift shop, we were thrown for a loop. If Tasmanians historically had not cared much for the thylacine, they obviously liked it now. Tasmanian tiger T-shirts, jerseys, and hooded sweatshirts lined rack after rack. There were tiger snow globes, decorative plates, pewter figurines, sun visors, key chains, refrigerator magnets, collectible spoons, shot glasses, tea towels, and "stubbie" holders for keeping beer bottles cold. One long, multi-binned shelf was devoted exclusively to stuffed animal versions of the tiger. There were also numerous tiger books—from children's stories to scientific treatises. And there were even little striped jackets you could buy to dress up your dog as a thylacine. Apparently being branded extinct was no barrier to marketing.

We couldn't decide if the tchotchke-ization of the tiger was cute or disturbing. The Tasmanian devil ran a close second as the icon of choice. The devil toys had red tongues and big white fangs. Alexis quickly began criticizing the form, coloring, and texture of the stuffed animals. "What is this? This looks like a dog. What's wrong with these people?"

He picked up a book that showed a mummified version of a Tasmanian tiger. It had been found at the bottom of a cave in the Nullarbor Plain on the Australian mainland in the 1960s. The dry air and constant temperature in the cave had desiccated and preserved the body. Though the tiger was shrunken and dried-out-looking, you could still see its weird wolfy shape, several dark brown stripes, rows of sharp teeth, and even its tongue. When the tiger mummy was first found, some people thought the animal had died in recent times, which would mean that thylacines had somehow survived on the mainland. But when scientists radiocarbon-dated the mummy, they discovered it was more than four thousand years old.

Alexis pointed at the photo. "I have a mummified fox that looks exactly like that."

"Where'd you get that?" we asked.

"It was a present."

We spent the rest of the evening sampling Tasmanian wines from the bar on the foredeck. When we went to return our glasses, a tipsy woman at the bar was whispering to a friend and leaning her head toward Alexis and Dorothy. "Those two there. Wasn't he one of Carrie's boyfriends? And she's the rich one. Not Miranda, but—"

"Charlotte."

"That's the one."

They had mistaken them for actors on *Sex and the City*.

Around midnight, we decided to retire to our cabin and fell asleep immediately. After what seemed like twenty minutes, a tiny intercom positioned next to our heads tinnily blared, "We have arrived. It is six A.M." This announcement was repeated every few seconds until we were finally rousted.

Looking and feeling haggard, we trailed behind Alexis and Dorothy to the outer deck and looked out expectantly as the ferry approached the island and the city of Devonport. In the distance, mist shrouded a low mountain. In the foreground were a medium-sized industrial port, a McDonald's, and a multiplex cinema.

Alexis looked at the McDonald's. "We may have more to fear from globalization than we do from land leeches," he said.

Straggling off the ferry, we passed an old-looking beagle. This canine cop was the last line of defense in the effort to stop the importation of exotic species. As we filed past, he wagged his tail and panted at us. Alexis smiled at the beagle and patted the sleeping bag strapped to the bottom of his backpack. When we were just out of earshot he muttered, "That dog should retire if it can't sniff out this shit. He should be put out to doggy pasture."

6. DAY OF THE DEAD

We had arrived in Tasmania, the land of the tiger. And along with intense fatigue, we felt a sudden sense of urgency.

"Alexis," we said blearily. "We need to get out into the bush . . . to walk where the tiger walked . . . watch its stripes melting into the forest." Our eyes must have looked slightly wild.

"Wake up!" snapped Alexis. "You're babbling. You need some strong coffee." He pointed at a tour bus parked next to the ferry with a picture of a thylacine on the back. "See. The thylacine's right there. Go commune."

"I wonder if there's anywhere good to eat breakfast," Dorothy mused. She looked fresh as a daisy in a new pair of hiphugger jeans she had bought specially for our trip.

We went to pick up coffees in the ferry terminal. As we walked off, we observed Alexis beginning a series of stretching exercises. They looked like yoga positions crossed with the moves of a contortionist. He laid his palms flat on the ground and stuck his butt in the air. Then he tucked a foot behind his ear. The people on the thylacine tour bus looked on with interest.

After getting some caffeine, we found the car hire agency and rented a big white four-wheel-drive Mitsubishi Pajero. Then we drove with Alexis and Dorothy to the Backpacker's Barn, a local camping store. We had agreed to meet Chris Vroom there after he flew in from Melbourne, and we needed to purchase a few supplies. The proprietor of the barn greeted us heartily. "Welcome to paradise," he shouted in our faces. The veins in his forehead looked like they would pop with enthusiasm. "Tasmania *is* paradise," he added. We weren't ready for this so early in the morning.

His name was Carl Clayton, and inside the store, he kept a white sulphur-crested cockatoo as a pet. This is a raucous species of parrot given to decibel-bashing screeches. But Carl's cockatoo also knew how to talk, and it was one of those parrots that seemed always to be making snide remarks in our direction. While we were browsing amid the flashlights and water bottles, we thought we caught it saying, "Polly wanna—SCREW YOU!"

We bought some topographic maps and a compass. Most compasses made in the Northern Hemisphere don't work properly Down Under. The compass needle, which is counterweighted for use in the north, bogs down and doesn't rotate. We didn't want to risk getting lost: the Tasmanian bush is full of hazards. You could be fanged by a tiger snake, jabbed by a venomous bull ant, drained of your blood by land leeches, chewed on by a Tasmanian devil, or even spurred by a rogue platypus. More common (*much* more common) though was getting lost on a hot summer's day while hiking and dying of hypothermia when Tasmania's mercurial weather suddenly turned freezing.

Alexis didn't seem to share our concerns about the hazards of the bush. In fact, he looked like all his problems had been solved now that he'd brought his stash safely into Tasmania. He bought a lighter that looked like a tiny blowtorch to use with his pot pipe. Dorothy bought hundreds of dollars' worth of camping equipment—sleeping bag, inflatable sleeping pad, backpack, hiking boots, thermal socks, and a thick woolen shirt.

As we made our purchases, Carl goggled at us and waggled his head. "Am I your first two-headed Tasmanian?"

Two heads? We looked at him blankly.

"You came from the mainland, didn't you? Didn't they tell you that Tasmanians were supposed to have two heads?" He seemed disappointed.

We knew mainlanders typecast Tasmanians as being backward and inbred—kind of like Appalachian hillbillies. But we weren't aware it was a stereotype Tasmanians promoted. We wondered if Carl would appreciate hearing that several people on the mainland had advised us to "watch out for Tasmanians with six fingers."

Carl seemed to forgive our ignorance and informed us that in addition to running the barn, he was an environmental activist. He was working to get a nearby rain forest protected. It was called the Tarkine, and he had a novel idea for preserving it. Under his plan, the Tarkine would not only be maintained as a roadless area, it would also be a "no go" area. People—even hikers, his own clientele—would not be permitted to enter the Tarkine under any circumstances. "Humans," he informed us in a low voice, "are dirty, dirty, dirty animals." We were inclined to agree and promised to stay out of his rain forest.

When Chris showed up with a green compact he had rented, we suggested that he, Dorothy, and Alexis take the day off and explore some of the north coast's beaches. We told them we would scout ahead and meet up with them the following day. We wanted to get our heads together to think about the best way to pursue our quarry. Plus we had to see a man about a devil.

From Devonport we drove onto the Bass Highway, a long stretch of two-lane blacktop that runs along the northern coast of Tasmania. Tasmanians, like all Australians, drive on the left side of the road, a practice we found disorienting even while driving in a straight line. Every time we signaled to turn, the windshield wipers came on.

Our destination was the far northwest corner of the island, and once we left the port cities behind, we saw nothing but rolling pastureland, occasional glimpses of the Bass Strait, cows, and a few sheep. The only other attractions worth noting were the huge logging trucks that barreled toward us and the numerous roadkills—many of which we pulled over to examine. Though unable to identify any of the flattened remains, we perceived that most had fur, four legs, and a tail. These creatures had literally been pounded into the pavement. We diligently checked the bodies for stripes, but there weren't any as far as we could tell.

Back at the ferry terminal, we had picked up a copy of the local *Visitor Gazette*, which tried to put a positive spin on the roadside carnage:

> *One of the few sad things about this beautiful district is the roadkill.... The animals are sometimes impossible to avoid.... It is not because the locals are heartless or cruel with no compassion for wild things; they despair as much as you will. However, nature wastes nothing and these animals in their turn provide sustenance for Tasmanian devils, crows, hawks, and ravens, which are continually cleaning up.... One animal's death is another's life. Nature's way.*

We weren't keen to participate in "nature's way." Each time we drove away from one of our roadside autopsies, we scanned the highway for animals that could end up as flattened fauna. But no Tasmanian wildlife was waiting to dash beneath our wheels. In fact, the only creatures we saw were ravens picking at the flesh of animals that were already dead. We identified them as native Tasmanian forest ravens, *Corvus tasmanicus,* and checked them off in our bird book.

As for the rest of the scenery, it was lullingly monotonous. Brown pastures baked beneath the summer sun. Hereford cattle swished their tails. Except for the occasional splattered beast, nothing struck us as stopworthy until we came across a farm field filled with strange-looking plants. Bloated, anemic-blue bulbs floated atop unusually long brown stalks. A sign on a low fence read, "DANGER. KEEP OUT. TRESPASSERS PROSECUTED. ILLEGAL USE OF CROP MAY CAUSE DEATH."

The plants were opium poppies—the kind used to make heroin and morphine—and the bulbs were seed heads very close to harvest time. A field of the same crop in Afghanistan or Asia's Golden Triangle would draw down the wrath of international drug agents. But this was legal. Tasmania had a United Nations sanction to grow poppies for making medical-grade morphine and codeine. The island produces about 40 percent of the world's supply.

The poppy field spread out before us like a blue mist. Just a little slash in one of the bulbous seed heads would produce a sap that would soon harden into highly potent opium. We would see plenty of tigers under those conditions. We were tempted to lie down in the field and take a long, opium-induced nap. But we kept driving—mile after lonely mile.

As we passed signs for the towns of Black River, Smithton, and Marrawah (and roads named Devil's Elbow and Dismal), the pastures gave way to stands of forest dominated by eucalyptus trees. Signs of civilization dwindled to the vanishing point. We had nearly run out of highway, when we reached a ramshackle farmhouse, standing alone at the side of the road and surrounded by brush. A man in a polo shirt, blue slacks, and Blundstone boots was waiting out front. He was accompanied by an excited gray dog.

"Meet Scratch," he said. "I'm Geoff King."

Geoff was a sturdily built man, with wavy, auburn hair graying slightly at the temples. His face was red from being out in the sun, and it was immediately noticeable that he was blind in one eye. The blind eye drifted to the left, and it gave him a waggish expression—as if he was thinking of a good joke.

He ran his good eye over us. "You look a bit done in," he said.

We explained that we weren't used to driving on the left side of the road, and were actually feeling a bit dizzy. He congratulated us on not crashing. "Good on ya. You did a wonderful job."

We had heard Geoff King was an expert at finding Tasmanian devils in their wild state. In the absence of the tiger, the devil earned the title of being the largest marsupial carnivore in the world.

He inspected our four-wheel drive. "That's a lovely bus," he said. "If you're not too tired we could take a ride over to my property."

"Would you want to drive?" we suggested.

"Absolutely . . . mind if we just put this in the back?" "This" was a black plastic recycling bin—the size of a big milk crate—covered by a tarp. Dozens of flies swirled around it. We looked at it apprehensively. "It's for the devils," Geoff explained.

As he lifted the mysterious black box into the back of the Pajero, we attempted to ignore the rank odor emanating from inside.

Geoff drove the Pajero down to a T where the highway ended and turned left onto a narrow strip of blacktop. "This lonely outpost is the Arthur River Road," he said. At first the road was paved, but it soon turned to gravel. As we crunched along, Geoff explained that he hadn't always been a devil specialist. He had been a cattle farmer. In fact, the King family had been running cattle in this far corner of Tasmania for more than one hundred years. Geoff and his brother, Perry, were the fifth generation of Kings to work the land.

Geoff, however, was a strange bird by the standards of most people in this farming community. For one thing, he was more interested in wildlife than livestock. For years, he tried to run cattle on his family's coastal property with an eye toward conservation—attempting to reduce the cattle's impact on the fragile foreshore and sensitive seaside plants. But in 1997, he decided to go his own way. He gave up on running cattle, split the family property with his brother, and turned most of his half (830 acres) into a wildlife preserve. Once the cattle were removed, the habitat started to revive—and all sorts of creatures moved in.

Geoff would camp out on his property at night and watch wallabies, wombats, and devils. With income from the cattle gone, he started offering wildlife tours—and he focused on devils, black-furred, four-legged marsupials that screamed like banshees in the dead of night. These fierce animals lived only on the island of Tasmania, having been driven extinct on the mainland several hundred years ago—probably, like the thylacine, by the dingo. Geoff learned the devils' habits, what they liked to eat, and how best to observe them. Until then, he had never really seen a devil up close. "Most of the time you only see them dead on the road or running across the road very quickly. Just being able to sit down in the darkness with these animals and learn the males from females has been terrific."

We decided this was a good time to raise the tiger question. "You don't ever see any tigers while you're out looking for devils, do you?"

"Nahhh," he said. "But you are in tiger country."

Northwestern Tasmania had been the location of some of the most credible tiger sightings in recent years. It was also the place where a bounty was first put on the tiger's head.

In 1825, Geoff said, the Van Diemen's Land Company—a London-based concern—was granted hundreds of thousands of acres on which to raise sheep by the British crown. The company's main holding was Woolnorth, a huge parcel that made up the entire northwest tip of the island. Convicts from the island's jails were brought in to herd sheep, and contract workers from England (including Geoff's great-great-grandfather) were shipped in on long, perilous ocean voyages to help run the station.

In its first few years, the Van Diemen's Land Company suffered huge stock losses. Its sheep were killed off by bad weather and disease. And some were killed by animals—wild dogs, Tasmanian tigers, possibly devils. But tigers were targeted as the main culprits. It was a typical story. The British and their descendants had systematically gone after the top predator in most places they lived—particularly if it was considered a threat to livestock. In 1830, the company offered a bounty of 5 shillings for each male tiger and 7 shillings for each female tiger. The bounty would be increased to 10 and 12 shillings respectively as more tigers were killed. In 1836, the company hired its first "tiger man"—the first in a long series—whose job was to help eradicate the animal. Eventually, other groups of landowners began setting up their own organizations to pay tiger bounties, and the Tasmanian government set up an island-wide bounty system in 1888, paying £1 for each dead adult tiger.

As the bounty years wore on through the latter half of the nineteenth century and into the twentieth, tigers were seen less and less in the settled areas. In fact, they became so rare that if one was captured or shot, people would come from miles around to take a look.

One of the most famous photos of the Tasmanian tiger was taken in the nearby community of Mawbanna in 1930. It shows a young man, named Wilf Batty, holding a shotgun and squatting on his knees next to the stiff body of a tiger. The body is leaned up against a fence and the tiger's eyes are closed. It's believed that this was the last tiger ever to be shot in Tasmania.

"What about the sightings?" we asked. "What about all the people who say they've seen them?"

"I've spoken to people who say they've seen them or heard them. Lots of people believe the tiger's still around," Geoff said.

"What do you think?"

"I'd have to say that based on the evidence—or lack of it—that it's probably gone. But then you never know." He thought for a minute. "Tomorrow I'll take you to a place where there was a famous tiger sighting. It was taken very seriously because the fellow who reported it was a wildlife expert employed by the government. It sparked an extended search."

Geoff stopped and engaged the four-wheel drive. Then he made a sharp right and drove off the gravel road straight into the bush and onto a narrow, barely discernible track. As the Pajero lurched forward into a shallow sandy ditch, we remembered the woman at the car rental agency saying something about not taking the vehicle on unmapped roads.

As the Pajero squeezed through a corridor of tiny-leaved tea trees, rough branches scraped along the sides of the car and poked in through the open windows. The sandy track was rutted, dipping and cresting in a series of small waves. As we jounced along, we felt like we were back on the pitching ferry. Geoff worked the wheel in ways we had never imagined.

"You're a really good driver," we said, our teeth rattling.

"Well, I have a bit of a reputation. I used to be the designated driver after parties and other spirited events."

"You don't drink?"

"I do. But if you only have one eye, you can get pissed, and you won't see two lines going down the middle of the road. No double vision."

Reaching a small crest, Geoff jammed on the brakes and ran around to the back of the vehicle. In every direction, the knobby landscape was covered with tufts of native grass.

Geoff hauled out the foul-smelling black bin, removed the tarp, and pulled up a limp creature. He held it up by the tail to give us a better look. A patch of dried blood marked its chest. We were by turns fascinated and revolted, but we tried to play it cool. "What the hell is that?" we blurted.

"It's a pademelon."

"What kind of melon?" we asked, swatting away a few flies.

"It's a Tasmanian pademelon—also called a rufous wallaby. It's a small type of kangaroo, or macropod. This one was killed on the road we just drove down. I picked it up last night."

He laid the pademelon down on the sandy track. We studied its soft brown-gray fur, and its long, carrot-shaped tail. Its head unfortunately was too squashed to give any sense of its original shape.

We practiced the name, muttering "pademelon, paddy-melon, pad-eee—mell-uhn."

Geoff took a length of rope and tied it around the pademelon's legs and neck. He tied the other end to the back of the four-wheel drive. Then we drove off along the rutted track with the carcass bouncing along behind us.

"What we're doing is creating a scent trail," Geoff said. Tasmanian devils, he explained, can smell the perfume of death from a mile away. So by laying down the alluring scent of Eau de Dead Pademelon, we would draw devils—out on a night of scavenging—to follow this road, too. "Devils like to hunt along streams and creeks, and they treat roads the same. So they'll wander along this track, follow this scent trail we're dragging—and know that food will be out there."

"Is this what they like to eat?" We glanced back at the pademelon.

"Devils are carnivores, or meat eaters," he said. "But they prefer to feed on animals that are already dead."

"Do they ever hunt?"

"They can. Younger devils hunt more than older ones. A young devil coming out of the den could survive on a feed of moths for a night. They eat quite a variety of foods. Moths. Lizard eggs. Wallabies . . . Americans. They'll devour a carcass bones and all."

Being dined on by devils is actually one of the things Tasmanians fear about the bush. Not really that devils would attack you—but that they might eat your body if you died in a remote area. There's also the vague concern that a devil might try to gnaw on you if you were injured.

"Naaaah," Geoff said when we asked about this. But then he added, "Devils certainly have a very good sense of when other animals are weak and infirm though." With their incredible noses, they follow or track sick animals—sometimes showing up before an animal is quite dead. He paused and lowered his voice to a stage whisper. "That's why we call them the auditors of the dark."

He poked his head out the window and abruptly stopped the Pajero. "This is encouraging. I can see Tassie devil tracks here in the sand."

We pulled out one of our guidebooks—*Tracks, Scats and Other Traces: A Field Guide to Australian Mammals* by Barbara Triggs—and turned to the "Tracks" section. It said, "The Tasmanian devil has squarish footprints, distinctive because the four forward-pointing toes that are visible on the front and hind foot tracks are evenly spaced and level." The tracks in the sand looked like little bear claw prints.

We walked around to the back of the Pajero to see if the pademelon was still attached. Some of it was. We wondered when we might see an animal with all its parts.

"At night, we'd have seen two hundred animals by this time—wallabies, bandicoots, possums, wombats," Geoff said. "This is wonderful habitat for devils because there's so much food."

"So most of the animals in Tasmania come out after dark?"

"That's their time."

It was hard to believe we were in a wildlife paradise. Besides the dead pademelon, there wasn't an animal in sight.

Geoff drove on through the pale grasses until we reached the coast and saw waves crashing against a rocky beach. Fractured outcrops of pink quartzite jutted from the sea and formed ramparts on the shoreline.

"Welcome to King's Run," Geoff said. His property stretched along three and a half miles of undeveloped coastline. It was stunning. An enormous block of bright blue sky hovered over a sea of beach grasses waving in the wind. Blue-green waves shot into fountains of spray and foam as they broke against the rose-colored rocks.

Some of the outcrops were as big as houses and covered with multicolored lichens—living organisms that are a combination of algae and fungi. They were rust red, burned orange, and pale green. Usually these vivid encrustations are considered a sign of good air quality.

Geoff confirmed that this was true. He instructed us to look toward the west, past the rocks and surf. "See anything?" he asked.

"The ocean?"

"Heaps of ocean. If you set off from here, you wouldn't hit land again until you reached South America." From Geoff's it's seven thousand miles across the water to Argentina, one of the longest stretches of open water in the world. It's swept by the Roaring 40s, the powerful western wind that confounds ships and blows the air clean.

On the old Woolnorth property at a coastal headland called Cape Grim, the Australian government runs the Baseline Air Pollution Station. At times, Cape Grim has registered the purest air in the world.

Geoff left us to explore the rocky, lichen-encrusted shoreline. The beach was covered with small, swirling shells; huge strips of brown and green kelp; abalone shells inlaid with silvery mother-of-pearl; and cuttle bones. The air smelled fresh and briny, with a note of decaying seaweed. Inland, eucalyptus trees, bent by ocean gusts, lined a low cliff. We walked into the tufts of grass behind the beach. The landscape was windswept and desolate, and it seemed devoid of wildlife. But then we began to look more closely. In between the tussocks of grass—everywhere—were piles of animal scat.

We pulled out our copy of *Tracks, Scats and Other Traces* and read from the introduction: "For many people who visit the wild places of Australia the mammals that live there are an unknown presence, rarely seen. But the signs of the presence are all around, if one can read them." The signs included tracks, scratchings, scrapings, burrows, bones, and scats.

The abundance of scat led us to conclude that this place was profoundly alive. We had just worked this out when Geoff reappeared on the beach, wearing a black, full-body wetsuit and brandishing a sharp, serrated knife. He looked like a murderous seal. "Can't you just imagine a tiger walking along here?" he shouted.

Despite the chilly water temperature, he was about to leap into the sea in search of abalone. Abalone is the most expensive shellfish in the world—and one of Tasmania's most lucrative exports. Geoff dove into a salty pool ringed by rocks and came back with five big black shellfish. Each was the size of a tea saucer. We began to salivate.

"We'll eat well tonight," he promised, prying open the shells and cutting the flesh free from the pearly interiors.

Before taking off from the beach, Geoff unhitched what was left of the dead pademelon from the back of the Pajero and left it for the local devils to snack on. "I only take out little bits of food on these nights," he said. "So we don't give a complete feed to an animal. It just lures them into the area. Tomorrow night, after the rest of Team Thylacine arrives, we'll lay down another scent trail, conceal ourselves in a hide, and—if all goes well—watch the devils come down to feed."

Just before we left, we saw a pair of long-legged shorebirds flying across the beach. As they disappeared, we heard them calling. *Heh, heh-heh-heh-heh-heh*. It sounded like a grating, staccato laugh. "Those are masked lapwings," Geoff said. They were nesting on the beach. "When you hear them calling out at night, it might mean a devil's approaching."

Not far from Geoff's house, we saw a small prickly object in the middle of the road.

"Wouldn't want anyone to hit that," he said, pulling the Pajero to the side.

The prickly object was in motion, slowly ambling across the blacktop. "That's an echidna. It's a bit like your porcupine."

The echidna was a hunchbacked creature—about sixteen inches long—with a hairless needle of a snout. Its back was covered with long black hairs and white spikes.

Early settlers and explorers in this part of the world, not knowing what to make of the animals they encountered, often named them for creatures they were already familiar with. The echidna was originally called a porcupine because of its spiky back and sometimes a spiny anteater because, like South American anteaters, it had a long sticky tongue that darted out to eat ants and termites.

The name "echidna," given to the animal by scientists, comes from Greek mythology. In ancient myth, Echidna was a hybrid monster—half beautiful woman and half snake—in other words, half mammal and half reptile. That seemed like an apt description for this animal. Though the echidna is placed firmly in the mammal camp (class: *Mammalia*), it has some reptilian characteristics. For example, a female echidna does not give birth to live offspring but actually lays an egg—a leathery, soft egg like a turtle's or snake's—and she lays it inside a pouch on her own belly. The egg incubates in this little pouch and when it hatches, the baby echidna (called a puggle) is only the size of a jellybean. The developing puggle remains in the pouch for two or three months until the growth of spikes makes it necessary for the mother to evict it.

Echidna sexual relationships are among the most unusual in the mammal world. At the beginning of the breeding season in winter, a single female echidna may be followed for weeks by as many as ten males in single file, each hoping to father the one puggle she will have that year. This strange procession is known as an echidna train, and the males are usually lined up from largest (at the front of the line) to smallest (serving as the caboose). After weeks of rejecting their advances, the female will finally select one male—usually the largest—although rival males may need to engage in a head-butting contest in order to defend their ascendancy. Mating includes lengthy foreplay during which the male probes the female for several hours with his snout and strokes her spines, followed by belly-to-belly coupling to avoid mutual spiking—an event that can last as long as three hours. Afterward, the male and female go their own ways, with the female preparing to lay her egg and the male possibly joining another echidna train in the hopes of mating again.

The echidna is a charming and enigmatic animal—and one that we gathered, by the calm manner of its rolling gait, is not easily intimidated. Geoff waited until the echidna had safely crossed the road, and then we got out to take a peek. It must have sensed us coming, but instead of running away, it showed off a simple but impressive defense strategy. As if it were on an elevator, the echidna seemed to literally sink inches down into the ground. "It's digging in," Geoff said. "Not much can get at it now." The echidna had used its sharp-clawed feet to burrow rapidly downward, and all that remained of it on the surface was its spiky back. It looked like a huge ball of black yarn stuffed with knitting needles.

Although echidnas are sometimes killed on the road, they are the only Tasmanian animals that can have revenge on a hit-and-run driver. In return for being sent to echidna heaven, they can retaliate with a spike in the tire.

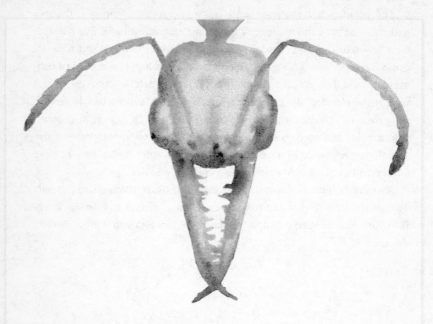

Geoff had invited us to spend our first night in Tasmania at the King family home. His wife and two young sons were away on vacation, so he had the one-story sprawling wooden farmhouse to himself. When we went inside, we saw that his living room was lined with an assortment of natural history ephemera. A plaster cast of a Tasmanian devil's footprint. Skulls of various animals. Seashells and dried-out sea sponges. Driftwood painted with intricate designs. There was also a small library of books on Tasmanian flora and fauna. He had field guides on birds, mammals, shells, reptiles, trees, wildflowers, and rain forest fungi. There were also books on aboriginal history, as well as a government report dating from 1980 called *The Tasmanian Tiger,* which analyzed the possibility of the tiger's survival. It was full of charts and graphs.

In the kitchen, Geoff cut the cream-colored, tonguelike abalone meat into thin pieces and quickly sautéed them in butter, with a touch of fresh garlic. He presented us with two small plates. "I wanted you to taste the most tender bits," he said. Then he returned to the kitchen to warm up some homemade curry. We gobbled down the abalone in between sips of sauvignon blanc we had bought in Devonport. The abalone's clamlike flesh was ambrosial—sweet and meaty, with a hint of the ocean it had just been pulled from. After these appetizers, Geoff joined us at the table, bringing over plates of chicken curry and rice. He had prepared the curry using a free-range chicken, or "chook" as he called it.

After a few bites, we reminded him that the other members of our expedition would be arriving the next day at noon.

"Now, who are they exactly?" Geoff asked.

Alexis, we explained, was an artist. He was going to be making images of Tasmanian wildlife. Dorothy was an art critic and Alexis's new love interest. And Chris . . . who was Chris? We didn't really know him.

Geoff stopped eating. "He's not an ax murderer, is he?"

"No, he's a wealthy art collector from Manhattan."

"Oh well, that could be more dangerous."

After dinner, we switched over to a carton of Shiraz that Geoff brought out from his pantry and watched a cricket match that went on for hours—which still wasn't long enough for us to understand the rules. When we finally jumped into our sleeping bags around 2:30 A.M., we discovered that the guestroom had been invaded by an army of small brown beetles. They made soothing clicking noises and occasionally plopped down on us throughout the night.

In the morning, we drove over to have a cup of tea with Geoff's mother, Dulcie. In front of her white clapboard ranch house—which was as isolated as Geoff's—she kept peacocks as pets. Four small brown peachicks pecked the ground in her front yard.

"Aren't they lovers?" she cooed.

She was a wiry, energetic woman, about seventy years old, sportily dressed in black shorts, striped ankle socks, and sandals. Geoff had told us that in her twenties, Dulcie had been the all-Tasmanian badminton champion and came close to representing Australia in the Commonwealth Games.

She fixed us tea with lemon from her lemon tree. And we sat down in a room decorated with framed drawings of horses. (A family-owned horse had won the Tasmanian pacing championship in 1979.) Geoff had hoped his mother would have some stories to tell us about the Tasmanian tiger. But when she heard the word "tiger," she said, "Ooooh, the tigers are traveling at this time of year—the tiger snakes."

Our ears perked up. Getting lost, land leeches, and hypothermia were high on our list of bush dangers. But tiger snakes were higher.

"My first memory is of snakes," Dulcie told us. One day when she was a young girl, she was helping her brothers drive cattle through a field when a tiger snake bit her. "It banged like a hammer on my leg," she said, pointing to her thigh. "It just stood up and struck. The poison went off on my trousers. I remember they were new blue jeans."

The snake's fangs hadn't broken the skin, but her family called in the doctor anyway. "He said even a little bit could do you in. If you stay calm, you can last eighteen hours, but if you run around . . ." She trailed off.

After finishing our tea, we all went for a drive. Geoff took backroads to the top of a nearby hill, where we had a panoramic view of rolling green pasture and stands of native forest. Occasionally, we could make out a lone eucalyptus tree, with its angular skeleton of forking branches and blue-green leaves growing in flat tufts on top. These oddball trees were the epitome of Down Under.

"What we have here," said Geoff, "is a very English pasture system grafted onto a very Tasmanian landscape." English ryegrass and clover grew fitfully in the fragile sandy soil. Tasmanian farmers are highly protective of these pasture grasses, surrounding them with fences to stop native animals from grazing—and frequently resorting to shooting.

On the way down the hill, we drove along a shady, wooded road. Geoff pointed out some huge gray-barked eucalyptuses. "Smithton peppermint gums," he said. There were also dark, thick-trunked wattle trees called blackwoods with heavy spreading branches covered in long green leaves. "Very good for making furniture," Dulcie commented.

As we drove, we passed a tract of forestland. Something terrible had happened: the land was a black hole of uprooted tree stumps, gouged earth, and small scattered limbs. It looked like it had been bombed.

"What happened?" we asked.

"It's a clear-fell," Geoff said. "It's crown land—it belongs to the government. They're wood chipping it for export to Japan. The wood chips are used for making paper." He pointed out a few remaining piles of branches, broken logs, and brush. "They pushed those together to be burned."

"This was always my favorite road," his mother added sadly. "We would drive cattle down here through these lovely trees and listen to the birdsong."

At the bottom of the hill, Geoff opened a gate in a wire fence and drove into a green pasture filled with Dulcie's cows. Geoff made a bellowing noise and dozens of Black Anguses and brown-and-white Herefords began following the Pajero.

Most of this grazing land, he said, had been painstakingly cleared by hand by the early settlers. There had always been a history of logging and land clearing in the Northwest. But that was when trees were felled by determined men using axes and double-handed crosscut saws. "A lot of Tasmanians were in these isolated areas, and they would chip away at the land year after year." These days logging had a more industrial quality. The logging companies used chainsaws, bulldozers, mechanical log loaders, and excavators. After clear-cutting a parcel of forest, they would torch the land, burning off the remaining debris. It didn't seem to matter if the local community was opposed to a forest being cut down. The government had a quota system—a certain amount of public forest could be chopped each year, including a certain percentage of old-growth forest. Now, the logging companies were chopping the trees as fast as they could. Geoff said it was as if they had switched the bounty from the thylacine's head and put it on the forests.

By the time we got back to Geoff's house, the other members of Team Thylacine had already arrived. Chris was playing with Scratch, while Alexis and Dorothy were leaning against the hood of Chris's car. They looked sleek and tanned from their day at the beach.

Geoff looked relieved. "Well, this isn't too bad," he whispered, glancing sideways at Alexis. "I've never met a New York artist before. I was expecting a seedy character with a goatee and leather pants. These people look relatively normal."

Everyone shook hands, and Chris presented Geoff with four bottles of wine.

"Welcome to the Northwest," said Geoff.

"The roadkill here is unbelievable," Alexis said as if he were raving about the quality of the local tomatoes.

Dorothy made a face. "He made us stop to photograph them all."

We asked Alexis if he had been able to identify any of the creatures.

"No, but they all had a marsupial gesture."

He got out his digital camera and showed us a rogue's gallery of dead animals.

"This one's completely flattened," he said, clicking on a torn-up object we would have taken for a shredded bit of old carpet if there hadn't been bone and muscle protruding. "It must have been run over by one of those logging trucks."

He continued to click. "This one's a triptych—it's in three sections. I think it's some sort of kangaroo-like creature. And this one is totally unfamiliar. It's got a furry tail though. Any ideas about this one, Geoff?"

Geoff had a look. "Hard to say, really."

Alexis clicked through a couple more portraits. Then he put down his camera. "What about tigers, Geoff? Have there been any tiger roadkills?"

"None that have been documented."

In a place suffused with flattened fauna, the absence of a single, verified tiger roadkill in more than half a century was used by skeptics as more proof that the tiger was extinct. True believers had their own argument, however. The surviving tiger population had simply become adept at dodging cars.

That night at sunset, we would return to Geoff's property in an attempt to see Tasmanian devils. Meanwhile, Geoff suggested we all head out to the scene of the famous tiger sighting he had mentioned the day before. The sighting had been made by a man named Hans Naarding about twelve miles north of Geoff's in a remote area called Togari. On the way, we stopped at a small roadside store, where we picked up the local newspaper, the *Advocate*. The big story was that a man had gone wood chopping and never came back. There was a search party out looking for him. We wondered if the devils had eaten him.

Alongside the newspaper, the store was selling a black-and-white charity calendar, titled the "Men of Marrawah." Mr. April was the proprietor himself, a bald and beefy gentleman, standing naked and stocking grocery shelves. Mr. September was Geoff's brother, Perry, angling for fish in only his birthday suit. For a small town, Marrawah had a surprising number of pinup boys. We ordered some sandwiches and picked up bottles of water and a few Cadbury chocolate bars. Mr. April was very solicitous about our sandwiches. He didn't think we'd want lettuce because it wasn't quite fresh. But he did put on sweet purple beets. It was hard not to imagine him nude while he was spreading the bread with butter.

We leafed through the calendar looking for Geoff's photo, expecting to see a caption that read, "Geoff King and Pademelon: The Naked and the Dead." But he wasn't in there.

"How come you're not in the calendar?" Dorothy asked, flashing him a knockout smile.

"I'd have loved to," he responded. "But I wasn't invited."

We thumbed through the newspapers and found a full-page ad for Tasmanian-made Cascade Premium Lager. It showed a bottle of beer with a pair of tigers prominently displayed on the label. Under a blurb that said "Out of the Wilderness . . . Pure Enjoyment" was a thylacine lapping suggestively from a misty, jungle-like stream.

The island was filled with such representations. The sides of tour buses like the Tassie Link and Tigerline Coaches were painted with stylized tigers. Tourist brochures were filled with them. Tasmania's state cricket team was named the Tigers, and their cricket caps were emblazoned with aggressive, toothy-looking thylacines. We reached into one of our pockets and pulled out a 50-cent piece.

"Alexis! Heads or tails?"

"Tails," he said, then added with a trace of wariness, "What are we flipping for?"

"A Cadbury bar."

We twirled the coin into the air and it landed on heads: the profile of the Queen of England. We turned the coin over. Tails was two thylacines standing on their hind legs and holding up the Tasmanian coat of arms.

Alexis bought us a chocolate bar from Mr. April. But then he upped the ante. "That's nothing," he said. "What about all the license plates?"

License plates? We walked around to the back of the Pajero. Behind the license number was the Tasmanian government logo, a tiger in a circle of green, peeking out of the grass. The thylacine had been right behind us all the time, and we hadn't even noticed.

We headed north toward the Naarding site and after about ten miles, Geoff turned off the highway onto an unpaved logging road that cut through a low-growing eucalyptus forest. Eucalyptus leaves have a waxy coating that reflects sunlight and produces a hazy glimmer. At first it's dazzling, but after a while the reflection tires the eyes. We began to feel sleepy and dazed. White dead spars poked up through the canopy, reminders of an older forest, one that was taller. As we drove, the Pajero kicked up a thick cloud of dust, and we lost sight of Chris's car behind us until Geoff rolled to a stop at a deserted fork in the middle of the trees.

"He was parked right here," said Geoff, pointing at a triangular wedge of land where the roads met.

We waited for the dust to settle before stepping out into the crossroads. Beneath our feet, the sandy soil was the consistency and color of flour, with particles as fine. A light wind rose, covering us all in a thin layer of white.

"The story is that Naarding was out doing a snipe survey," Geoff continued. "He got up in the middle of the night to take a piss, and then saw a tiger. He claimed he had time to count the stripes and that he saw its testicles as it retreated."

That had been in 1982. Hans Naarding was a wildlife biologist, originally from South Africa, assigned to do fieldwork in the Northwest. He said he had parked at this isolated spot for the night and planned to sleep in his vehicle. It was raining hard. Around 2:00 A.M., he woke up and, out of habit, swept the area with a small spotlight. Through the rain just twenty feet away, he saw a tiger standing, its eyes shining yellow in the light. He observed it long enough to count twelve stripes on its back and to see it open its jaws and flash its teeth. But when he reached for his camera, the tiger disappeared into the forest.

Naarding's story wasn't that different from hundreds of other sightings that had been reported, except for the fact that Naarding worked for Tasmania's Parks and Wildlife Service—and a lot of his colleagues believed him.

The Parks and Wildlife Service is charged with the protection of rare and endangered animals, and it seemed imperative to make a thorough investigation. If the tiger still survived in this remote part of Tasmania, perhaps it could be saved from extinction. But the wildlife officials didn't want to stir up a lot of publicity. Newspaper reporters, TV cameras, and tiger buffs of all kinds would pour into the Northwest if they got wind of Naarding's story. And that wouldn't be very scientific. It would be best, they decided, to conduct the search in secret. A wildlife officer named Nick Mooney (the same one whom we had called for advice before leaving the States) was chosen to investigate.

In the months after the sighting, Nick began a methodical search that covered more than 250 square kilometers of forest, farmland, and coast around the area of the Naarding sighting. He created sand traps in an attempt to document the impression of a tiger footprint; he monitored camera traps along animal trails in the hopes of snapping the tiger's picture; and he baited traps with animal meat. He examined countless scats and rooted out possible dens. And he also ran into Geoff King.

Fairly early in the investigation, Geoff wandered into Nick while he was doing fieldwork. Being a chatty type, Geoff began questioning him about what he was working on. Nick was vague. Not long after that, Geoff ran into Nick again at the local pub. He went up to him, slapped him on the back, and said, "So, have you found the Tassie tiger yet?"

"I'd only been joking," Geoff told us. "But he pulled me aside and said, 'You've found me out, mate. Would you mind keeping it a secret?' I was flabbergasted."

Nick's search was spread over fifteen months in 1982 and 1983. Sometimes Geoff would accompany Nick on his investigations. One method was simply driving around at night, shining a spotlight into the darkness and hoping to see a pair of eyes shining back at you. Some animals' eyes reflect yellow in the dark, others green or blue, and others red. Most wildlife experts in Tasmania can identify an animal by eye shine alone. Although Naarding had said the eyes of his tiger had flashed yellow in the dark, no one could confirm the color of a Tasmanian tiger's eye shine. So Nick and Geoff would drive around looking for something unusual gleaming out of the night.

One night, they saw something. "Nick said, 'That's not quite right.' And we began to get excited. It was a very unusual color. We crept up on those eyes in the dark, so as not to scare the animal off—whatever it was. Of course, it wasn't scared of us. It turned out to be a cow."

Nick's sand traps were similarly unfruitful, turning up the tracks of nearly every Tasmanian mammal but the tiger. And so were the camera traps—although they did get some great candids of surprised wallabies, annoyed devils, and stealthy possums. But as far as the tiger, no concrete evidence emerged.

In 1984, Nick Mooney wrote up his findings in *Australian Natural History* magazine. Although the search had failed to turn up conclusive physical evidence of the tiger's survival, he remained "optimistic that more of us will see this mysterious and beautiful animal." He wrote:

> *The recent sighting confirms that the search area was used by thylacines at least irregularly up until autumn 1982. If irregular use was normal, this may not have changed. If regular use was normal, the only factor changing this would have been disturbance, such as intensified forestry. . . .*
>
> *The problem of what should and should not be done is perplexing. Before rational decisions can be made, we must decide on certain basic facts about the animal. We know very little of its ecology. When the thylacine was common, all efforts were to kill or capture, not study it, a common attitude to predators in those days. We have little fact, much hearsay, and some folklore. Unfortunately, most of the bushmen who had frequent first hand contact with the thylacine are now dead. . . .*
>
> *Whether a "wait and see" policy or a more active long term searching policy aimed at active management should be adopted is under careful consideration. A contingency plan is being prepared in the event that elusive extant thylacines are finally found. Hopefully this will occur in secure areas involving sufficient numbers to allow study and a population recovery in the near future.*

The Naarding sighting had stirred up a near frenzy of hope that the Tasmanian tiger somehow—against all odds—had survived. But every year since, that hope had dimmed another watt. When we talked to Nick on the phone, he was far less optimistic than he was in 1984. Still, Tasmania's Parks and Wildlife Service continues to record and occasionally investigate tiger sightings.

As Geoff finished his story, we began to look around. The Naarding site was nothing like the lush, misty forest we had seen in the beer ad. It was nearly 90 degrees Fahrenheit outside, and the intersection of the barren roadways looked like a dusty truck stop. We wondered how many tiger seekers had visited this spot before us and started to feel slightly self-conscious.

Dorothy and Chris stood around in the baking sun. We imagined they were wishing for margaritas and beach towels (though they were too polite to say anything). We began taking copious notes, making sketches of the site, snapping photographs, rubbing our chins and speculating, and pacing around in the dust.

In the heat and white light of the day, there wasn't an animal in sight. Not a bird. Not a skink. Not even a tiger snake. The scrawny trees around us looked drained of life.

Alexis took a bottle of water, and poured a thin line of liquid into the white floury dust of the road, just where Naarding had parked. We looked over his shoulder. He had drawn a Tasmanian tiger—and we watched its watery stripes evaporate in the flaming summer heat.

"Now you see it, now you don't," he said.

We walked over to the spot where Naarding said his tiger had disappeared into the forest. The vaguest suggestion of a trail dipped down from the road and was flanked by two large tree stumps that looked like jagged, rotting teeth. Behind the stumps was a tangle of bracken fern, leading down into a patch of young eucalyptus forest.

We leaned against one of the big stumps and wondered what Naarding had really seen, if anything. We considered the possibility that Naarding had been right. It was easy to imagine a tiger emerging from this scraggly forest into the crossroads and being blinded by a beam of light. He might well have turned tail, flashed his balls, and said, "Later, pal." But then what happened to him? Did he breed? Did he die alone in the bush? The white roads leading off in three directions suggested the possible fates of the tiger: extinct, surviving, or wavering in between the two. We thought about the "in between" road. Maybe Naarding hadn't seen a flesh-and-blood tiger. Maybe he had seen a ghost, an apparition of Tasmania past. Being the victim of species-cide might incite the tiger to come back from the dead and haunt the island. The Northwest seemed like a promising breeding ground for ghost stories.

Alexis interrupted our ruminations. "I don't think you want to put your hand there," he said. We turned around and saw a phalanx of large black ants boiling up from the stump we had been leaning against. Their legs and backsides were painted red as if they were wearing war paint. And the pincers jutting from their oversized heads were so large, we could actually see their toothy outlines as they waved them at us menacingly.

Geoff peered down. "Inchmen," he pronounced. "They can be very nasty."

Inchmen, also called bull ants, didn't take kindly to intruders near their nests. Each had a retractable stinger with which it could jab a victim repeatedly and inject venom that caused instant pain. It could last for days. And if you were unfortunate enough to be allergic, you could go into anaphylactic shock and die.

We thanked Alexis and promised to give him back the Cadbury bar.

"No problem," he said. "The road to Tigerville is paved with angry creatures."

We drove off in another cloud of dust. We had ended up feeling a little embarrassed about our interest in the Naarding site. But really it had been kind of exciting—our first contact with the thylacine. Or at least its habitat. Had we not needed to rush back to go on devil patrol, we would have employed Team Thylacine in recreating the whole episode. Geoff would have been drafted to play Naarding. We would have been the Latham's snipes—migratory birds that breed on Russian and Japanese islands—which Naarding was observing. Alexis could have been the tiger. Chris and Dorothy could have been panicked pademelons fleeing the scene.

"Do you think there will be any time to go to the beach?" Alexis asked as Geoff turned the Pajero back onto the highway. Dorothy looked hopeful.

We glared. "The devils live on the beach at Geoff's," we said between gritted teeth.

"Just asking."

Geoff jumped in. If we wanted to see Tasmanian devils, we would need to be hidden well before dark, so the devils wouldn't suspect our presence.

Before heading out to his seaside property, Geoff stopped in front of his barn to pick up a few supplies for the night. It was a rectangular building, made of corrugated iron sheets.

"Coming in?" Geoff asked.

We decided to wait outside while Dorothy, Chris, and Alexis accompanied Geoff to look at the horses, chooks, or whatever animals he kept inside. We took in the last heat of the day and looked up at the wide-open, pale blue sky.

We wondered if the real-life Tasmanian devil would bear any resemblance to the cartoon character of the same name. The character—nicknamed Taz—had started as a minor player in Bugs Bunny cartoons in the 1950s. Taz was depicted as a dull-witted, hairy, slavering beast that whirled like a tornado and had an insatiable appetite for everything and anything, including mountainsides, elephants, and of course rabbits. Although Taz had originally costarred with Bugs only three times, he had come back in recent years as a star in his own right—not only having his own Warner Bros.–produced Looney Tunes series but spawning an industry of toys, T-shirts, and other swag. Often Taz was the only reason geography-challenged Americans had even heard of Tasmania. And it was frequently confused with Tanzania.

Our thoughts were interrupted by the sounds of Geoff cursing and Dorothy emitting a shrill cry. We rushed into the dimly lit barn.

Sunlight filtered in through gaps in the roof, illuminating a gruesome tableau. What looked like a dead kangaroo was hanging from the rafters. It was swaying slightly, a noose around its neck and its tail hanging straight down. On the floor nearby, a rough sack partially covered the body of another dead animal. The body and the sack were smeared with blood and covered with lumps of shit. The second victim was mangled beyond recognition, but probably another kangaroo-like creature. It looked like the scene of a marsupial murder-suicide. Alexis, Chris, and Dorothy bathed the dead animals in a strobe light of camera flashes as they rapidly clicked photographs.

Alexis pushed a button on his digital camera and showed us a photo of

Geoff—taken minutes before—removing a stiff creature from a dingy white freezer at the back of the barn. Geoff was holding it upside down by its tail.

What kind of barn was this? It certainly wasn't used for keeping horsies. It was more like a meat locker.

Geoff was in a foul mood. He quickly explained what had happened: In the freezer, he stored a small supply of roadkill. That way, if he did a devil viewing, he would always have meat for creating a scent trail or feeding the devils. The day before, in preparation for our arrival, he had removed a Bennett's wallaby, a medium-sized type of kangaroo, from the freezer and placed it in the sack to defrost. But something had gone wrong. Some kind of carnivorous animal had gotten into the barn, torn through the top of the sack, and gorged itself on the wallaby meat. The attack had been ferocious. Geoff pointed to the wallaby's head. Its face had been eaten off. To add insult to injury, the ravenous beast had crapped all over the wallaby's corpse.

Geoff's anger was rising. He knew who the perpetrator was. The key evidence was the distinctive shape of the turds on top of the dead wallaby. It was cat shit.

A cat?

"Ferals," said Geoff bitterly. In Tasmania—all across Australia—house cats had gone completely wild. There were tens of thousands of feral cats living in the bush. They were the same species as the domestic cat (*Felis catus*), but these feral cats survived without the help of people and preyed on native wildlife. "They're savage," Geoff said. "Horrible."

Alexis surveyed the carnage. It was a bloody mess. "That was one bad pussy," he said. "Was it marking its territory?"

"No, it just shitted it out, so it could eat more."

To thwart the cat's returning for another meal, Geoff had hung another frozen wallaby from the barn's rafters. Hopefully out of the cat's reach. That explained the creature swinging by its neck. But it also presented a new problem. The hanging wallaby wouldn't be defrosted for hours. What would we use for devil food?

As we had learned, roadkill was not exactly hard to come by in Tasmania. Early that morning a visiting biologist whom Geoff had befriended had deposited the dead bodies of a wallaby and a possum outside his barn. *Thought you could use these.*

The donations were fresh and ready to go. Geoff quickly retrieved them and put the carcasses into a familiar-looking black bin, which he loaded into the back of the Pajero. Chris offered to bring his car, too. Fitting all six of us plus the carcasses into the Pajero was a bit of a squeeze.

As we caravanned out to Geoff's property and turned onto the Arthur River Road, Alexis pulled out his wallet. "Hey, Geoff, do you want to see a picture of my girlfriend?"

Dorothy rolled her eyes. When Alexis handed over a small photo, Geoff's face instantly lit up.

"Ahhh, she's lovely," he said. "What's her name?"

"Beatrice."

It was a photo of Alexis's pet cat stretched out Cleopatra-style on a faux leopard-skin rug. She was a Maine coon with thick, luxuriant gray fur and tabby markings. It was hard to believe that this pampered pussy was the same species as the wild beast that had savaged the defrosting wallaby.

A few years ago, Alexis had spent $5,000 to save Beatrice's life. She had fallen from the window of his third-floor loft apartment in Manhattan and suffered a collapsed lung, a broken pelvis, and two broken legs. She had to have her left front leg amputated and was now a three-legged cat.

As Alexis stared at the photo, he curled his right hand into a paw and made a batting motion. Then he said, "Meeeew, meeew."

We gave him a look.

"What?" he said. "I miss my puss-'ems."

When we arrived at the edge of Geoff's property and the start of the narrow dirt track that led to the coast, Geoff advised Chris to abandon his car and join us in the four-wheel drive. The only way Chris could fit was to cram into the luggage area and sit on the floor next to the dead animal bin.

As we squeezed through the tea trees on the bumpy track, our vehicle began, more and more, to fill with the rank, sweet odor of decaying flesh.

"How're you doing back there?" we asked Chris.

His voice had taken on a resigned quality. "It's really humming," he said.

We felt bad for him. "Have you ever seen a Tasmanian devil before?" we asked to get his mind off the smell.

"I've seen the cartoon."

"Good on ya," Geoff said. "This will be far more terrifying."

A few minutes later, Geoff stopped the Pajero on a grassy rise, and we all got out. He pointed to a few devil footprints in the sand. This suggested devils had followed the scent trail we had laid the night before.

Geoff took the top off the bin, removed one of the limp carcasses, and dropped it on the sandy ground. "That's a brushtail possum," he said.

Despite the odor, we bent down to take a closer look.

"There's nothing quite like the smell of marsupial braised in its own enzymes," Alexis said, plugging his nose.

The opossums that lived back in the United States (the only marsupials that lived in North America) were unattractive animals. They had naked scaly tails, ratlike mugs, and hoary white-and-gray fur. But this possum was beautiful. Its slinky body was two and a half feet long, and it was covered with a plush black coat that was thickest on its bushy tail. Chris and Dorothy wisely kept their distance as Geoff tied a rope around the possum's dead body and attached it to the back of the Pajero.

"So why exactly are we doing this?" Chris asked.

"We're going to lay down a scent trail to attract *Sarcophilus harrisii,* the Tasmanian devil," Geoff said. "The species name *harrisii* refers to Harris, the man who first scientifically described the devil. And the genus name, *Sarcophilus,* means lover of dead flesh."

Geoff knelt down in the sand and slit the dead possum's belly open. With his one clouded-over eye, he looked like a cross between the Grim Reaper and a deranged pirate.

"We want to drag the guts along the ground," he said, wiping his gore-covered knife on a patch of ferns next to the track. "Hopefully, a devil will follow the scent."

"So," said Alexis, "we're chumming terrestrial-style."

With Geoff at the helm of the Pajero and the possum dragging behind us, we drove out across old pastureland and scrubby heath. On the way, we passed some landmarks of King family history, including the spot where Geoff's great-great-uncle first ran cattle in 1880. "My old uncle Charlie set up camp here for the first two years," he said. "You can still see an old chimney."

After a mile or two, we reached the sea. The waves of the Southern

Ocean were bigger than they had been the night before and crashed mightily against the rocky outcrops that lined the shore. The rocks, made of pink quartzite crystals and covered with patches of orange lichen, glowed molten red in the rays of the setting sun. There wasn't another human being in sight.

Geoff drove up to a tiny house about one hundred feet from the shoreline. It was slightly dilapidated, made of weathered asbestos siding, with a small brick chimney. The ground around the structure was sandy, covered with beach grasses, small wind-stunted trees, and massive outcrops of jagged rocks. Friends of Geoff's family had originally built the house as a fishing camp. Geoff called it "the shack." And he used it as a blind from which to observe devils after dark.

While the other members of Team Thylacine went to look at the seashore, we watched Geoff detach what was left of the possum from the back of the Pajero. He threw the remains in the bush. Then he took the dead animal bin and heaved its contents onto the ground behind the shack. "We'll use this little morsel of flesh to attract the devils," he said.

It was a roadkill wallaby. The body was still largely intact—muscular jumping legs, soft gray fur. However, its head was missing. *Severed in the collision? Eaten off?* We never found out.

Geoff took a two-pronged metal stake and pounded it—*thump, thump*—through the furry animal's back and belly to hold it in place. We were reminded of a passage from *Dracula* when Professor Van Helsing destroys a gang of beautiful female vampires by driving wooden stakes through their hearts and cutting off their heads. It was "wild work," the vampire killer wrote in his diary.

Although devils don't come out until after dark, Geoff wanted us to be concealed an hour before sunset. "Once we're inside the shack," he said, "the devils won't be able to see or hear us." He seemed anxious not to spook the devils, so we rounded up the group and went into the little house to hide. Inside, the fishing shack was roughly furnished with two bunk beds, a large table, utensils, and a brick fireplace. A well-used dartboard surrounded by puncture marks hung behind the door.

Geoff gathered some wood and lit a fire. Once it was roaring, he produced the skulls of various animals—a platypus, an echidna, two spotted-tailed quolls (carnivorous marsupials, also called native cats), and a devil—and displayed them along the table. In the flickering firelight, it was a ghoulish scene—an ossuary of Tasmanian wildlife. The platypus skull was toothless and dominated by V-shaped bones outlining the strange beak; it looked like a dowsing rod. The echidna's skull was also tooth-free and elongated into a tube that supported the creature's snout and housed its long, ant-catching tongue. The quoll skulls showed those animals' meat-eating preferences, with four sharp fangs and a series of serrated, razor-sharp molars. But the heads of these predators were dwarfed by the devil's.

The devil's skull was thick, solid, and powerful-looking. Its three-quarter-inch-long canines were pronounced, sharp, and curving. But the eight molars in the back of the lower jaw were the skull's most impressive feature. They were solid, designed for the heavy work of bone-crunching, and the two molars in the very back had sharp, arrowhead-shaped extensions for tearing flesh. Geoff pointed to the thick layer of bone that made up the jaw. "There's an enormous amount of area here to attach muscle to, and that's what gives them their incredible jaw strength." A twenty-five-pound Tasmanian devil, he said, has the chomping power of a hundred-pound dog.

We considered the box office potential of *Jaws V*—starring a Tasmanian devil instead of a shark.

Chris uncorked two bottles of Shiraz, and after pouring everyone a glass, we made a toast. "To the devil," Alexis said. "To the devil," we chorused. Geoff twirled the red liquid in his glass.

In a drawer, we found a collection of magazines. Beneath some recent issues of *Boating* were soft-core porn magazines dating from the 1960s and 1970s with titles such as *Man* and *Adam*. Chris began reading an article titled "Are Blue Movies Doomed?" Dorothy settled down with "A Penny for Your Pants."

A picture window faced out the back of the shack. As night slowly fell, we stood looking out with Alexis. Through the glass, we could see the headless wallaby laid out on a patch of dirt. It was surrounded by beach grasses rustling in the coastal breeze. Behind the wallaby, a triangular outcrop of pink quartzite—shaped not unlike the back tooth of a devil—jutted into the dark blue sky. Geoff had set the stage well, training a small spotlight on the carcass. We waited in the near darkness, pondering all the roadkill we had encountered.

"Look, I see something!" Alexis whispered.

A Tasmanian devil was standing in front of us on a little rise. It stood in profile, sniffing the air, in the last remnants of fading light. It was the size of a big, husky bulldog and was covered with sleek black fur with a thin white band crossing its chest. Its chunky barrel of a body was supported by remarkably short, stout legs. Its neck was so thick as to be almost nonexistent—a heavy bearish head seemed to take up nearly one quarter of its overall body size. This fat, hulking head was topped by tiny, round, reddish pink ears.

Geoff had a look of bliss on his face. "She's a lovely girl, isn't she?"

We studied the devil's features. She had a big, black round nose at the end of a short, nearly hairless snout; beady black eyes that were set wide; and an abundance of long, messy whiskers.

Alexis squinted. We could tell he was trying to put the devil into some familiar animal category—without much success. "That is a crazy-looking predator," he said after a while. "It's like a child's drawing of a scary dog."

"See how she has a tear out of her left ear?" said Geoff. "If she turns round, you can see there's a wound on her right side." Geoff knew this devil. She had denned under the shack the previous year, and five months earlier he had seen her with four devil babies in her pouch. He had nicknamed her Shacky. "She must have a den not far away, so she's prepared to take a risk with a bit of light still about."

Shacky trotted down to survey the carcass, her glossy coat shining in the light as she approached it. There was a hint of stealth in her movements. Before venturing to take a bite, she lifted her head and appeared to look right at us through the window. "She can't see you," Geoff whispered. Her pink ears twitched ever so slightly, as if she were listening for an approaching threat. Then below the wallaby's tail, she tore off a gob of flesh and chewed it in the back of her jaw. We could see her fangs flashing as she cut through each bite with her molars.

"This is a typical way that they'll enter a carcass," said Geoff. "In through the anus. They find a soft bit that they'll work and work until they get it open enough, and then they're right into the rich meat of the rear legs."

We heard the sound of teeth chewing on flesh amplified behind us— and jumped. *What was that?* Geoff had hidden a baby monitor in the grass near the wallaby carcass and placed the speaker over the fireplace. *Rip. Smack.* "I like to leave that as a little surprise," he said. Through the window, we observed Shacky using her muscular neck and jaws to yank off tidbits of fat, flesh, and gristle.

"In the morning there won't be anything left of the carcass . . . except the bottom jaw with little teeth in it and maybe some crushed bits of bone."

We asked Geoff what the devils would be eating if we hadn't left the wallaby out for them.

Devils, he explained, are incredibly adept at finding food. They'll troll up and down the beach, sniffing for the washed-up carcasses of seals, birds, and fish. Inland, they'll smell out dead wallabies, pademelons, platypuses, wombats, frogs, even dead farm animals. They also dine on Tasmania's endless supply of roadkill.

"Do they ever eat human remains?" we asked.

Geoff assured us that if we ended up dying in the remote bush, where so many things can go wrong—hitting your head, breaking your ankle— Shacky or one of her pals would take care of us. "There's no worries at all," he said cheerfully. "A lot of the bushwalkers who go missing in Tasmania are cleaned up by devils."

But did he know of any actual cases where devils had eaten a person's body?

Geoff thought back. "There was a guy who hung himself up in New Norfolk and his legs were missing," he said. "And then there was another case where all that was left of a body was bones—strewn over a large area."

Perhaps because of their carrion-eating ways and the fact that they occasionally snacked on dead humans, devils were never very popular in Tasmania. The pejorative name "devil" was assigned to them by the earliest English settlers. It's only recently that the devils' evolutionary value and role in the ecosystem have been appreciated. Today, the devil is the official symbol of the Tasmanian Parks and Wildlife Service. But many of the farmers who live near Geoff still think devils are foul beasts. "One of the things I'm trying to do is show that devils aren't as evil as they're made out to be," Geoff said. "They're pretty rough with each other, though they don't often hurt each other in their contests. And with people, they're actually quite timid."

They also might have some medical benefits. Geoff pointed at the small open wound on Shacky's right flank. "She's had that now for two years. It doesn't seem to heal. But it hasn't seemed to harm her either. Devils have an incredible antibacterial quality to their blood, similar to crocodiles. They've done a little testing. So you might be sitting in New York in a few years' time and rubbing 'devil blood cream' on your hands."

For all the gore, Shacky was rather elegant. She was particular about the way she tackled her meal and occasionally even dainty in her movements. Taking a break from her feast, Shacky lifted up her blood-drenched maw and sniffed the air with her sensitive nose. Satisfied that no other animals were sneaking up on her, she returned to her repast of raw wallaby. Over the baby monitor, we began to hear the sounds of crunching bone.

"That's so adorable," whispered Alexis, as Shacky gnawed on the wallaby's leg bone.

"She's still got a bit of a pouch," Geoff said. Like other marsupials, devils give birth to embryo-sized young that have to crawl through their mother's fur to get to the safety of the pouch where the teats are located. Although there are only four teats available, female devils give birth to as many as thirty rice-grain-sized, naked young. Survival of the swiftest takes place as the newborns scramble to reach the pouch. Since only four can get teats, the rest perish. The ones that survive do most of their developing in the pouch, which is like a second womb. After a few months, the young devils venture out for the first time, but still return to the pouch for milk and protection for several more weeks. "The pouch should shrink when the young go off on their own," Geoff explained. "She looks like she might still be taking care of her young in a den somewhere."

Shacky gave a little twitch. It was clear that she sensed something out there in the dark. "Could it be a tiger?" Geoff whispered.

Suddenly, the quiet of the shack was ripped by a guttural demonic screaming, a combination of rabid dog and Linda Blair in *The Exorcist*. It was shocking, otherworldly, bizarre—thrilling. It ranged in pitch from deep throaty snarling to insectlike sibilation. A devil with a huge head ("that's a male," Geoff said) charged down the hill and insinuated himself between Shacky and the carcass. An aggressive, whirling dance began, accompanied by a series of screams, hisses, and growls. First, the male tried to ram Shacky with his rump, but she turned on him howling and feinted at his face with her teeth. Then he turned his back on her and tried to gain a position on the carcass. But she whipped around shrieking and snarling, and butt-bumped him off. To counter, he tried to rump-ram her, but she bit him, and he dashed offstage, with a small bloody wound on his left flank.

It had all happened in less than ten seconds—and we were left with the shocked, slightly guilty exhilaration one feels after witnessing a bloody bar fight.

"I guess that's why they call them devils," Chris said.

Even Geoff was impressed. "That big male was at the top of the ranks."

Shacky ambled back to her feed as if nothing had happened. Although female devils are considerably smaller than males, they regularly win such battles.

"You see it a lot with females, particularly when they've got young," Geoff said. "They can be half the size of a male that will approach, but they defend the carcass and stay. It's about who's hungriest."

We couldn't help but notice that Shacky was supersizing it. "How much can one devil eat?"

"On average, devils consume 15 percent of their body weight every night, but they can take in as much as 40 percent. This one belies the statistics. The amount of food I've seen Shacky eat over the last couple of months, she should be as fat as mud."

We did a few calculations on a notepad. An average male devil weighing twenty-three pounds can, on a hungry day, eat more than nine pounds of meat and bone. That's comparable to Alexis, a 180-pound human male, eating 70 pounds of food in a twenty-four-hour period. We'd seen Alexis chow it down—particularly when he was high—but never quite like that.

"Why do devils eat so much?"

For one thing, Geoff said, devils have to cover long distances at night in search of food. If they haven't eaten, they're constantly in motion. Radio tracking has shown devils traveling as far as twenty miles in a single night. During these sojourns, they typically jog at a rate of six miles per hour. All that running requires energy. Plus, when females are nursing their young, they need much more food than the average devil.

Geoff pointed out that Shacky was beginning to gnaw on the wallaby's tail. "There's some really juicy and nourishing food in the tail," he said. "They go to the tail when they want a bit of a delicacy. Generally, they leave the intestines for last."

Even without its head, the wallaby must have weighed at least twenty pounds. "She couldn't eat the whole thing, could she?"

"She could eat the bulk of the back end of that wallaby and she would be a very big, round girl. She'd be really bloated."

We asked Geoff if he had a name for the male devil that Shacky had vanquished.

"Oh no, I don't give them names. She's the Shack Mother because she denned under the shack. But I find it hard to give them names because I might find them dead on the road the next day."

He looked at Shacky with affection. "It's a bit sad. Most devils only live to age five or so. I estimate she's about four now—but she's had a pretty easy life around here, so she might live a bit longer. In wildlife parks, they can live till they're eight."

Shacky had abandoned the tail and gone back to work on the hole she'd been excavating in the wallaby's hindquarters. Then her entire head disappeared inside. For a moment, she looked like she was wearing a big, furry, bloody hat.

"She's really Down Under," said Alexis. "She's going in through the anus and coming out the belly button. Do you think if the carcass were big enough, she would just climb right in it?"

"Sometimes people will see a cow they thought was dead—and it moves," said Geoff. "It's because a devil eating the carcass has worked its way inside."

"Ghost cow . . ."

"Zombie cow . . ."

"Elsie gets it the wrong way . . ." said Alexis. "You know what we're going to need to do, Geoff? I'm going to have to put an intestine in a bag and make pigment from it. Can we arrange that?"

Geoff's eyes opened wide. "Fantastic," he said.

Shacky was still gorging when a new devil appeared on the scene. He was coal black except for a single white marking circling the top of his foreleg. He stood at the top of the hill like a general preparing for battle and studied the scene. Shacky clearly knew he was there. The General's head was massive. (As they get older, the males' heads become proportionally bigger, and the head and shoulders can be as much as 25 percent of a male devil's body weight.) By comparison Shacky looked petite. We heard the far-off peep of a bird—a lapwing or plover—and out of nowhere a third devil raced across the field of combat, screeching and heading straight for Shacky. She merely looked at this would-be interloper and hissed—causing the intruder to zigzag into a complete retreat. On top of the hill, the General continued to stand his ground and sniff the air. Just as Shacky was preparing to take another bite, he charged down the hill, screaming what sounded like the battle cry of hell.

"Lovely, lovely," Geoff whispered as they engaged in their whirling devil-match. "He's in wonderful condition." *EERRERGEEE. AHGH. RARRGH.* Either Shacky had finally eaten her fill or the big male was too much for her. With a final roundhouse booty-bash, he forced her from the carcass. Shacky skulked away into the night.

The screams from this last battle had unnerved us. But Geoff told us we didn't know the half of it.

One night when Geoff was a young boy, neighbors on the farm twenty miles down the road had been out shooting wallabies. They were culling them to prevent them from grazing on stockland. There was a shooting accident, and a neighbor boy was killed. While the family made arrangements in town, Geoff was asked to look after their deserted farm. The dead wallabies—about thirty or forty of them—had been left in a pile a few hundred feet from the farmhouse. In the night, the devils came for them. "I'll never forget lying in bed, listening to the cacophony—the devils, I don't know how many there were, screaming and yowling. It was the most bone-chilling thing I'd ever heard."

By the time the General got to work on the carcass, the wallaby's bones were sticking up through the flesh. Muscle and sinew dribbled out of his mouth. His muzzle was covered with blood. Then, without even being challenged, he simply scampered off. We looked at the empty stage.

"That's not usual," Geoff said. "But then who knows? Maybe there's a tiger out there after all." Tigers were more than twice as big as devils— and the only animals in Tasmania that could kill an adult devil. Even if tigers had truly breathed their last as a species, devils would still be hard-wired to keep an ear out for the tiger's approach. "It's like they're listening for a ghost," Geoff added.

After a minute or two, the General returned to the edges of the spotlight and very tentatively licked the wallaby. Then he perched alongside the carcass, gripped the mangled body tightly with his front paws, and hauled up gob after gob of wallaby flesh. Suddenly, he reared back as if summoning all his strength, and like a weightlifter using a clean-and-jerk motion, he lifted the carcass . . . up . . . up . . . up . . . Geoff looked stunned. "He's pulled it free!" he shouted. The General's black eyes gleamed as he scuttled off backward, dragging the carcass and metal stake into the darkness.

Geoff grabbed a pair of work gloves and flashlight and raced out of the shack. *Where the hell was he going?* A gibbering panic broke out among our ranks as we watched Geoff disappear over the hill and out of the range of the spotlight. We imagined him returning with ten devils attached to his arms and legs, screaming for help.

Instead, Geoff reappeared, holding the mangled wallaby triumphantly over his head. He had won the tug-of-war with the devil—and this was his bloody prize.

"Wild work" was all we could think.

After Geoff's horror movie turn, we decided to pack it up for the night. As we washed out the wineglasses and put the animal skulls back on their shelves, Geoff shared some disturbing news about the devils.

Over the last fifty years, Tasmanian devils had enjoyed a population boom—and a measure of protection and positive publicity. That wasn't always the case. For years and years, from settlement times onward, these creatures of the night were hunted, poisoned, drowned, and shot. As late as the 1960s, there were concerns that the devil might be headed for extinction. Now, Geoff said, devils were facing another threat.

A mysterious devil disease was racing through parts of Tasmania. The disease was lethal, causing disfiguring facial tumors, and appeared to be spreading from devil to devil. Before the disease was detected in the mid-1990s, the devils' overall population was estimated at 150,000. Since then, the population had dropped by one third. In areas where the disease was most virulent, devil numbers were down 85 percent.

Although the disease had not yet reached the Northwest, Geoff was concerned. "It's worrying," he said. On an island, species are more vulnerable and things can change very quickly. He couldn't imagine Tasmania without those bloodcurdling screams.

With the ocean at our backs, we left the shack and rode through the darkness across Geoff's property. The headlights and moon cast misshapen shadows over the landscape.

We hadn't traveled more than a hundred yards when we turned a corner and a small, squat, furry animal came into view. The animal stood motionless, bottom-heavy and stooped over. It was a little hunchback kangaroo. For a moment, it was frozen in the headlights, a cowering marsupial Quasimodo. Then it sprang into life, and with a series of short quick hops, zigzagged away into a small tangle of trees.

"That's a Tasmanian pademelon." It was a live version of the creature we had dragged behind the Pajero the day before.

"Wow, that's my first one," said Alexis.

"Mark the date," said Geoff. "You're no longer a virgin."

Geoff stopped the vehicle on top of a small rise looking out over an expanse of grass. "This is a nice little spot. It's quite juicy," he said. The grass was clipped short, but not by cows or lawn mowers. "It's basically a marsupial lawn. It's kept short by the amount of animals that are here. Look at that mob." He pointed at five kangaroo-like animals that were munching grass in the middle of the field. These were bigger and sleeker than the chubby pademelon—and they weren't intimidated by the Pajero. Their eyes glowed yellow in the headlights.

"Those are Bennett's wallabies," Geoff said. "What we fed to the devils tonight." The biggest wallabies stood over four feet tall and had two-and-a-half-foot-long tails that stretched out on the ground behind them. Their triangular faces were marked by tiny white mustaches, and their long ears twisted and turned so they could listen for predators in two directions at once.

It was startling to see wild animals in a landscape that had been desolate just a few hours before. It was, as they say, hopping.

"Where do they go during the day? Into the woods?"

"Yeah, just into the verge."

As we slowly jounced over the undulating track, a wallaby or pademelon would occasionally *boing* across our path. In the silvery moonlight, we picked out the forms of dozens of grazing, nibbling, hopping animals.

Pademelons and Bennett's wallabies were just two of the forty-five species of macropods that live in Australia. Macropod means "big foot." These animals have huge hind feet, as well as powerful hind legs and long thick tails. Following this basic kangaroo body model, Australia's macropods had evolved to live in every landscape and habitat, including deserts, swamps, rain forests, and rocky terrain. There are even two that live in trees.

Just a few feet away, we saw a tiny creature on its hind legs, hopping next to a dark outcrop of rocks. It looked like a furry overgrown mouse.

"Is that another species?" we asked.

"Nahhh, that's a joey—probably just out of the pouch."

It was a young pademelon—about eight inches high and apparently about thirty weeks old. It hopped tentatively on tiny macrofeet, staying within one or two hops of its mother's pouch. Then it hopped back in and poked its tiny head out. It would spend about four months in this half-in/half-out stage before heading off on its own.

At one time, Geoff said, Tasmanian pademelons had also lived on Australia's mainland. But a combination of factors—clearing of their forest homes, persecution by British settlers, and predation by foxes—proved too much for them. By the early 1900s, this small kangaroo species had vanished from the mainland. Now it survived only in Tasmania.

Our observations on the marsupial lawn were cut short when Alexis burped loudly. It was one of those drawn-out, deep-from-the-belly belches that, while gross, is worthy of respect. Dorothy gave him a look of dismay. He shrugged. "I'm imitating the distress call of the over-the-hill devil," he retorted.

When we reached the edge of Geoff's property, Chris retrieved his car, and we hit the gravel road that led back to the highway and Geoff's house. Within a minute, we saw a dead wallaby on the roadside. Geoff stopped the Pajero, picked up the wallaby, and threw it into the brush.

For devils, Geoff explained, this road was a tempting smorgasbord—

a little taste of possum, a little pademelon, even a little devil. Devils aren't ashamed to eat their own brethren and often get run over while intent on a little roadside cannibalism. To protect the neighborhood devils from speeding cars, Geoff did a nightly roadkill run, tossing most of the dead animals to the side and taking some back for freezing.

"About twenty Tasmanian devils are killed on this road every year and I expect when it gets the tar or bitumen on it, it'll get worse," he said. The gravel road was in the process of being paved.

"The main thing you can do is get people to slow down at night. If you drive down here at sixty kilometers an hour, you won't hit anything. In the 230 times I've done devil viewings, I've had maybe four animals hit me. At sixty kilometers an hour, you get down here in fourteen minutes. At a hundred kilometers an hour, you get down here in eleven minutes, and you would probably kill an animal a night."

He stopped again to pick up a brushtail possum.

"It's quite fresh," Alexis pointed out.

"Yes, it's been killed in the last couple of hours. We're just going to give it mouth-to-mouth . . ."

"It's gorgeous," Alexis said, looking at the possum's thick, luxurious fur. "Too bad we've only seen dead ones."

Geoff put the dead possum in the back of the Pajero—he was keeping this one for freezing—and Alexis took this opportunity to light his pipe. The smell of weed and the freshly dead possum combined to create a heady perfume. And it wasn't Chanel No. 5.

A little further along, the headlights illuminated something fairly large resting in the middle of the road. As Geoff maneuvered around it, lighting up a trail of blood, he identified it as a dead wombat—a big vegetarian marsupial that burrows like a woodchuck and is related to the koala. "I'll come back for that one later," he said.

A moment after, we hit a sharp bump in the road. The possum in the back flew up and landed with a thump.

"It's ali-I-ive," Alexis sang.

Geoff dropped Alexis and Dorothy off at his house and picked up another recycling bin. We rode back with him to where the wombat lay in a blind spot between two crests. "This is going to be a quick salvage operation," Geoff said. "We don't want to become roadkill ourselves."

We scuttled onto the moonlit road, and Geoff lifted up the poor beast, unveiling a pool of blood beneath the body. He placed the animal in the black bin, wound-side down. Geoff's hands were drenched in blood. It took two of us to carry the wombat over to the car. It felt like we were hauling a sack of flour. The wombat's short, bristly fur was rough to the touch, and the body gave off an intense, musky odor.

"That's not the smell of it being dead," Geoff said, wiping his blood-covered hands on a rag. "That's its normal smell. Smelly animal the wombat, but much loved by the Tasmanian devil—for eating."

Back at Geoff's, in front of the house, we examined the wombat with a flashlight. In the black recycling bin, it was curled up on its side. Its husky body was covered with coarse silver-gray hairs and its thickly padded feet were generously clawed. We studied the wombat's flat furless nose and its left eye, which was small, deep-set, and closed in death. The black container made the wombat look like it was in a little casket.

Alexis came out to sit vigil with us. "I should do a drawing of this," he said. "It's poignant."

In fact, the scene reminded us of a drawing we had once seen by the painter and poet Dante Gabriel Rossetti. A lover of animals, the nineteenth-century artist kept a wombat at his house in London—he had obtained his pet from an animal dealer—and would frequently hold it on his lap and scratch its belly. It's said he even allowed his wombat to sleep on a "silver serving dish" at the dinner table. (Some scholars believe Rossetti's mealtime menageries were the inspiration for the mad tea party in *Alice in Wonderland*.)

In a letter Rossetti wrote to his brother in 1869, he said, "The wombat is a Joy, a Triumph, a Delight, a Madness." When Rossetti's beloved pet died just a few months later, he was heartbroken and memorialized it through a combination poem-and-illustration. Rossetti drew himself weeping, his face covered with a large hankie, with the chubby-bellied wombat lying dead on its back, looking remarkably like the specimen we were mourning. And he wrote these lines beneath his picture.

I never reared a young Wombat
To glad me with his pin-hole eye,
But when he most was sweet & fat
And tail-less, he was sure to die!

10. sexy beast

T he next morning we were driving with Alexis back down the Bass Highway, past pastures, cows, and the occasional sheep. He was still talking about the dead wombat and how he might make pigment from its flesh. "I'll pulverize it and mix it in with acrylic medium," he said. Then he added, "Tell me again, what are we doing today?"

"We're going fishing for the freshwater thylacine."

So far, we had hugged the coast. But inland, Tasmania was covered by wet forests and sliced by thousands of rivers, streams, and creeks.

"Oh yeah," said Alexis. "Just so you know, I told Chris and Dorothy there wouldn't be room for them in the boat."

"What boat?"

"I don't know." He sighed. "I didn't know what to tell them."

We had advised Alexis the day before that Chris and Dorothy should find something else to do today. After their politely bemused response to our visit to the Naarding site, we didn't think they would have the patience for our little fishing expedition. Our quarry? *Astacopsis gouldi,* one of Tasmania's most bizarre and elusive creatures.

"Is it rare?" Alexis asked.

"Very."

If it weren't for the Internet, we probably never would have heard about it. We'd been doing Google searches to find out more about Tasmania and its wildlife and discovered that certain combinations of keywords led to unexpected material. When we put in "Tasmanian tiger + sightings," Google spit back hundreds of Web sites about cryptozoology that lumped the tiger in with such mythical creatures as Bigfoot, the Loch Ness Monster, and the Chupacabra, a goat-sucking monster. Other keyword combinations led to a number of amateur science fiction stories and online role-playing games in which the Tasmanian tiger was a character (usually a futuristic hybrid or mutant with special powers). Living or extinct, the Tasmanian tiger had a pretty active life in cyberspace.

Further Googling served up scientific information—providing new leads in our search for strange Tasmanian beasts. That's how we found *Astacopsis gouldi* ("Tasmania + invertebrate"), an absolutely gargantuan species of crayfish. It was an extreme animal—the largest freshwater invertebrate in the world—and it lived only in Tasmania. Its rareness combined with the fact that it was the fiercest animal in the river ecosystem had earned it the nickname of freshwater or invertebrate thylacine. But most Tasmanians just called it the giant lobster.

We were driving down the Bass Highway to meet Todd Walsh, a freshwater biologist who's made saving the lobster and Tasmania's rivers his personal business. We had arranged to meet him at a turnoff near Wynyard about seventy miles back down the highway from Geoff King's house. Actually Geoff had arranged it. (He and Todd used to play footie together.) When we pulled up, Todd was waiting beside a red four-wheel-drive Terrano, wearing dark sunglasses and a gray T-shirt with a kangaroo on it. He was in his mid-thirties, with a bright-eyed open countenance and small slightly elfin features.

"G'day," he said. "So you're the ones who want to see the famous lobster? Are you feeling fit?"

"Er . . ." We admitted we hadn't visited the gym recently.

"You're all right," he said. "Gyms are for fuckwits anyway."

Then he jumped into his four-wheel drive and we caravanned inland through rolling farm country. Eventually Todd stopped in front of a locked metal gate that blocked a gravel road. It was a logging route, but Todd had permission to go through. He pulled out his lobstering gear—traps, buckets, and bait—and distributed it among us. "We'll have to walk along here a bit."

"So how come I've never heard of the lobster?" Alexis asked as we crunched along the gravel. "It's such an extreme animal."

"It's the location, isn't it?" Todd said. "Tasmania's very isolated. The thylacine's popular because we shot 'em, and they died out. The devils are popular because of the cartoon—and the name. *Devil.* It's all marketing."

But the lobster was getting to be somewhat well-known, he said, certainly among crayfish experts. "I've had crayfish people from all over the world fly in specifically to come to Tassie. It's like the Holy Grail."

"What do they say when they see one?"

A smile flickered across Todd's face. "*Fuck!* That's what they say."

We crunched along beside parched, brown pastureland. The temperature was climbing toward 90 degrees. After half a mile or so, trees began appearing on each side of the road. On the right were small, scrubby pines, all growing at a uniform height. *What a weird little ecosystem,* we thought. "That's a tree farm," Todd said.

"Jesus," said Alexis, looking at the evenly spaced trees. "It's like an invading army."

Trees, Todd explained, had been cleared in order to grow trees—faster, stronger, better trees that had been imported from outside Tasmania. They would be cut down in a few years for wood chips. On the opposite side of the road, a wall of native forest loomed up. The trees were tall, and the forest looked thick and impenetrable. Todd indicated that this was our destination.

This would be our first journey into the Tasmanian bush. "Anything we should watch out for in the woods?" we asked.

"A lot of people are worried about the snakes. But on the whole, I'm more scared of bears."

"Bears?" *There were no bears in Tasmania.*

"I went to America for a crayfish conference and I was shit-scared of going into the American woods. It's the unknown . . ."

"I saw a bear on the porch of my country house—" Alexis began.

"Bugger that! A nine-foot grizzly coming at me? I'll take a six-foot tiger snake. Now that's all right."

Six feet?

"So," Alexis said, "the tiger snake is the one to be concerned about?"

"All the snakes are poisonous over here. If you stand still, they'll go right past you."

"What happens if you get bit?" we asked.

"Ninety-nine times out of a hundred you won't be. But if you are, the tiger snake's venom delivery system isn't all that effective. Its fangs are really small. The mainland's a bit more deadly. They have some nasty ones over there." He brushed a few flies from the bait bucket he was carrying. "Taipans are pretty aggressive," he continued. "They're probably the only snake you've really got to watch. That's an angry snake. A lot of people say tiger snakes are angry at this time of year, but they're just more active."

What exactly was the difference between "active" and "angry"? We wished we had worn thicker pants.

Todd pointed out some tall clumps of grass growing on the edge of the forest. They had two-foot-long, dull green blades. "Watch out for cutting grass. It's more common than snakes," he said. "Don't grab it. Even if you're falling over, don't grab it." We looked more closely at the cutting grass. Each blade had paper-thin, finely serrated edges. "It's like a scalpel," Todd said. Just then he turned off the road and into the trees.

As soon as we pierced the wall of forest, we were enveloped in shade and damp. Thick-trunked trees climbed up high overhead and fanned out into a leafy mass. Ferns covered the sloping forest floor, and dead trees lay where they had fallen, wearing thick coats of luxuriant green moss. A moment before, we had been in a virtual desert. This was lush, primordial. We felt like we had entered a time warp.

"There's no trail," Todd explained, hopping over a fallen log and starting down a steep slope. "See that creek? We'll follow that down to the river to avoid the undergrowth."

As we bushwhacked down, a thick layer of decaying wood, rotting leaves, and mud sucked at our boots. Huge, decomposing logs blocked our way. Looming overhead and making up the understory were tree ferns—twenty-foot-high holdovers from the Age of the Dinosaurs with massive green fronds sprouting like hair from the tops of weird, spongy trunks.

"I feel like I'm on Skull Island," Alexis said, looking up into a parasol of seven-foot-long fern fronds. We all gazed upward but there was no sign of King Kong or his brother and sister apes.

"This is wet sclerophyll," Todd said, "which is almost rain forest, but not quite."

Sclerophyll means "hard leaf" and referred to the waxy coating on the leaves of the eucalyptus trees that dominated the canopy. But this forest was anything but hard.

It was a riot of growth and decomposition—living and dying, slippery and rough. Fallen logs and dead spars practically melted into the ground. As we took each step, the forest floor shifted in ways we didn't expect. We clutched at tree trunks, logs, and branches for support.

"A lot of the trees are rotten," Todd warned. "Don't grab a dead tree. Things tend to fall away."

You'd think telling the difference between a live tree and a dead one would be easy. It wasn't. When we grabbed on to one reddish-colored tree trunk, it literally crumbled away in our hands, and we toppled backward, sliding down into the mud.

"No worries," Todd said. "You'll get your bush bearings in a minute."

As we proceeded over ground that was often the consistency of the inside of a Three Musketeers bar, we quickly discovered it was a good idea to keep moving. If we stepped on top of a fallen log and paused for too long to plot our next step, one of our legs would crash through with a crunch, leaving us knee-deep in decaying wood.

Todd himself moved through the wet forest with ease. As he effort-lessly sprang onto logs and over the wet, shifting ground, he looked like some kind of nimble forest cat. Slender with a light, athletic build, he seemed designed for the bush.

In flat sections when we dared to look away from our feet, we studied the woods more closely. The canopy was more than one hundred feet overhead. Mixed in with the eucalyptus trees were rain forest species like myrtle and sassafras. These tree species were ancient, Todd said, with fos-sil forms dating back 80 million years. They had small, leathery green leaves, and their trunks were tall, straight, and solid—good for holding on to.

"So is this a good place for lobsters?" we asked Todd.

"It is. Trees are very important to river systems. Lobsters mainly eat rotting wood. But if they find a dead roo or a fish on the river bottom, they'll eat it. The biggest ones are fourteen pound and a bit over three foot long."

Alexis whistled.

"Yeah, they're pretty big. 'Course, I haven't seen any over ten pound."

The biggest lobsters, he said, had all been trapped and eaten. Freshwa-ter lobsters were a delicacy in this part of Tasmania—so much so that the Tasmanian Parks and Wildlife Service had declared the lobster a vulnera-ble species. Lobsters could live until they were forty years old, and they just kept growing year after year. But the biggest, oldest, meatiest lobsters were now extremely rare. In 1998, the government had imposed an all-out fishing ban to give the giant lobsters a chance to recover. "It will be a few years before we see those sizes again," Todd said. He began to pick his way across a boggy flat.

We followed and our boots plunged into soft, wet mud. Then we slid down a muddy embankment on our backsides and found ourselves at the river's edge.

When we left the dim light of the forest, the sunlight on the river was dazzling.

"It's called the Hebe, H-E-B-E," said Todd. He pronounced it "he bee," as in heebie-jeebies. "It comes from a place called Dip Range and it runs into the Flowerdale River, which runs into the Inglis River." Geoff had told us his great-great-granddad had drowned in the Inglis River while crossing it on horseback.

We looked down at the water. It was the color of freshly brewed tea. "Why's the water brown?"

"It's tannin." Most of the rivers in Tasmania are this color, he said, stained by natural runoff from the buttongrass plains covering Tasmania's hills.

The Hebe was slow and meandering, twisting out of view every couple hundred feet. Huge eucalyptus logs fell over it and across it and lay half submerged. Branches hung down over its steep banks, which were overgrown with trees and ferns. It was the most pristine river we had ever seen.

"This is as good as you'll see anywhere," Todd agreed. "It's one of the lobster's last strongholds. Lobsters only live in northern Tassie and only in rivers that flow into the Bass Strait, except for the Tamar. They're also in the Arthur catchment, which flows near Marrawah where you just came from. But that's it."

Todd laid out his fishing gear, four collapsible basket-shaped nets, and unwrapped his bait, rainbow trout heads and a local saltwater fish called stripey trumpeter. "This will be a treat for them," he said. With a piece of wire, he skewered the fish heads and tied them to the nets.

We asked him if he did a lot of fishing.

"I'm a fisherman from way back. My grandfather, father, and myself used to catch and eat lobsters."

Back in the 1940s and 1950s, his grandfather told him, you couldn't walk for three feet in a river without coming across a lobster. Local people would take home pots of them. Two-foot-long lobsters could be found lurking in streams hardly larger than puddles. Their massive claws would be mounted as trophies and hung on walls just like a buck's antlers. But then the population began to dwindle.

"They taste so nice that a lot of people still go out and catch them, even though the maximum fine is now ten grand."

"When was the last time you ate one?"

"Two weeks before the ban," he said. "They're sensational."

Now, instead of fishing for lobsters to eat, Todd had a scientific permit to catch and release them to monitor the health of their population.

"We'll go upstream and set some traps," he said. "And we'll drag some big lobsters out."

Where we entered the Hebe, the water was only a foot deep and very slow moving, barely making a sound as it trundled over small stones. We followed Todd over islands of gravel to where he dropped down the first trap beside a submerged log.

Since the banks were made impassable by the thick green vegetation, we walked in the middle of the river. Our hiking boots were designed to be waterproof even in ankle-deep water. However, this feature was rendered moot when we stepped into a hidden pool and the river came streaming in over our boot tops. Pretty soon the water was up to our thighs. From then on, things felt rather squishy.

We sloshed for a quarter mile up the Hebe, and Todd laid the second and third traps in deep, shaded pools. Then he jumped up on a huge rotted log—which lay like a bridge across the river—and dropped the last trap down on a length of blue twine. The trap and bait slowly sank, disappearing into the tea-dark water.

"We'll give each trap about three quarters of an hour."

As we reversed direction and slogged back downriver, Todd picked up the pace. He was no longer a forest cat. He had turned into a river otter. And we were having trouble keeping up. We tripped over snags concealed beneath the dark water, plopped into hidden holes, and lost our balance on slippery rocks. Often his voice would trail off as we floundered behind.

"Some people might look at this and see a messy river," we caught him saying. "It's full of snags, fallen logs, fallen leaves and branches. In some parts it's shallow and in other parts there are deep pools. But it's a healthy river. Lobsters eat the wood and detritus. Juveniles occupy the shallower parts, and the older lobsters like to lurk in the pools . . ."

We lost him again for a few minutes, but then made a huge effort to catch up, churn-clomping through the calf-high water. "Another thing that has to be considered is the lobster's lifestyle," he was saying. "Some animals are very adaptable. They reproduce quickly, mating frequently and having lots of young. The lobster's the opposite of that. Lobsters are slow to move into new areas and slow to reproduce. Male lobsters don't start breeding until they're nine years old and females not until they're fourteen. And the females only breed once every two years."

When we reached the shallows again, Todd slowed the pace. He flipped over a few small rocks and put a hand net in the current to trap anything that had been hiding. On the fifth or sixth try, he caught a tiny lobster that easily fit in the palm of his hand. Olive brown and shiny from the water, its shell was delicate and nearly translucent. "This is their typical color," he said. "But they go from blue to black. You can actually find them sky blue in other stream systems."

The baby lobster had a jointed mermaid tail that ended in a fan, two miniature claws it was waving, and two long antennae. Todd said it was a female. He pointed out two circles by her second set of legs where eggs would form when she matured.

"This one is probably just two years old, heading into her third season. So it'll be another twelve years before she's sexually mature. She'll hang around this area for another three or four years yet. This shallow area is safe because platypus and fish can't really swim that well in here and get under the rocks."

Platypuses? This was another reminder that we were in a strange-ass place.

Todd took out a measuring tape. "She's ten centimeters all up. They're pretty vulnerable at this stage. Probably only about 10 percent would survive to even this size."

She didn't look like a giant—but then again, this youthful crayfish was already the size of an average adult crayfish in America. In Louisiana and Mississippi—America's crayfish capitals—crayfish typically reach sizes of about three inches, and they're considered a delicacy, served up as crayfish étouffée, crayfish bisque, and crawdads in clarified butter. On mainland Australia, crayfish are called yabbies—and eaten with similar zeal—barbecued with garlic or put into salads with mango and avocado. When we thought about all this, we began to get a little hungry. It was getting toward lunchtime.

Todd must have sensed what we were thinking. Conservationists, he told us, have been advocating that the lobster be rechristened as *tayatea*, what's believed to be their original aboriginal name, in the hopes that if it isn't called a lobster anymore, people won't be tempted to eat its sweet, delectable flesh.

Todd put the crayfish down on the stream bank and she backed away from us. Crayfish everywhere walk backward, keeping their eyes—and claws—facing the enemy. As she back-stepped into the water, she looked like a gunslinger exiting a bar with both barrels raised. Then she took on the color of the stones—and melted away.

Todd said it was time to check the traps. We churn-clomped back upriver—and checked each one: Empty. Empty. Empty. Empty. The bait hadn't been touched. So we headed downriver again and set up on a dry, gravelly bank to eat lunch.

We had brought chicken, or chook, sandwiches, garnished with butter, lettuce, and beets. Tasmanians seemed to prefer butter over mayo in their sandwiches, and sweet purple beets over tomatoes. As we ate we observed hundreds of butterflies and other flying insects swarming in the treetops above the riverbank. We listened for birdcalls, but didn't hear any—maybe it was too hot. We all sat silently for a minute.

"So have you ever seen a thylacine?" Alexis blurted.

Todd laughed. "Ahhh, no I haven't."

"What do you make of all the sightings?"

"Well . . . I think if they survived, someone would have a photo or a video or a dead one somewhere." He followed up with the rational, scientific viewpoint: "When they were shooting them for the bounty, they shot a hundred in one year, a hundred the next year, a hundred the third year, and then none or one the next year. Their stocks were down, and they reckon now that it's just bad luck that they decided to get a plague, like a flu, go through them. They couldn't handle it. The population just crashed."

He was probably right. We'd heard this argument before that the tigers had been pushed into extinction by the one-two punch of overhunting followed by disease. But we still felt a vague, tiny, ultra-minute glimmer of hope.

"What do you think of all the people who come to look for the tiger?"

Todd paused a moment before answering. "Ah, well, they're in a dreamworld," he said. "It's like the Yeti or Bigfoot, isn't it?"

Tasmanians, he said, needed to get more involved in protecting the native animals that were still around. And sometimes that meant using tough measures. He cited the feral cat problem as an example. "They kill birds, they kill small mammals . . . and they're bloody big, big as a possum. Savage. They get to six kilo. That's fourteen pounds."

"What's the best way to get rid of them?" Alexis asked.

"I had a steel trap, but I've given it back to the Parks Department now. It had a trip lever inside and when the door shut, they couldn't get out. Then I'd take the whole thing, put that in a big plastic bag, and then put it on the exhaust pipe. It might frighten them a bit, but they certainly don't have any pain. They just get knocked out and die. I reckon thirty seconds and they're unconscious, so I think it's a great way to kill them. I only do that because it's a painless way to go. The RSPCA [Royal Society for the Prevention of Cruelty to Animals] wouldn't see it that way. You're supposed to take them to the RSPCA and have them put a needle in."

Todd mentioned that he hadn't been feeling too kindly toward his local Animal Rescue group. They had kidnapped his dog. He had been letting the dog run around unleashed on the property of a fish farm where he was working, and one day someone came and lured his dog into their car. "He jumped in and went for a ride, as you do, being a dog. He thought it was great fun." Then they took the dog to Animal Rescue and when Todd called, they refused to give the dog back, saying that it was being mistreated. "He was lean, very lean. They thought, since its ribs were showing a bit, that we'd been starving it. We got him back after a fight. When I took him to the vet, the vet said he was as fit as a race-horse—in prime condition."

From up above, we heard the distant whine of an engine. It was a pro-peller plane—though we couldn't see it behind the curtain of trees. "It's either for fire spotting or dope spotting," Todd said. "The cops have a really big dope task force."

Alexis's ears perked up. "I have some pot that I got in Melbourne—it's really strong shit."

Todd gave him an inscrutable look. "It probably came from here," he said finally. "Tassie supplies Sydney and Melbourne."

We began to slog up the river again. The sun was bright, but the tea-brown water seemed to absorb all the light and our legs were invisible be-neath the surface. The forest along the banks was like a shimmering green wall—ferns, tree ferns, ancient trees dripping with moss and lichens. From the air, the Hebe must have looked like a tiny crack in the forest's armor. It wasn't easy pushing through the thigh-deep water—it was like exercising on an underwater treadmill—but it was pleasant being heated from above and cooled from below.

Up ahead, emerging from the undergrowth, we saw what looked like a chicken on stilts. It was creeping through the fern fronds along the bank. "That's a Tasmanian native hen," Todd said. Like the lobster and the devil, the native hen doesn't live anywhere in the world except Tasmania. It stood about eighteen inches high, its plump, brown-feathered body supported by long gray legs. Its beak was yellow, short, and stout, and its eyes were bright red. With only rudimentary wings, Tasmanian native hens are flightless. Their only defense against predators is their running ability. In short bursts, they've been clocked at speeds up to fifty kilometers per hour. Their main predators are harrier hawks, eagles, feral cats, and Tasmanian devils. And they have also been killed by farmers for grazing on newly planted crops. But people didn't care much for their taste—at least Todd didn't. "You want to know how to cook a native hen?" he asked. "You boil it in a pot with a rock. When it's cooked, you keep the rock and throw away the chook." Such lack of culinary appreciation was good for the hen. Another of Tasmania's flightless birds, the Tasmanian emu—a long-necked avian giant that stood five feet high on stilt legs—was tasty enough to be eaten to extinction by the island's early colonists.

Tasmanian native hens also have another interesting quality. They're one of the world's few polyandrous birds, *poly* meaning many and *andr* meaning men. That is to say, females typically have multiple mates—and these female-dominated family groups are usually bound for life. Bird scientists call this type of family arrangement—whether headed by a male or female—a dynasty. Female native hens may have one, two, three, or four husbands in their little setup—and they mate with them all.

"I'm digging this chook," said Alexis.

The native hen took one look at our splashing and high-stepped off into the ferns.

As we continued our trek upriver, we checked all the traps again. They were still empty.

Todd assured us the lobsters were all around us. But hidden in the dark waters, camouflaged to blend in with the color of the rocks and stream, they might easily go undetected.

"Would you say they're a cryptic animal?" we asked.

"Cryptic is the perfect word for them," he said and led us further up-river to find a better location for one of the traps.

We began what became a routine, tromping up and down the river, checking the traps each time, and occasionally moving them. We were having absolutely no luck—although once Todd pulled up a trap and found the bait had been stolen. An entire rainbow trout head had gone missing. "Bastards!" Todd mumbled admiringly. Then he rebaited the trap. "He'll be back."

We continued our circuit and when we stopped to take a break, we calculated we had been searching for four hours. Our waterlogged boots felt like lead weights. And we had discovered new hazards: sharp sticks poking us from underwater, exposed tree roots that tripped us up, and a poisonous caterpillar that Todd warned us not to touch. He also mentioned that there were bloodsucking, heat-seeking terrestrial leeches lurking in the trees—but our legs were so chilled from the cold river water, they probably couldn't sense us. "Horrible animals," Todd said, cringing. "I hate leeches more than anything. They make me itch for a month."

It occurred to us that though we had been traversing the same half-mile stretch of river over and over, we had only the vaguest clue where we were or how to get back to the road. If something were to happen to Todd, we might end up as lobster bait ourselves.

Behind us, we heard Alexis chanting, "*Tayatea* . . . come out and play-uh."

Todd turned over a few stones and showed us a stone fly larva, a sleek black bug with red stripes. It was an indicator species, meaning that it was vulnerable to pollution, and symbolized the overall healthiness of the Hebe. Not every river in the lobster's range was in such good shape. "In some rivers, lobsters have been wiped out or nearly so," Todd said.

Apparently being delectable wasn't the lobster's only problem. "The worst thing is land clearing for agriculture," he said. "When they clear the trees, the soil just runs right into the rivers and covers up the lobsters' homes."

The glare of the sun had become less intense. A bird called from the treetops. Time was passing—and just when we started thinking this fishing expedition was going to be a bust, the Hebe began to unveil its secrets.

On our next circuit, lobsters were in two of the first three traps. Gingerly, Todd held them up for us to examine. Both were young males, about six inches long. Their shells were olive brown, and one had sky blue markings on its underside. They looked a little roughed up. The first had a scar on his flank, and the second was missing a claw. Todd told us these injuries might have been the result of lobster-on-lobster violence. They flailed and clapped their inch-long claws as if to emphasize his point.

"They're pretty territorial," he said. "You put a couple in the bath together and they'll tear each other apart."

We watched as the young giants scuttled off into the Hebe. They looked like little gladiators.

Although sunset wasn't until nine and it was only five o'clock, the light was already beginning to fade in the river valley. We could have been satisfied with the two young males—but Todd clearly wasn't. There was only one trap left on this run, and he couldn't let go of the big lobster. "I've got to keep trying," he said. "It becomes an obsession." If this last trap didn't deliver the goods, he thought we should stay and keep looking even if it meant hiking back in the gloom. We all agreed—although Alexis was getting nervous. In addition to telling Dorothy that there would be no room in the "boat," he had said we would be back at 2:00 P.M. Now he was torn between the potential wrath of his girlfriend and seeing a once-in-a-lifetime biological oddity.

The last trap was set beneath a giant fallen log. Todd looked positively Lilliputian when he stood on top of it. He leaned over the edge for more than a minute, peering down into the submerged trap, assessing the situation. Finally, he slowly pulled the line up. As the trap became visible just beneath the surface, we saw a shadow, something large and dark. It was a big male—more than twice as big as the two we had caught earlier. Todd held him up, and he waved his husky claws. This crayfish was more than a foot long.

"He's a buck, a sexually mature male, about fourteen or fifteen years old. Watch out for the claws. He'd break your finger."

Biggie had incredible body armor. His hard, crusty shell was dark bronze and reinforced with various serrations and barbs. His claws were surrounded by spikes. Still glistening from the water, he angrily waved his five pairs of brawny legs. He looked like he was hopped up on steroids.

"It's a pretty well-defended animal," Todd said, quickly measuring him. "Not too much can get at it."

From the tip of his claws to the tip of his fanlike tail, Biggie was thirteen inches long. Todd placed him on the ground, so we could get a better look.

Biggie's eyes were like black beads, sitting atop quarter-inch-long

stalks. His eyes had a distinctly intelligent look about them. For a hulking crustacean, they were profoundly expressive—and what they were expressing was outrage.

Clearly Biggie had never experienced such effrontery in his life. If the tiger was once the king of Tasmania's terrestrial realm, the lobster was the king of the rivers—at least this river—and he was going to assert his dominance.

He leaned his antennae back and reared up, his claws poised to strike. Alexis stuck his nose down to get a closer look and Biggie clapped his claws together.

We held a pencil right next to Biggie as a measure of comparative size and got ready to take a picture. But then he grabbed the pencil in his right claw and waved it as if to say, "How'd you like me to write a book about you?????" *Three American fuckwits travel to Tasmania on an ill-defined journey in search of a long-lost tiger and are eaten by a rare and amazing lobster, God's gift to crayfishdom.*

"Hopefully," said Todd, "this is the animal that saves our river system."

"He's kind of sexy," Alexis pointed out.

Todd looked thoughtful. "They have been called sexy before," he said, studying Biggie's claw. "That's a hell of a nipple clamp."

11. SUICIDE HEN

When we got back on the Bass Highway, Alexis tried to call Dorothy and Chris. They had arranged for us to stay at the Sunset Holiday Villas in Arthur River, a few miles south of Geoff's property. When he reached the proprietor, she told him that Chris and Dorothy had gone out to dinner. Alexis was worried about not getting back on time, but we figured we had better eat, too. This was not a part of the world where stores and restaurants stayed open late. Since the Bass Highway offered nothing to eat but pasture, we veered off toward the town of Stanley.

Stanley is situated at the end of a four-mile-long finger of peninsula that juts into the Bass Strait. A huge, steep-walled rock called the Nut hovers over the town. From a distance, the Nut seemed to rise like a biscuit and looked like a big, fat Pillsbury Grand. About 12.5 million years ago, the five-hundred-foot-high Nut started out as a lake of boiling hot lava inside a volcano. At some point the lava lake cooled down, solidifying into greenish basaltic rock. Ultimately, the softer rock of the volcano's cone eroded away, leaving this squat cylindrical landmark.

As we sped up the peninsula toward the Nut, twilight began to descend. The narrow roadway unfurled like a black ribbon in front of us. We wanted to get there before the little town shut down.

Suddenly in the dimming light about fifty feet ahead, we saw three native hens standing on skinny legs beside the blacktop. All three started to cross, but then two of the hens saw the Pajero coming and skittered to a stop. The third native hen put on a fabled burst of speed, dashing across the road like a sprinter. *It made it!* But then it looked back. When it saw the other birds hadn't followed, it started back and dived right in front of us.

"Suicide hen!" Alexis shouted, as we slammed on the brakes.

We heard a thunk and looked out the back window to see its lifeless body rolling away. When it came to a stop, one of its little wings was pointing upward, the feathers ruffling slightly in the breeze.

It's one thing to see a dead animal on the side of the road. It's another thing to be responsible for it. We had vowed not to kill any animals in Tasmania. Now we were responsible for the end of a dynasty.

Alexis pulled out his *Field Guide to Tasmanian Birds.* He put a checkmark next to the native hen's picture. Beside it he wrote, "KOR." Killed on road.

When we got to Stanley, we stuck our heads into a little café called the Stranded Whale. It was a tearoom that served plates of scones with pots of jam and clotted cream. But there was something incongruous about the decor. The walls were decorated with photographs of whales—all of them dead or dying. They had washed up on Stanley's beaches, which appeared to be a magnet for strandings. By way of explanation, the waitress said the Stranded Whale was owned by an oceanographer.

"What's with the predilection for giving out-of-the-way watering holes morbid names like the Slaughtered Lamb and the Bucket of Blood?" we asked Alexis.

"I don't know. I thought that was only in the movies. Maybe we should open a bar and call it the Asphyxiated Cat."

A little girl sitting at one of the tables—she was about three years old—pointed at one of the dead whales. "Mama, look at the big fishie!" she said.

Alexis immediately corrected her under his breath. "It's a cetacean," he muttered. Then he pointed over our shoulders. "Hey, that's *Astacopsis gouldi*!"

We turned around. On the wall hung a monster-sized pair of claws. They were mounted trophy-style and posed to point menacingly toward the café's ceiling. The claws alone were fifteen inches long.

We remembered what Todd had told us about crayfish specialists and what they said the first time they saw the lobster. *Fuck!* we thought.

These claws were big enough to pincer us by the ears. We knew Biggie hadn't really been all that big. But these claws suggested a gargantuan lobster—one that probably measured a yard long from the top of the claws to the tip of the tail. Nothing that big could have lived in the Hebe. Could it?

"Maybe they should rename this place the Killer Crustacean," Alexis said.

On the drive back down the peninsula, we couldn't stop thinking about *Astacopsis gouldi*. The giant claws spoke to us of possibilities, of phenomenal creatures and strange beasts that were just out of our reach.

We thought about the Tasmanian tiger. The evidence—or lack of it— pointed to the tiger's extinction. But on the flip side of the facts was faith—a lot of people had it. Probably half the people in Tasmania.

A few years ago, we had met a Buddhist monk. He was from the Himalayan country of Bhutan. More than most countries, Bhutan is untouched by Western influences. The king of Bhutan employs an official Migo hunter, and there is a national park devoted to this animal's preservation. The Migo is better known to most people as the Abominable Snowman or Yeti. It's a cryptozoological creature—a mystery animal—meaning that people report seeing it all the time, but there's no scientific evidence that it actually exists. We asked the monk if the Migo was real. He said of course it was real, as real as anything. It simply didn't exist in *our* reality.

Was the Tasmanian tiger like this? Here, but not here? Had it passed on to another realm? Or was it just hiding?

When we turned back onto the Bass Highway, nightfall began to descend. It was a slow process, a progression of flame-colored clouds parading across miles of pale purple sky, finally fading to black. In the diminishing light, the sharp forms of eucalyptus trees stood out across glowing pasturelands until they finally dissolved into darkness. This transition, from day to night, was captured long ago by Bernard Cronin, a Tasmanian writer. His poem "The Way to Marrawah," written in 1917, included a section about evening on this very stretch, the thirty secluded miles between the regional center of Smithton and Geoff's remote community.

> From Smithton to Marrawah the shadows fall awry,
> From half-light to twilight the changing moments fly;
> The tea-tree and currant-bush are nodding in the breeze,
> And wondrous is the yellow moon that peeps between the trees;
> While soft sounds the lullaby of waves upon the bar,
> Of the grey lands, the coast lands,
> The dream lands, the ghost lands,
> The lands that steal from Smithton away to Marrawah.

Except for our headlights, the road had gone completely dark.

"I think Dorothy's going to be pissed," Alexis said from the gloom of the back seat.

"We're getting there."

As we drove, flecks of white began softly striking our windshield. At first, there were just a few, but then the intensity began to increase.

"This is the strangest thing I've ever seen," said Alexis.

We peered into the darkness. Small, delicate white moths in swarm numbers were fluttering, falling through the black sky. It looked like it was snowing.

We wondered where the moths were coming from. Had a migration blown in off the Bass Strait? Or maybe they had just emerged from their cocoons en masse. When Geoff had told us that young Tasmanian devils could live off moths, we thought that was pretty slim pickings. Apparently not. This would be a feast.

Pale wings thwacked softly against our windshield, coating it with body parts.

"Roadkill," said Alexis each time one struck. "There's another roadkill. You killed it." We tried to turn on the squirter to spray them off, but the windshield wipers came on instead, smearing insect gore across the glass.

As we drove through the nocturnal moth-storm, it was as if we had entered a combination carnival ride and shooting gallery. It was almost like a cartoon. Strange little animals kept popping up on the side of the highway, threatening to run out in front of us. A young pademelon tried to cross the Pajero's path and then leapt back to safety. A Bennett's wallaby dashed out and managed to get past before we smashed it. We clenched our teeth: *We will not kill a marsupial, we will not kill a marsupial* . . .

"Hey, do you think you could drive any slower?" Alexis asked.

Although Geoff had recommended sixty kilometers per hour as a safe nonlethal speed, we were barely pushing forty.

By the time we rolled up to Geoff's house, it was 10:30 P.M. We apologized for coming by so late to pick up the rest of our gear, but he seemed thrilled to see us—or at least Alexis. During the day, he had looked up Alexis's artwork on the Internet and seen some paintings Alexis had made of Pleistocene creatures such as saber-toothed cats and the American mastodon, using tar from the La Brea Tar Pits. They were shadowy, fossil-like impressions. Geoff had also located some Rockmans of cockroaches, seagulls, and a Norway rat. The paint had been made using leachate from a garbage dump in New York City.

"They're absolutely fantastic, mate. I was stunned," Geoff said. Alexis's plan was to use similar materials to paint Tasmanian wildlife. In the spirit of things, Geoff presented Alexis with two half-gallon-sized plastic bags filled with animal scat. "It's probably more than you can use . . ." he said apologetically.

One bag was filled with cube-shaped wombat scat. The other bag contained Tasmanian devil shit, and it was pretty fresh—oily and covered with what we took to be white mold. "That's actually bone fragments," Geoff said.

We knew Alexis had asked Geoff for these materials, but we wondered if he had been high at the time. The idea was that Alexis would mash the scat up and mix it with acrylic medium, thereby creating a unique pigment. We imagined Geoff out on his beautiful seaside property, picking up pieces of wild animal dung and inspecting them to see if they were painterly.

Alexis's reason for drawing the island's wildlife with forest soil, river mud, and animal by-products was surprisingly academic. "The materials," he had explained, "have a relationship to the history, geography, or direct interaction I have with particular organisms. They come out of the tradition of diaristic travel. They have a sense of intimacy."

They also smelled. We buried the bags of scat deep beneath our gear inside the Pajero, and Geoff said he would see us the next day.

It was still another ten miles to our motel in Arthur River, which is sometimes referred to as "the Edge of the World." This last leg of the trip was even more nerve-racking than the trip from Stanley to Geoff's. We were dead tired. The gravel road was pitch black and completely devoid of traffic. Potential roadkills lurked everywhere, and several times we had to slow to a crawl to avoid actual ones littering the road. After crossing a narrow, one-lane bridge, we finally reached our destination. In the headlights, we saw a sign for Sunset Holiday Villas pointing toward two wooden buildings off in the gloom.

Alexis nodded toward a lone pademelon standing in the parking lot. "If the tiger is still out there, there's a shitload for it to eat."

The lights of the two buildings were dark and the curtains were drawn. Inside, there was no sign of life. We found ourselves whispering.

"Is this the place?"

"Why isn't anybody here?"

"There's Chris's car."

"How come there aren't any lights on?"

We weren't even sure which building was the motel. We persuaded Alexis to canvass one of them while we waited in the car. He came back and hissed, "It's somebody's *house*."

Now it was our turn. We made our way up the steep plank stairway of the other building. After deliberating for a few moments, we knocked on one of the doors. Dorothy, dressed in a white nightie, opened the door, revealing a square of light. She looked livid and thrust a key into our hands. We went back to the car and took out our gear, lingering on the gravel while Alexis went upstairs to face the music. We guessed we were in the room next to theirs. We went up, tried the key, and knocked several times. Where was Chris? We couldn't get the door open.

"Do you think it's the wrong room?"

"It must be the wrong key."

We tiptoed back toward Alexis and Dorothy's room. Inside, we heard Dorothy yelling at Alexis for being so late.

"Maybe we should just sleep in the car." As we stood outside, we noticed that the night air smelled of the sea.

Finally, we knocked again. Alexis opened the door, looking harried. Behind him, we could see Dorothy pacing and red-faced. Alexis held out a key without saying a word. In her state of exasperation, Dorothy had given us the wrong one.

As we slunk back to our room, we considered that perhaps love unleashes the fiercest beast of all. We had a sense we had just witnessed the emergence of a new species. In the morning, we vowed to announce our discovery to the world: *Pradasuccuba amiphagi*. Translation: The boyfriend-eating devil who wears Prada.

That night, we dreamed about wombats and feral cats and devils and pademelons and giant lobsters and tea-brown rivers and pitch-black highways. In one of the dreams, a group of rowdy marsupials and motley Tasmanian creatures were riding in the back seat of the Pajero.

"Don't go so fast," a native hen criticized.

"You're driving on the wrong side of the road," a bristly wombat screamed.

"Ahhhhhhghghhghghg!!!!!!!!" We nearly collided with a giant white moth.

Just as an echidna began to berate our poor driving, we were awakened by the sound of Alexis, Dorothy, and Chris entering our suite.

They had a kangaroo with them. It looked a little out of its element among the furniture and stood there politely.

Chris was beaming. "It's a Bennett's wallaby," he said.

The owners of the motel had found this kangaroo on the roadside inside its dying mother's pouch, and they were raising it themselves. Chris had offered to watch her for half an hour.

"Her name's Ruby," he said. "Although it might be Roo B. That's her rap name."

She took a few tiny hops and sniffed one of our mud-encrusted hiking boots. Then she began to lick them.

Chris held out a big woolen stocking cap, with a small label stitched on the side that read "Billabong." "It's her pouch." As he held it open, Ruby hopped in and flipped herself over. With her little gray snout peeking out, she looked like a human baby in a sling.

"So where were you last night, Chris?"

"I slept in there," he said, indicating Alexis and Dorothy's room.

He would have gotten the full brunt of the battling devils. But with Ruby, it seemed like everyone had taken a chill pill. Dorothy and Alexis looked cozy again. The lovers' tiff was over.

We took turns holding Ruby and tried feeding her with a long-nippled bottle the owners had given Chris.

"We won't let that mean Tasmanian tiger eat you, Ruby."

"You need some milk, don't you?"

Alexis cuddled Ruby against his bare chest as if he were modeling for the Marsupial Edition of *GQ.* "Who's the baby?" he goo-gooed at her. "Do you want to go back to New York with Daddy?"

Ruby was the same species of wallaby we had seen nibbling on Geoff's marsupial lawn. Her fur was dewdrop soft, like a silk cloth, and it was pale gray with spots of chestnut on her back and neck. The tips of her paws, nose, ears, and tail were black as if she had dipped them in soot. Stroking her fur was profoundly calming. It felt like we had taken a sedative.

When the motel owners first rescued Ruby, she was considered to be about six months old—although it's hard to know when to start the clock on a marsupial's age. In a certain sense, marsupials are born twice: first when they emerge undeveloped and hairless from the womb and make their desperate crawl to the pouch, and again many months later when they take their first peek out of their protective shelter. At the time her mother was killed, Ruby was still nearly hairless. To save her, the motel owners had to feed her specially made marsupial baby formula. They put her in a makeshift pouch and kept her out of the light, otherwise she could have gone blind. Ruby stayed in her surrogate pouch for three weeks without ever attempting to come out.

By the time we met her, Ruby was a year old. At sixteen inches high, she was about half-grown, and we observed that her feet were already enormous, one quarter the length of her body. (The foot-to-body ratio in humans is typically about one sixth to one seventh.) Wallabies are not called macropods for nothing.

Ruby soon became restless with all our canoodling (at her age, she was growing less dependent on both the pouch and the formula), and she squirmed away. She poked tentatively around on the carpet for a few minutes and then began hopping through the room as if she had springs in her backside. *Boing.* Next to Alexis's backpack. *Boing.* On the couch next to the remote. *Boing. Boing. Boing.* And then she took a dump, five neat round pellets. No problem. We scooped them up and plunked them into the toilet. Ruby followed us into the bathroom, snooped behind the john, and took another dump on the tile floor, and then hopped into one of the bedrooms and effortlessly hopped from the floor to the middle of the bed, where she pooped again.

The sedative was beginning to wear off.

Alexis picked up *Tracks, Scats and Other Traces* and flipped it open. There were fifty pages of glossy photographs, many in color, of scat—tiny marsupial mouse shits, hearty echidna poops, kangaroo dumps, even cow patties. He looked carefully from the book to the five round brown pellets Ruby had just deposited. "Yup, she's definitely a Bennett's wallaby," he said. Then he looked at the bedspread. There was a damp spot where Ruby had just peed. "Maybe you better take her home before I turn her into pigment."

After returning Ruby to the Sunset's owners, we headed outside. *Where were we exactly?* The panic of night driving had not left much room for observation. It turned out the Sunset stood at the mouth of the Arthur River, one of the longest rivers in Tasmania. The Arthur started out up in mountain streams above the Tarkine and ran down one hundred miles until it met the Southern Ocean. From the one-lane bridge we had crossed the night before, the river looked slow-moving and sleepy. We walked down to a narrow, sandy beach that marked the river's mouth. The beach was littered with sun-bleached logs that had washed down from the forests upstream. It was as if a giant had swept his huge, beefy paw through a swath of tall trees, plucked up a handful, and casually tossed them down again.

We sat with Chris for a while on an old log and watched a fishing boat motor out into the ocean. The day felt sleepy like the Arthur. Maybe we were turning nocturnal.

Chris mentioned that the day before, while we were out lobster hunting, a tire on his rental car had burst. He had taken it to a tire service next door to the Sunset. "You should talk to Murph," he said of the repairman. "He knows all about tigers—and he doesn't like devils very much."

We headed up to the tire service—it was the same building we had mistaken for the Sunset the previous night—and walked up the wooden stairs. Through the window, we spied a man and a woman, who looked to be in their late sixties, eating breakfast in a room decorated with plump wombat figurines and furry wombat stuffed animals. We knocked tentatively, and the couple—who introduced themselves as Betty and Warren ("Murph") Murphy—immediately invited us to join them.

"You must really like wombats," we said.

Betty admitted she was a bit of a wombat fanatic. She had hand-raised several young ones found, just like Ruby, in their mother's pouches on the side of the road.

"Wombats are the nearest of animals to a human baby," she said. "When they drink from a bottle, they close their claws around your little finger." They can also be very naughty. Young wombats like to play fierce nipping games. We could imagine Betty—who was wiry and feisty looking—getting tough with a rambunctious adolescent wombat.

We explained that we were interested in Tasmanian wildlife and the Tasmanian tiger in particular.

"Ahhh, tigers . . ." said Murph in a hardy Tasmanian brogue. "My mum's brothers snared a tiger and caught three cubs in 1921 . . . I think it was in Brittons Swamp, near Smithton. The skin of the mother was in the family up until about ten years ago. My mum used to keep it as a rug on the bed. When we were kids, we used to play lions and tigers with it. Then my old uncle panicked, because someone told him it could be worth a pile of money. He put it in a bag and stored it at the bank for security—and the weevils got to it. So it ended up just a bagful of fur and chewed-up leather."

His uncle had been right about the skin being valuable. About six months before we arrived in Tasmania, a hand-stitched rug made of eight tiger pelts sold at auction for $270,000. The family that originally owned the rug had used it to warm their piano bench.

"What happened to the three cubs your uncles caught?"

"One died and it's mounted at the museum. The other two went to the zoo," he said.

Although that had been before Murph's time, he himself had spent years in the bush, working as an axeman and sawyer felling trees and later as a saltwater crayfish fisherman.

"Did you ever see a Tasmanian tiger?" we asked hopefully.

"No, but I've heard them." Suddenly, he made a sharp cry. "Cay-yip!" It was startling. Betty merely sipped her tea.

"About twenty-five years ago," Murph continued, "we camped out for a fishing weekend up the Arthur River. We heard one on the hill above us and another one coming down toward the Arthur. They were calling to each other. They couldn't have been more than a couple hundred yards away. Sounds like that don't carry far in the bush." He cay-yipped again.

His dog had been terrified by the encounter, which he said was further proof. "According to old-timers, dogs were absolutely petrified of tigers. I had never heard tigers before, but I had heard everything else we've got in the bush, and we have some *very* strange sounds."

"Like the devil? That's a weird sound."

"Bizarre," he agreed.

Murph had snared wallabies for their pelts in his youth, and one time he accidentally snared a Tasmanian devil. He took the devil home and kept it alive in a big wooden crate. He said it was a vicious little beast—and warned us to be on our guard in the bush.

"If you were injured and had nothing to defend yourself with, that would be the end of you. A devil would come at you and take a nip." Murph thrust his head forward devil-style. "A hard wooden broom handle—they can just bite that off like a guillotine. And they don't leave anything."

We asked if he thought the Tasmanian tiger was still out there in the bush.

"Yes. No reason why it shouldn't be. All the sightings can't be false—especially considering some of the people who've made them. Parks and Wildlife have as much as admitted that. I'm quite convinced."

Here was a man who had lived in Tasmania all his life, who had intimate contact with the bush. And he was certain that thylacines survived. Our hopes surged wildly. Murph must have seen the evangelical look in our eyes. With all the attention the tiger gets, he said, you had to have some perspective on it, a sense of humor.

To be blunt, we weren't the first people to come to the Edge of the World asking about the thylacine. In the mid-1980s, not long after the Naarding search ended, an old bushman named Turk Porteus—who ran a tourist boat on the river—fueled the fire when he reported seeing a tiger on the Arthur where it intersected with the Frankland River, fifteen miles upstream from where we were staying. Turk said he and his father had trapped a mother tiger and her cubs when he was a boy and meant to keep them as pets, but they needed money and ended up selling the tigers for £11. Taking some of the last tigers out of the wilderness had plagued Turk's conscience, and after his sighting he told the local papers that he was relieved to see the tiger still out there in the bush. Some locals thought Turk had made up the story to stimulate business, but others weren't so sure. Either way, Turk's sighting brought even more tiger seekers into the Northwest—all hoping to be the ones to rediscover it and bask in its Grail-like light. That's where Murph and Betty stepped in.

"We had a film crew up here a few years ago looking for the Tasmanian tiger on the Arthur," said Betty. "So we decided to oblige them."

She pulled a photo album off a shelf and opened up to a page with a color photograph of a shaggy Tasmanian tiger crouched in riparian foliage. "We made it up of pieces of carpet," she said. "Then we put it up on the riverbank, so that as their boat went up the river, they would go right past it." She and Murph chuckled. "We couldn't help ourselves." They never found out if the filmmakers were fooled. But when some of their neighbors went on a duck-hunting trip up the Arthur, they were ambushed by a furry, striped predator. "BOOM, BOOM," said Murph, taking aim with an imaginary rifle. "They blasted it."

Early that evening Geoff drove up in his pickup to take us spotlighting for animals on his property. Alexis slung a pair of binoculars around his neck and Dorothy topped off the woolen shirt she had purchased at the Backpacker's Barn with a chartreuse silk scarf.

"They are a lovely couple," Geoff said. "I wonder if it will work out?"

We all caravanned out to the coast, Chris being relieved that he didn't have to share space with a rotting marsupial. When we got there, Geoff set up a telescope facing the ocean. "Have a look," he said, shouting above the sound of the waves. We peered through the lens, and an off-shore scene leapt into view. A line of black birds streamed through the circle of light, some of them flying just inches above the water's surface. "They're short-tailed shearwaters—also called muttonbirds." They had plump bodies and long, thin wings (more than twice as long as their bodies) that were in constant motion. They poured through the circle of light in a never-ending procession.

Each spring, 18 million muttonbirds migrate to Tasmania's coasts and offshore islands to breed and nest. There are more than 150 colonies, one of which has at least 3 million muttonbirds in it. Such numbers were hard to comprehend. Tasmania's aboriginal people had hunted the mutton-birds for food—and so did the European settlers, who called them flying sheep. As we gazed through the telescope at the procession, we felt like we were looking back in time at the preindustrial world. The muttonbirds had spent the day diving for fish, squid, and krill to bring back to their young in their nests. "They're heading back to their burrows for the night now," Geoff said.

We headed in, too. As we walked inland, the ocean sounds receded. Geoff led us along a two-foot-wide path that cut through the coastal grasses. The path was sandy, and along the edges the grass was tramped down. "This is a wallaby run," Geoff said. "Once wallabies settle on a trail, they tend to stick to it. They could have been using this same track for ages. It may be hundreds of years old."

We thought about the Tasmanian tigers and aboriginal people who had lived and trafficked through here hundreds of years ago. There were several aboriginal sites on Geoff's land—middens along the foreshore, mysterious arrangements of stones and depressions where huts had once stood. But Geoff wasn't completely comfortable talking about them. "It's not appropriate for Europeans to interpret aboriginal sites," he said. "But I do think they're important. It connects me to the past going back six thousand years."

Aboriginals lived on Geoff's land and all along the northwest coast until the early 1830s when a missionary named George Augustus Robinson came through and convinced the people to follow him and resettle on islands in the Bass Strait. His idea was that if the aboriginals were rounded up, they could avoid deadly confrontations with the white settlers. Robinson thought he was saving them, and he wanted to convert them to Christianity. Their destination was a concentration camp on Flinders Island—and almost all the aboriginals he took there died within a short time.

Tasmanian tigers lived and hunted on Geoff's land, too. Robinson wrote in his diary about seeing a mother "hyena"—one of the early names for the tiger—and her three cubs on a beach a few miles away. They must have stalked pademelons and wallabies along this very path. According to the recollections of old bushmen, tigers would follow their prey on a slow chase, trotting after them relentlessly until their victims got tired, at which point they would chomp them on the neck with their mighty jaws.

Along the ancient wallaby track, there was a fork—a natural wallaby crossing—that was strewn with dozens of cylinder-shaped scats in various degrees of decay. We studied one of the fresher ones closely. It was gray and white, and made up of fur and bone fragments. It looked familiar.

"It's a devil latrine area," said Geoff. "They leave their poo here to communicate with each other."

We waited quietly to see if the devil poo would communicate anything. Then underneath the sound of rushing wind and the muffled crash of waves, we began to hear something. It was a slow-rhythmed whirring noise. *Whzzz . . . Whzzz . . . Whzzz.* The sound was rising up from the ground all around us.

We looked at Geoff inquiringly. "Native dung beetles," he said.

Tasmania has many species of native dung beetles—and they're all programmed to dispose of the scat of Tasmania's native creatures. Devils, wombats, pademelons. It's a natural solid waste management program. And it worked pretty well until the settlers brought in cows and sheep. The native cleanup crew turned up its mandibles at the huge, sloppy dung of these introduced beasts. Over the years, cow and sheep patties built up. They would dry out and sit there, turning fertile pasturelands into giant muckheaps. To prevent the loss of grazing land and the resulting proliferation of flies, a visionary entomologist came up with the idea of bringing in cow-patty-loving dung beetles from Africa. The scheme was successful—but given the volume of dung generated by livestock, new dung beetles have to be imported all the time.

We continued inland, walking through tufts of grass, across old pastureland, and short-cropped marsupial lawns. Geoff's land was vast, and dusk was a long process. Colors and shapes changed moment by moment. The sky was enormous, and as we walked, it subtly shifted from ultramarine to gray-purple.

Alexis pointed to a grassy rise topped with skinny, windswept tea trees. "What is that?" he said.

A creature was moving slowly toward us, its body black against the tan grasses. It looked like a bear cub cut off at the knees.

A look of bedazzlement lit up Geoff's face. "Fantastic," he said. It was the devil in the flesh. And it was meeting us on our own turf—daylight or what was left of it. "You don't see this often."

Though we had seen devils just two nights before, there was something different about this encounter. We hadn't lured this one with dead wallaby treats. This devil was just walking through, sharing the landscape with us, a rare intersection between two worlds.

The devil stopped and raised its head to sniff, almost lifting itself into the air. Every part of its body was in that sniff. The fading light shone dully on its sleek, glossy fur as it determined its next move.

Whatever scent was in the air—shifty humans or the irresistible odor of carrion—the devil determined to change course and headed off at an oblique angle. It trotted away with a herky-jerky lope—like the rocking gait of an Indonesian shadow puppet—and exited into the tea trees.

Seeing this ambassador from the nocturnal realm was auspicious and slightly transcendent. It even took Geoff a while to shake off his amazement. Wild devils don't make a habit of coming out in the light—and certainly not in the vicinity of people. But he came up with an explanation that was simple enough. It was a young devil out pushing the envelope, taking risks an older devil might not.

We were struck by our good luck. If we were visited by the elusive devil, could a tiger be next? "Do you think it means anything?" we asked Alexis.

"Yeah," he said, lighting his mini-blowtorch. "It's Miller time." Intoxicating smoke wafted into the Tasmanian twilight.

Geoff stopped to show us a tall green grass called a cutting rush. It looked like the cutting grass we had seen with Todd. "It's a species of *Gahnia*," Geoff said. "The white pith is edible." Careful not to cut himself on the sharp edges of the blades, he cut from the bottom of a few flat stalks and peeled back the green sheaths. The white inside tasted like a buttery potato.

"Delicious," Chris pronounced.

"It's good bush tucker," Geoff agreed.

Alexis wandered off down one of the crisscrossing wallaby tracks. When we caught up with him, he was staring intently at a small cluster of yellow flowers. "These dandelions are freaking me out," he said. "Are they freaking you out?"

"Um—"

Just then, a sleek black animal streaked through the grass ahead of us. It moved about three times as fast as the devil.

"What is that?" shrieked Alexis. "A devil on crack?"

"That was a feral cat," said Geoff.

"It looked like a fucking tiger."

The way the cat was bounding through the grass, fully extending its muscle-bound body, it looked like a miniature black panther. It must have been chasing its dinner and was miles from any human abode. Geoff listed some of the creatures that would make easy prey for a house cat gone bush. Skinks, antechinus, swamp rats, and ground-nesting birds like

superb fairy wrens. On small islands, the introduction of feral cats has caused animals—from parakeets to wallabies—to be extirpated.

We continued to walk, and Alexis asked us to hang back behind the group. His eyes had grown bloodshot and his pupils were cavernous.

"You know that Vroom has a lot of cash?" he said. His tone had become conspiratorial. "I have the perfect project for him. I'm going to ask him to fund a feral cat eradication program for Tasmania."

We considered the resulting headlines. "Yank Millionaire Wants Your Cats Dead." "Kitten Killer to Pussums: I Want Your Blood."

Then we had a flash of the future: the Vroom Museum in Smithton. At the main entrance would stand a bronze statue of Chris, with one hand raised in a fist and the other holding up a limp, lifeless cat. Hanging on the museum's walls would be hundreds of tiny mounted cat heads, with inscriptions like "Ginger, two-year-old domestic cat, killed at Johnson's Farm."

"There could be a publicity problem," we suggested. "The locals may not share your healthy antipathy toward feral cats—some of which are their pets."

"It would cost just a fraction of his wealth," Alexis argued. "Remind me to ask him about it."

We decided to test his commitment. "What about Beatrice?" we asked.

"Mew," he said, batting his imaginary paw. "Beatrice isn't a cat," he added. "She's my kitteny mittens."

Our walk ended at the back end of the devil shack, where the picture window faced out on scenes of nocturnal butchery. It was almost dark and Geoff suggested that Team Thylacine have a fortifying glass or two of wine before heading out to look for creatures of the night. While Geoff led the others inside, we examined the spot where Shacky & Co. had devoured the entrails of a wallaby like they were saltwater taffy. All that was left were dried bloodstains and a few bits of gristle.

Suddenly, we felt a tug of inspiration—or maybe it was possession. Our backs hunched. Our hands squeezed into claws. We began to bare our teeth. Then we charged up and down the hill in back of the shack, spinning around and thrusting out our butts to repel each other's attacks—all the while doing our best *Exorcist* impressions: "Ra ra ra ra ra ra raaa, yahhhh, arrrrgggg."

We took turns playing Shacky and pretended to gnaw on giant joints of wallaby meat, while occasionally sniffing the air. As a finale, we devoured an imaginary pademelon tail, using only our canine teeth—occasionally booty-bumping for position—and extended our bellies in satisfaction.

Exhilarated, we entered the shack. "What did you think of our Devil Play?" we asked. It had failed to draw applause.

Geoff had disappeared into the back, and Chris and Dorothy were both engrossed in reading magazines—seemingly.

Alexis looked up momentarily. "No comment," he said.

Maybe we needed better costumes. Black turtlenecks or some rouge applied to the earlobes.

When Geoff reappeared, he told us about his own wildlife theatricals. Not long ago, a German documentary crew had visited the Northwest. They wanted to re-create a scene in which two fishermen supposedly captured a Tasmanian tiger.

The story was that the two fishermen were sleeping in a hut on the beach about thirty miles south of Geoff's place. In the middle of the night, they heard growling sounds. When they went to investigate, they found an animal eating fish from their bait bucket. To drive it off, one of the men hit the animal with a chunk of wood—and the creature collapsed. When they came back at first light, the animal was dead. And that's when they realized it was like nothing they had ever seen before.

Before leaving to go fishing, the two men weighted the body down with wood and sheet metal—so that other animals wouldn't drag it off. Sometime during the day, they told a fisherman with a two-way radio that they had killed a Tasmanian tiger and were planning to alert the authorities when they got back. The third fisherman circulated the story and it spread like bushfire.

When the two men returned to their camp that evening, they discovered it had been raided—the animal was gone, along with a new pair of boat paddles. To prove their story was true, one of the men collected hair and blood samples, which were turned over to Tasmanian wildlife authorities for analysis. Eric Guiler, a thylacine specialist at the University of Tasmania, concluded that the hair was not that of a devil and strongly resembled that of a Tasmanian tiger. An extensive search of the area was launched, but no tigers were found, though footprints, believed to be those of a tiger, were collected. The body of the missing animal never surfaced.

This incident occurred in 1961, and it was still one of the most hotly circulated tiger rumors in Tasmania. In some versions, the fishermen had been drinking heavily and been so smashed that they mistook a Tasmanian devil for a tiger. In others, the tiger was stolen by a government black-ops squad devoted to keeping the tiger's survival secret.

In the German dramatization, Geoff and one of his cousins were drafted to play the fishermen. Geoff's dog, Scratch, played the Tasmanian tiger, or Beutelwolf (as it's called in German). Scratch was filmed in silhouette, his triangular ears doubling for those of the tiger. In their scene, Geoff and his cousin pretended to bash Scratch with a boat paddle. They were paid for their performance in beer.

"When they first came to Tasmania, the filmmakers said they were convinced the thylacine was extinct," said Geoff. "But by the time they left, they weren't so sure anymore. Tasmania has that effect."

Outside the sky had turned black, and a nearly full moon hung low over the grassy terrain. Geoff hooked a spotlight up to the battery in his pickup, and we jumped into the bed of the truck.

"Let's party," said Alexis as he fired his pipe.

"I'm not going to start until you're holding on tight," yelled Geoff.

We gripped the back of the cab, and the pickup began bumping across the dark, undulating landscape. It felt like we were on a slow-moving roller coaster. Geoff switched on the spot, and dozens of creatures were illuminated. It was like a surreal Serengeti. Pademelons and Bennett's wallabies bounded in every direction. Seeing this burst of hopping life made us laugh wildly, and we tried not to lose our grip and go flying off.

Alexis did a play-by-play of the action. "Nibbler at one o'clock." He pointed at a wallaby joey munching grass. (Nibbler was a word he usually reserved for young women who worked at Manhattan art galleries.) "You can't see me, I'm hiding. I'm a little pademelon."

Close to the car, a dark furry animal was slinking away from us. Geoff put on the brakes and yelled that it was a brushtail possum. Moving low to the ground, it looked like a mink stole scuttling across the grassland. "Isn't that gorgeous?" Alexis said. "She's so sumptuous showing off her fur coat."

Geoff's truck continued to jolt along, and as we looked out over the moon-glazed grasses, we saw something hefty trotting beside a line of bushes. It was a wombat with a bristly gray coat and stumpy tail. Besides the possum, the wombat was the only creature among the mass of hopping things that was moving on all fours.

The wombat put on a burst of speed and easily outpaced Geoff's pickup. For a fat and cuddly-looking thing, it moved fast. Apparently, a wombat's short legs can take it to speeds up to twenty-five miles per hour.

Geoff explained that wombats emerge at night to graze on grasses and plant shoots, and spend their days in burrows. The long curving claws on all four of their feet make them accomplished diggers. (The pouches of female wombats face backward so that dirt won't get in during their excavations.)

He stopped to point out a wombat burrow—a giant mouse hole in a soft hummock of earth—and advised us never to crawl inside. Woe, he said, to the unwelcome visitor that tries to follow a wombat into its underground home. For defense, wombats have a thick plate composed of bone and cartilage on their backs. A wombat can use this plate to block the entrance of its burrow and crush the skull of an interloper. Occasionally, wombats kill one another in subterranean turf wars, squashing each other like deranged linebackers. They can also inflict serious bites with their strong, chisel-like incisors.

In the spotlight, the wombat's stout body and the way it trundled along with a heavy step gave it the look of a hippopotamus. We watched the wombat's backside quiver enticingly as it moved off.

"What a butt," said Alexis.

Roving across Geoff's land, we observed more hoppers, diggers, and nibblers. It was marsupial heaven, the Outback crossed with Middle Earth. We felt slightly melancholy at the thought that in the morning, we would be moving on to explore other parts of the island, other thylacine haunts. When the pickup hit the gravel on the Arthur River Road, we crammed back into the Pajero and prepared to go our separate ways.

"Okay, Team Thylacine," said Geoff. He knocked on the hood for emphasis. "You're finished here." The next day we would begin searching for more people like Murph, people who believed the tiger was still out there. It was after midnight when we said goodbye to the one-eyed man who had ferried us through the realm of the devil.

"If we're going to keep wombat hours, I really need to crawl into a dark burrow," Alexis said, unrolling the window of the Pajero as we drove down the Bass Highway. It was mid-morning—just hours since our magical marsupial tour had ended—and about 80 degrees. The sun was beginning to beat down relentlessly. Dorothy and Chris had gone off to do some exploring and would meet up with us later.

We were becoming almost intimate with the two-lane Bass Highway—

the sparkling ocean waters in the distance, the dry brown grasses of the cow paddocks, blocks of blue poppy fields, patches of eucalyptus forest, the logging trucks that shook the blacktop. Even some of the roadkills were beginning to look familiar.

While Alexis dozed off, we mulled over the tiger. Before coming to Tasmania, we had been nearly convinced that the thylacine no longer roamed its old haunts, but after talking to Murph we weren't so sure. It's true there was no convincing physical evidence. But there were those niggling eye- and ear-witness reports.

About ten tiger sightings a year are reported to the Parks and Wildlife Service in Tasmania. However, there are many more that don't make it into official statistics. Sometimes rather than calling the government, tiger spotters call someone they know will be more open to their claims. That was the man we were going to see.

We passed a road construction crew on the bridge over the Black River, and turned inland. Our destination was the home of James Malley, and after a few wrong turns into isolated homesteads, we pulled up to a large, nineteenth-century wooden farmhouse surrounded by paddocks. A sheep next to the immaculately groomed front walk gazed at us quizzically as its owner came out to meet us. James wasn't the twitchy conspiracy theorist we had expected. He was tall, big-shouldered, and rosy-cheeked, just over sixty. And his expression was sunny and affable.

"I'm just working on a new tiger trap," he explained as he ushered us inside. "It's an intricate snare with a trip wire—a tigers-only trip wire that won't catch smaller carnivores. It's baited with a blood scent that frightens herbivores. I've tested it with tracking pads, and so far wombats and kangaroos won't go near it."

Although James had never seen a tiger himself, he had been looking for them for more than forty years. "I get calls from all over Tasmania," he said, sitting us down on a pair of comfortable brown couches in his living room.

In fact, he had just investigated a sighting that he thought was quite promising. It had merited an article in the Hobart *Mercury* headlined "Tassie Tiger Alert After Reported Bush Sighting." James was quoted extensively.

The article reported that a man had stopped his car to switch into four-wheel drive on a backroad in Tasmania's Northwest. As he did so, he saw two wombats run across a track in front of him. To the man's surprise, the wombats were followed by a Tasmanian tiger. The man reported that the tiger then stopped and looked at him for about ten seconds from about fifteen feet away—and then continued the chase. When he got home, the man immediately called James.

"He couldn't believe his eyes," James told us. "It sent him right off."

James quickly went out to the location of the sighting to look for tiger tracks, but didn't find any. "The wallabies were all jumpy," he added. He took the wallabies' skittishness as a sign that a predator had recently been in the area.

So why, we asked, do eyewitnesses phone James rather than the Parks and Wildlife Service? For one thing, he said, "People get frustrated because they ring the authorities and they don't do a damn thing about it." For another, James didn't question their honesty or sanity. What he did do, though, was give them a good grilling. "I'm pretty ruthless when I'm culling out sightings," he said. Eyewitnesses were prone to making mistakes. Native animals, even dogs and cats, were sometimes mistaken for the tiger. "I ask them, 'How long did you see it? Did he have a bushy tail with plenty of hair at the bottom?' And if they say yeah, yeah, then *no,* they haven't seen one."

He's also careful to keep people's names quiet. Even in Tasmania, where a large percentage of the population believes the thylacine is still around, you are liable to be branded a nutter if you report seeing one.

Strangely, that was also the Tasmanian government's longtime excuse for considering records about tiger sightings exempt from Freedom of Information requests. Although the Parks and Wildlife Service maintained they were protecting the privacy of people who made the sightings, the refusal to release any information about the locations and types of sightings for many years made tiger enthusiasts suspicious. As James put it, "The authorities in the Parks and Wildlife Service, they'll tell you they're extinct, but they know damn well they're not."

James is not bothered by the lack of conclusive physical evidence, nor the fact that the tiger is officially "presumed extinct," nor the fact that most scientists disagree with his position. He made the leap of faith more than fifty years ago when he was thirteen years old and heard what he believed was a thylacine calling in the bush.

"That's probably the worst thing that ever happened to me," he said. "What did it sound like?"

James threw back his head—sending his thick mop of gray hair flying—and gave off a high-pitched "EeYIP! EeYIP!" It was a variation of the call Murph had produced.

"That was the end of me," James said. "That's why I started looking for this jolly tiger."

When James was nineteen, he started interviewing hundreds of old bushmen and trappers. *How had they snared the tigers? What did tigers eat? Where did they live?* James became a one-man thylacine lore encyclopedia.

Based on his research, he concluded that Tasmanian tigers had taken to eating sheep because fur trappers had emptied the bush of game. "The bounty came on because the natural tucker was taken away from them," he said. Thousands of thylacines were killed for the bounty, and it's theorized that in the late nineteenth and early twentieth centuries, a disease went through the already depleted tiger population, pushing it over the edge into extinction. Many trappers reported seeing weak, ill-looking tigers with thinning hair that made little attempt to fight when trapped in their snares. "They reckon there's a disease that went through them. A lot of the scientists think it was distemper. But the old-timers say it wasn't a disease at all. When the tigers came down to the coastal areas, they looked poor from lack of food." If there had been no disease, that meant tigers living in more remote areas, where the trappers hadn't penetrated, could still be around.

He also learned that a surprising number of Tasmanians had kept captured tigers as pets. "Ones taken at an early age made a hell of a good pet. There was no wagging the tail—they're physically incapable of it—but they would sit by the table while you were eating and they would follow you along. Very loyal." Of course, there were limits to what these wild predators would put up with. "There was a guy at Balfour, he had one. He thought he would take him out on a lead and the tiger bit him on the backside."

Then there was the tiger's incredible nose. "Evidently their brain—there's so much of it used for their smelling capabilities—they can smell further than any animal on the earth. One fellow had a pet tiger that he brought up with his dogs. It could smell nine kilometers down the track from where he lived. As soon as someone started on the track, the tiger's hair would bristle up."

Alexis's nose crinkled skeptically. "That's a helluva schnozz," he said.

And finally there were the tiger's culinary habits. "They're a blood feeder," James told us with obvious relish. "They always opened their prey up around the heart where the main of the blood was. They folded the skin back very neatly. Then they ate across the stomach down to the leg."

We got a little chill at the thought of a tiger lapping up our blood and wondered if the old bushmen that James had interviewed had been prone to exaggeration. We had read that tigers actually had an average sense of smell—relying more on sight and hearing for hunting. And the "blood feeder" thing sounded like a campfire tale.

Then again, *who knew?* Every predator has a preferred method for devouring its prey. And some animals are remarkably skilled in the art of selective butchery. A mountain lion eats the internal organs of its victim first, then covers the carcass with grass and twigs, and returns to it over subsequent days. When a grizzly bear preparing for hibernation catches a salmon, it carefully removes the fatty skin, brains, and eggs—the parts with the highest fat content—and discards the rest. A pod of killer whales will gang-attack another species of whale—sometimes one that's three times their size—only to eat the big whale's high-protein tongue, leaving the rest of the carcass behind. So maybe the idea that the thylacine drank its victim's blood wasn't really that unbelievable.

James brought out a huge cardboard box filled with tiger memorabilia. There were reports, photographs, newspaper clippings, drawings of tracks, and an astonishing amount of correspondence. Hundreds and hundreds of people had written to James over the years, offering advice about how to find the thylacine (*perhaps if he could devise a better trap, had he checked in the hollows of trees?*), inviting themselves along on searches, wanting to know more about the tiger's life, habitat, and habits. Some of the letters were official correspondence from museum curators, magazines, and television producers. Most were from private citizens fascinated or even obsessed with the thylacine. There were letters from Australia, England, Scotland, Germany, and the United States: *My desire is to come to Tasmania and find the thylacine. . . . I hope to get there soon. . . . I would sometime very much like to work with you.*

After a while, the longing in these letters became embarrassingly familiar. We started to go through the piles of photos. There was the famous black-and-white photo of Wilf Batty, the last man to shoot a Tasmanian tiger. There were photos of tigers in captivity, their powerful legs in midpace as they strode through makeshift enclosures. And there was a news photo from the Launceston *Examiner* headlined, "$2600 Grant to Tiger Men."

In it, we made out a young James, standing with two other fellows beside a Land Rover. In 1972, James had joined a tiger triumvirate. It was called the Thylacine Expedition Research Team, and it conducted one of the most thorough and best-documented searches for the tiger since the animal disappeared in the 1930s. It was a peculiar group. There was James himself, a dairy farmer from the Tasmanian Northwest and an expert in tracking; Jeremy Griffith, a young zoology student from the mainland, who spent every spare moment looking for the tiger and trying to drum up funding; and Bob Brown, a medical doctor, also from the mainland, who had come to Tasmania to get involved in environmental politics.

In the photo, a representative from the British Tobacco Company is presenting the three with a check for $2,600. James has muttonchop sideburns, a narrow tie, and a big-buttoned, wide-lapeled suede car coat. Jeremy is golden-haired, wearing a sport jacket. He looks like Ryan O'Neal in *Love Story*. Lean and lanky, Bob is the conservative-seeming one, with a square jaw, short hair, and a formal black suit. The photo looks like an album cover for an early 1970s British folk-pop band.

James had been looking for the tiger for ten years when he first met Jeremy Griffith in 1968. Together, they made some memorable treks in search of the tiger, carrying impossible loads on their backs through sucking swamps and junglelike bush. Their most ambitious adventure was a ninety-mile trek undertaken at the end of 1970. Believing thylacines in more settled areas might have died out from poisoning meant for devils, they focused on an area of the western coast between Macquarie Harbour and Port Davey. They believed this area was untouched by hunters and (unlike some other remote regions) had a reasonable amount of game for the tiger to live on. This section of the country was notorious. Tasmania's first prison had been located at Macquarie Harbour and brutal as it was for the convicts, the surrounding bush was worse. One in ten convicts escaped into the unforgiving landscape—and almost all perished in the attempt. In one famous case, a group of escapees—defeated by the relentless rains and confusing, rocky terrain—resorted to murder and cannibalism before the last survivor was finally captured.

James and Jeremy flew into the depths of this wilderness, hitching a ride in a small plane with an archaeologist looking for aboriginal carvings. And then they began looking for tigers.

James was a very physical person. He'd grown up in the bush and working on a farm. But Jeremy was indefatigable. At one point on the expedition, he took over half of the things in James's pack and was carrying 140 pounds. "He was still faster than me, and if he wasn't watching, I'd have popped a big stone in his pack just to slow him down. He got me to keep going by telling me stories."

The trip was grueling. "We were walking right up to our chest in mud and covered in leeches. One day when we were making camp, the leeches were so thick on Jeremy, he raked them off his face and threw down handfuls. There were bush fires, rivers we had to ford." They combed the coast north of Port Davey looking for tiger tracks, but found none. Then they turned inland cutting through buttongrass plains and rain forest to reach Macquarie Harbour. Despite all the hardship of the trip, the tiger was nowhere to be found. When James and Jeremy reached the coast again, they were spotted by abalone divers. "We were rough and ragged. Our clothing was torn to bits. When they first saw us, they turned the boat around. We looked like criminals on the loose left over from convict days," James said. They caught a ride back to civilization in the diving boat.

James's enthusiasm was not dulled one whit by the trip's lack of success. On his own time and money, he continued to investigate sightings and track the bush, laying down countless blood and scent trails, in the hopes of obtaining a tiger footprint. "I had to do it out of my own pocket," he said, "out of the scent of an oily rag." In May 1971, James found what he was convinced were tiger tracks in the north-central community of Beulah, an area where there had been many tiger sightings. Jeremy flew down especially from the mainland to look at them. While the tracks were proof to James that the tiger survived, Jeremy was less certain and they decided together that the tracks "were not clear enough to be used as evidence." Meanwhile, Jeremy wrote hundreds of letters and organized meetings with government officials. He also scrounged donations together to open a temporary exhibit in Launceston, Tasmania's

second largest city, to raise public awareness about the tiger and encourage people to report sightings. That's when Bob Brown, the third team member, got involved.

Bob had a medical practice in Launceston, and he spent less time in the bush and more on logistics. He rented the tiger hunters an office in Launceston and created maps plotting tiger sightings. The idea was that they would personally investigate every new sighting and rank it as to its quality and credibility. Not only would they interview witnesses in detail, they would go to the sighting locations and thoroughly search them for footprints, tiger scat, and actual animals. In addition, they investigated high-quality sightings from previous years.

To get the public involved, they created fact sheets, several of which James still had. One flyer titled "Reward $100 for Tiger Tracks" showed thylacine tracks drawn and initialed by Jeremy, alongside wombat and devil tracks for comparison. At the bottom of the flyer it read, "IF YOU FIND TIGER TRACKS, PLEASE GO TO ANY LENGTHS TO PRESERVE THEM AS WE DESPERATELY NEED THE EVIDENCE" and "To Find Tracks, we must be informed of Sightings Quickly."

As the search intensified through the later part of 1972, it seemed that there were explanations for many of the best sightings: A stray German shepherd with its ribs showing was found in the vicinity shortly after one well-known tiger incident. A striped feral cat was discovered in the vicinity of another. A set of footprints long assumed to be those of a tiger proved to be wombat tracks. Famous photographs of a tiger taken from a helicopter were actually of a dog.

The three tiger hunters logged thousands of miles following up on sightings and tracking the bush. But with no compelling physical evidence and the debunking of some of the best-known sightings, Jeremy and Bob eventually lost heart. In a fifteen-page report on the results of the search written in December 1972, Jeremy Griffith came to the conclusion that the tiger was extinct—though he encouraged Tasmanians to continue to report any sightings. In a three-page addendum, Bob Brown advocated that the tiger be classified as extinct. He concluded, "If a live thylacine were found at some future date the event, while joyous, would be remarkable."

James's contribution to the report was short and unambiguous. It read:

REPORT BY JAMES MALLEY:

After spending 3 of the past 12 years in the field in the actual pursuit of evidence for the existence of the Tiger I remain convinced it is not extinct.

The only evidence I can produce to back this claim is 20 photographs of indistinct footprints found after the sighting of a Tiger at Beulah in May 1971. These tracks were definitely those of a Tiger. However they were not distinct enough for anyone who was not thoroughly familiar with animal pads to recognize as such.

A plaster cast taken at Mawbanna in August 1961 is definitely that of a Tiger.

In recent years many clear sightings have been made by people whom I know personally. I have no doubt of any sort in their sincerity and honesty. The majority of recent sightings have been made in three areas of the State—the central East Coast, the northern part of the Arthur River Basin, and the northern edge of the Central Plateau.

The Tiger can be saved if the right policy and an attitude taken in its best interest is adopted for these areas.

In conclusion, I offer any future assistance I can give that might be helpful in ensuring this animal's survival.

JAMES F. MALLEY
TROWUTTA

After publishing their report, the three tiger hunters went in different directions. James continued to search for the thylacine. But he also went on to become a prosperous farmer, branching out from dairy cows into peas, potatoes, and even opium poppies. ("It was good money," he said.) He also worked in real estate and had staked a claim on an opal mine on the mainland. He had recently enrolled his daughter, Bronwyn, in a correspondence course to learn how to cut opals. When we visited, James was in the process of renovating his house. He showed us that his fireplace was made from "convict bricks," each one with the thumbprint of the man who made it while serving out his sentence. "I've done a lot in my life," James said. "The only thing that could make me happier would be to see a tiger."

Jeremy and Bob also continued to make names for themselves and stir up controversy. Jeremy finished his university degree and later founded a philosophical society called the Foundation for Humanity's Adulthood and wrote several books, including *A Species in Denial* and *Beyond the Human Condition*. Jeremy was the subject of a critical documentary titled *The Prophet of Oz* on the Australian news show *Four Corners*, and he later successfully sued the television network for defaming him. Bob Brown went on to become a senator, the first Green Party member elected to the Australian Senate, as well as the first openly gay member of Parliament.

"Did you vote for him?" we asked.

James looked slightly shocked. "Oh, I'm a conservationist, but I would never vote Green," he said. Bob Brown had been the best man at his wedding—but politics were politics.

James, of course, was the only member of the expedition who remained a believer. "There's no doubt, the tigers are there," he told us. "It's just a matter of finding them." From his perspective the tiger is a rare species—and it needed people's help. "Australia's got a lot to learn about conservation," he said. "Indigenous people knew how to take care of the land. Maybe we should give it back to them."

We showed James a map of the Southwest and pointed to the place we intended to hike, the South Coast Track. He gave it a glance and said simply, "That's hopeless." Though it was in one of the least developed parts of Tasmania, with 5,300 square miles protected in national parks and world heritage areas, it had never been rich in animals.

James pulled an old map out of the box and gave it to us. On it, Tasmania's rough coastline was surrounded by blue ocean. Inland, there were probably ten blue rivers for every yellow road and highway. And range after range of broken hills. James pointed to the place along the Arthur River where he had heard the tiger calling when he was thirteen years old. We marked it with a little blue X.

"What you need to do," he said, "is go south of the Arthur River, find a high ridge, and just sit there after dusk and listen."

14. fishy feast of the fairies

After saying good-bye to James, we found ourselves driving once again along the narrow peninsula that led to the stark-walled Nut. It was still long before sunset and the road was blissfully clear of animals. We had agreed to meet Dorothy and Chris in Stanley, where they had rented a cottage for the night.

"What do you want to do tonight?" Alexis asked.

"We were thinking of going to see the little blue penguins."

"I've seen those before."

"Where?"

"At the aquarium in Sydney."

We tried to ratchet up his interest level. "They're the smallest penguin species in the world."

"Yep, I know."

"They're also the only blue penguins."

No response. The extreme animal thing wasn't working this time.

We hadn't really had a chance to look at Stanley in the rush of our last visit. We'd been too rattled by our run-in with the suicide hen. Stanley turned out to be a historic fishing village of just a few winding streets. Its snug one-story, dormered houses—built when the town was founded in the mid-nineteenth century—now served mainly as restaurants, shops, and B&Bs. Though the human population of Stanley was stable at around six hundred residents, the village had undergone some demographic changes. Specifically, the local penguin population had skyrocketed from twelve to two hundred over the last six years.

Historically, little penguins had always nested on the shores of the Bass Strait, but as coastal towns like Stanley developed, fewer and fewer penguins came ashore. At one point, Stanley was down to just a few straggling penguins that were forced to reside under people's beachfront homes and beneath the tombstones at the town's seaside cemetery. To give the penguins better digs, Stanley residents built burrows on the lower slopes of the Nut, just a few hundred feet from the edge of town. As a result, Stanley's penguin population began to thrive.

We got the phone number for a penguin tour service from a flyer on the window of a local restaurant, and when we called, a cheery woman said a penguin van would pick us up at nine-ish. This was going to be another nighttime operation.

In the meantime, we decided to look around the town. Signs in pastel-painted tearooms and food shops offered Devonshire tea, abalone cakes, crayfish sandwiches, and fresh whole fish. At a shop called Hursey Seafoods, the fish were more than just fresh. Hursey's was more like an aquarium than a fish store. All kinds of fish—including tropical ones—were darting around giant Jacuzzi-sized tanks filled with seawater. A handwritten sign read, "BEWARE!! Please do not put hands in the tanks." While we were ogling the swimming seafood, Chris walked in.

Earlier, he had stopped by Hursey's and ordered two dozen Tasmanian rock oysters and a live fish called a bastard trumpeter. The proprietors had asked him to come back in twenty minutes. It would take them that long to net his purchase.

Back at our motel, a cottage called the Pol and Pen, Chris turned into a one-man episode of *Emeril,* making a fire in the fireplace, uncorking bottles of Tasmanian wine, and serving freshly shucked oysters and a locally made Brie warmed in the kitchenette's oven as appetizers. He then whirred around, making a salad (from locally farmed greens) and broiling the bastard trumpeter. Dorothy and Alexis snuggled on the couch in front of the fire.

"Wow, I've only got three days left," Dorothy said sadly.

"I'll miss you, paddypussums," said Alexis.

This was too public a display of affection for us. While gulping down the small, briny oysters, we shared some more information about penguins.

"What's interesting is that these penguins have a lot of different common names. They've been called fairy penguins. Blue penguins. Little blue penguins. But whoever arbitrates these things in ornithological circles finally settled on just little penguins a few years ago."

We felt a distinct lack of interest. "Sometimes the penguins wear sweaters," we added.

"Yeah?" Alexis said. "I thought they wore tuxedos."

We explained that there were sometimes nasty oil spills in the Bass Strait. It's a fairly heavily trafficked shipping zone. When a penguin swims into a slick and gets covered with oil, it can die of cold because the natural oils insulating its feathers are destroyed. Plus, if it starts preening itself, it can die from ingesting the petroleum. So what rescuers often do is pop oil-slicked penguins into tight-fitting wool sweaters. That keeps them warm and prevents them from preening until the oil dissolves or can be washed off. When they wear the sweaters, the penguins look like swanky 1960s ski bums.

After a big oil spill in 2000 an environmental group, the Tasmanian Conservation Trust, put out a call asking people to make penguin sweaters in preparation for the next disaster. They made available a knitting pattern that was published in craft magazines and promulgated on the Internet. And knitters around the world went nuts. Although the pattern was specific to size (the sweaters were nine inches long and four inches wide) and the location of holes for head and flippers, knitters could use whatever colors and designs they wanted. In all, the trust received fifteen thousand wool sweaters before they had to beg the knitting world to put down its needles. The sweaters came in every color from basic black to shocking pink. Some contributors even knitted designs into the wool, such as bowties around the neckline (formal wear) and the emblems of soccer teams across the chest. One knitting circle sent in penguin-size jerseys representing the colors and captains of each of the fourteen Australian-rules football teams.

Alexis wasn't charmed. "It's another case of survival of the cutest," he said.

He began rummaging among the supplies in the kitchenette, looking for something to eat for dessert. He came up with a chunk of Cadbury Dairy Milk bar and squeezed a layer of evaporated milk on top of a few squares. Then, still not satisfied, he took a spoon and plopped on a dollop of Tasmanian-made raspberry jam.

"Want one?" he said, holding out his goopy concoction.

"You know," we offered, "you don't have to come out to see the penguins—if you don't feel like it."

"No, no. Let's all stay together."

A minivan picked us up and drove us to the edge of the Nut. From there, we walked up the lower slope to the penguin rookery. Other visitors were silently filing down the trail in the dark, following guides who held flashlights covered with red filters. Our guide explained that the penguins were sensitive to bright light. In fact, white light and flash photography can temporarily blind them.

Although we couldn't see the burrows in the dark, they were currently occupied by five-week-old baby penguins. The parent penguins spent their days fishing in the Bass Strait and came back at nightfall to feed the chicks. Our visit was timed to coincide with their return. As we walked up the rocky trail, we heard the muffled sound of the Bass Strait washing against the beach below us and the tremulous cries of young penguins urging their parents to come in from the sea.

Our group paused to allow penguin watchers who had arrived earlier to go down. While standing beside the trail, we looked to our right. Just three feet from our boots was a small fluffy penguin. We could have accidentally stepped on it. The guide turned his red beam on the penguin. "He's waiting for his mother," he said.

In the weird red light, the young penguin looked like a bowling-ball-sized powder puff. He was hunkered down, lying flat against a sand patch, his thin black beak pointing expectantly toward the sea. Instead of a blue tuxedo, he was wearing a brown-gray down coat. This little penguin had never even been in the water. In a few weeks, the guide told us, he would get his swimming feathers, trading in the coat of down for a slick blue tuxedo—composed of ten thousand waterproof feathers. In his current position, he looked completely defenseless.

"Maybe he should be wearing a sweater," Chris whispered.

As we continued along the trail, we looked down the slope toward the sea and heard the parent penguins calling *huack, huack* as they prepared to come ashore. In the weak red light, we saw the dim forms of several foot-tall penguins slowly waddling up the rocky slope. They walked stooped forward slightly, their short flippers hanging by their sides. They reminded us of suburban commuters, straggling off their train after a late trip home and intoning, "What a day." Two fluffy juveniles came down to meet their parent—we weren't sure if it was the mother or the father—and the adult penguin began to regurgitate fish into their beaks. We detected the scent of anchovies.

Coming out of the sea like this is dangerous for little penguins, which is why they do it under cover of darkness. Onshore predators included sea eagles, Tasmanian devils, and introduced species like dogs and feral cats. "They're really much more comfortable in the water," said our guide. "Their scientific name is *Eudyptula minor,* which means good little diver." In fact, little penguins can spend weeks on the water without coming onto land. Having traded in their wings for flippers, they can "fly" underwater, diving to depths of 150 feet. They can even float while they sleep. And they actually sleep for only around four minutes at a time—they're big on quickie naps called micro-sleeps.

While they face sea predators like sharks and seals, their tuxedos provide ocean camouflage. When seen from above, their blue backs blend in with the color of the sea. When seen from below, their white bellies look like reflections on the water's surface.

For all the human traffic in this rookery, it was a small-time operation compared to other penguin tourism spots in Australia. There are approximately one million little penguins living along the coast and on islands in and around southern Australia and New Zealand, though their numbers have been cut nearly in half due to beachfront development. The biggest "Penguin Parade" is on the northern side of the Bass Strait at Phillip Island, about eighty miles from Melbourne. Phillip Island has five thousand penguins in its rookery and draws half a million tourists every year. The term "Penguin Parade" was even trademarked. That left us wondering what to call the Stanley penguin waddle. We drew up a short list of possibilities. Penguin Promenade. Penguin Perambulation. Penguin Pilgrimage. Penguin Pomp and Circumstance. Penguin Posse. Fairy Brigade. Fishy Feast of the Fairies.

None of them had the same ring.

"How about dinner bell for puss-'ems?" Alexis offered.

We began to feel that Alexis's position on penguins was parochial.

Up ahead, the guide had stopped and everyone in our group bunched up around him. He was shining his red beam onto the trail just ahead. A mother penguin had plopped herself down in the middle of the trail. She looked exhausted. In fact, she was probably taking a micro-snooze. "She's done in," the guide said. "We'll have to turn round."

"Can't we move her?" one of the tour participants asked.

The guide was shocked. "This is *their* place," he said.

Alexis took on the role of the penguin. "Go away," he said in a high timorous voice. "You're scaring me. I don't like you." Then he giggled.

We went back down the way we came. Perhaps as a form of consolation, our guide told us a little about the penguins' sex lives. "A few weeks ago during the breeding season, things got pretty noisy up here. You should hear the sounds they make calling to their mates." He made it sound like some kind of orgy.

"Ozzie and Harriet go wild," said Alexis.

On first glance, the little penguins seem to be the epitome of family life. Males and females "mate for life"—with a relatively low divorce rate of 18 percent, according to penguin researchers. (Not bad compared to a human divorce rate of 50 percent in the United States and 40 percent in Australia.) Husband and wife little penguins raise their young together, sharing the duties of sitting on eggs, watching young chicks, and feeding older juveniles.

But a closer look reveals a looser lifestyle. Partners frequently cheat—sometimes mating with four different birds in one night! Husbands do attempt to keep their wives from consorting with other males—but they're so easily distracted by their own infidelities that they have trouble successfully guarding their territory. Their cries during breeding season are sometimes described as wails, and the sound of all the nighttime calling in the rookery is thought to stimulate sexual activity.

Alexis seemed to be taking on a renewed interest. "Maybe someone should knit them some lingerie."

"Survival of the sexiest?" we suggested.

"You got it, baby."

The tour was officially over. Alexis, Dorothy, and Chris decided to walk back to the Pol and Pen, while we lingered at the bottom of the trail. Before the guide took off, we asked him whether Tasmanian tigers had ever preyed on little penguins.

"Maybe they still do," he said cryptically. Then he smiled and walked away.

With the shadowy hulk of the Nut looming above us, we envisioned a striped quadruped slinking down the beach with a blue-tuxedoed bird in its mouth. Anchovy ⇒ fairy penguin ⇒ Tasmanian tiger. It was an exotic food chain.

15. LISTENING FOR TIGERS

Tasmania's not very big, 177 miles from top to bottom, and 188 miles across at its widest. Some people told us we could drive across the island in a day and see everything there was to see in a weekend—but it just wasn't true. There are so many areas where roads, even trails, don't penetrate, so many folds in the landscape—forming countless hills and valleys. There's always something new to be found over the next ridge.

We looked at the map of Tasmania that James Malley had given us. The place-names provided a snapshot of the early-settlement era and were by turns quaint, romantic, and bizarre. Some were achingly British: Queenstown, Stonehenge, Northumbria Hill. Others were English spellings of aboriginal words—Marrawah (eucalyptus tree), Maydena (shadow), and Corinna (tiger). Some names described landforms or a place's most prominent flora or fauna—these included Frenchman's Cap (a high peak), Whale Head (a coastal point), Reedy Marsh and Rushy Lagoon (both townships), Black River (where James Malley lived), Opossum Bay, and the Tiger Range. And still others were testimony to the land's remoteness and the hard life of the first surveyors and settlers: Misery Plateau, Desolation River, Lake Repulse.

There was no name to describe the spot we had marked with an X, the place where James had heard a Tasmanian tiger calling when he was thirteen. It was in the middle of the South Arthur Forests on the edge of the meandering blue line that stood in for the Arthur River.

We decided to take James's advice. Find a high ridge in good tiger habitat on the south side of the river. Head up there at night and listen.

"Alexis, would you be up for a little tiger hunting tonight?" We were eating a breakfast of scones and clotted cream at the Stranded Whale. The claws of *Astacopsis gouldi* loomed up behind us.

He glanced at the claws. "Sure," he said. "Who knows what may lurk in the heart of the Tasmanian bush."

The area we had chosen for our tiger vigil was the Milkshakes Hills, a 690-acre forest reserve on a vast swath of land managed by Tasmania's forest service. It was on the south side of the Arthur, about eight miles upstream from where James had heard the tiger's call. The nearest town was Trowutta, the place where James grew up, ten miles north via the road. South of the Milkshakes, there were no roads at all. The nearest town was twenty-five miles away at Savage River.

As we drove south from the coast toward the Milkshakes, much of the road was unsealed. The day was hot and clear. The only clouds around were the dust storms kicked up by our speeding cars. Since we were following Chris, any scenery—dry pastureland, rain forest, and logging trucks—was obscured by a dirty brown scrim.

We stopped only once, pulling onto the gravel just past a wooden sign that read "Kanunnah Bridge—Arthur River." Kanunnah was one of the aboriginal names for the tiger. Below the bridge, the Arthur was surrounded by green temperate rain forest. Trees blanketed a sandbar in the middle of the river. A flock of white cockatoos flew over the treetops. Gazing at the dense forest, we began to appreciate the possibilities for concealment. It looked primordial enough to harbor an assortment of dinosaurs, not to mention a widely scattered population of dog-sized nocturnal predators. Maybe James hadn't just been hearing things.

When we arrived at the campsite, we pitched our tents under a pair of giant tree ferns, using some of the shed fronds to pad the ground. The facilities included a barbecue, a decent supply of wood, and a water tap marked "Not for Drinking." In the outhouse—which Australians called a dunny—there was a logbook in which visitors could write their thoughts about their visit. Most of the entries were pretty bland: "Beautiful drive!" or "Thanks for the dunny." But as we read further, we realized the little notebook was rife with references to snakes. "Another snake in the dunny," someone had written, accompanied by a squiggly drawing of a tiger snake. Since we had yet to see a tiger snake, we spent a fair amount of time holding our noses and peering down the hole of the pit toilet with our flashlights.

Much to our disappointment, the search of the outhouse came up empty. When we returned to camp, we saw Alexis crouched down next to his tent. We assumed he was doing some sort of butt-firming exercise, but then noticed that standing just a few feet away was a gray-furred pademelon—a very scraggly-looking one. We had seen dozens of these two-foot-tall wild kangaroos while spotlighting at Geoff's, but this was the first live pademelon we had seen in the daytime. They were supposed to be nocturnal.

Alexis was extending his arm to offer the pademelon a bit of bread and instructing Dorothy about the best method of photographing them in a moment of interspecies communion. "Wait a sec," he was saying. "Let's try to get . . . the money shot."

"That pademelon looks like it has mange."

Alexis ignored us. "Come on, Mangy, pose with Daddy," he cooed.

We had heard about macropods like this one. Hanging around campsites and getting sick on junk food. "You know, feeding processed food to kangaroos can give them a disease called lumpy jaw," we said.

Alexis didn't respond.

"It's an infection of the mouth. It's fatal."

Alexis withdrew the bread. "Sorry," he said to the pademelon.

With the offer of a snack rescinded, Mangy loped on all fours over to where Chris was cutting up strips of meat for the grill. Chris shooed him away, and Mangy sniffed hopefully at a locked garbage receptacle before retreating to the perimeter of the campsite. There he sat by the trunk of a eucalyptus tree, looking at us with brown, dewdrop eyes.

We cracked open one of our books, *Tasmanian Wild Life*, written in 1962 by the Tasmanian naturalist Michael Sharland. And we looked up his description of the pademelon:

> *Indeed, in neither its broad outline nor in its countenance is there anything distinctive or very pleasing. Its fur never seems to be well groomed or nicely combed, or sleek, or of a pleasing colour. The creature is more like a large untidy rat, the least presentable of the animals that comprise the kindred of the kangaroo. . . . The one good thing that may be said about it is that its flesh is the most delectable of that of any form of kangaroo.*

Ouch. Some of the pademelons we had seen were quite attractive. Yet Sharland had captured our camp pademelon perfectly. Mangy had greasy fur with matted clumps sticking out here and there. Hanging around the camp, hitting up hikers for handouts, Mangy was the macropod equivalent to a bum.

After Chris removed the steaks from the eucalyptus wood fire, we began to gorge on grilled sandwiches made with Tasmanian grass-fed beef. Mangy looked on longingly and moved slightly nearer.

In preparation for our thylacine stakeout, we paged through another one of our books, *Tasmanian Mammals*. Though conventional wisdom says the Tasmanian tiger is extinct, this field guide, published in 2002, was maintaining a hopeful stance.

We decided to share some of the information. "It says here that the tiger is 'mainly nocturnal but may bask in the sun in cold weather.' It also says it makes a 'coughing yap' when it's disturbed and a 'high-pitched yip or yap' when looking for prey."

"So we should listen for a yip or a yap?" said Chris as he poured Tasmanian pinot noir into our collapsible drinking cups. He was getting into the spirit.

"Yeah," we said. "But it might be difficult. The book says the tiger's very secretive."

Alexis gave us a hard stare. "Calling the thylacine secretive is like saying Elvis has 'kept to himself' for the last twenty-five years."

"Does Elvis have a range map?"

He leaned in. The range map for the tiger was an outline of Tasmania with four question marks on it.

An hour before sunset, the five of us began hiking the trail that led out of the campsite and wended its way to the hilltop above. Mangy escorted us for a few yards into the darkening forest, but then stopped, realizing that we weren't headed toward a pile of snacks.

"Do you think he'll follow us the whole way?"

Alexis stopped walking. "Why would a pademelon join a search for this island's apex predator?" he demanded.

We thought Alexis might be ascribing too much intelligence to this pademelon, but then Mangy looked at us suspiciously. "Hey, I was just looking for something to eat," he seemed to be saying. "I didn't want to *be* eaten." Then he hopped back toward the camp.

The trail that led out of the campground was a well-used one. First, it passed through what naturalists in Tasmania call a "mixed forest," a combination of eucalyptuses and rain forest trees. Boardwalks covered areas of the trail that would have been muddy in a rainier season. Fallen, disintegrating trees were hosts to young ferns, mosses, and lichens growing in bright green patches.

As we walked through the dark greenery, we thought about all of the expeditions that had been launched to find the tiger. Michael Sharland, the pademelon-hating naturalist who wrote *Tasmanian Wild Life*, had participated in one of the earliest searches in 1938. That was just two years after the last-known living tiger had died at the Hobart zoo. Led by Arthur Fleming of Tasmania's Animals and Birds Protection Board, the 1938 expedition went out into the goldfields near the Jane River, about ninety miles south of the Milkshakes. None of the miners working in that remote region had ever seen a tiger—but they thought they had *heard* tigers "making a curious yapping sound at night in the broken country around them—a sound they could ascribe to no other known animal." The 1938 expedition did not find a Tasmanian tiger, either living or dead, but it did find a set of footprints in the mud at a place called Thirkell's Creek. They took plaster impressions—and later the tracks were identified as those of a tiger.

Then there was the young naturalist David Fleay, who had an actual close encounter with the tiger. In fact, he was bitten on the ass by one in 1933 while taking the animal's picture. Fleay was fiddling with his camera while inside the tiger enclosure at the Hobart zoo, when the tiger snuck up behind him and took a bite. For the rest of his life, Fleay treated his tiger scar like a badge of honor, and he went on to become a renowned wildlife expert. He was the first person to successfully breed platypuses in captivity and one of the first to milk tiger snakes for their venom, so that an antivenin could be produced. In the 1940s he launched a full-on expedition to find Tasmanian tigers in the wild. He thought if he could capture the last ones and breed them in captivity, he could save the species. After months of futile searching, he found what were identified as Tasmanian tiger prints in an area called Poverty Plain. He also reported that he nearly caught a tiger in a trap, but that it escaped, leaving hair and feces behind. And he believed he heard Tasmanian tigers calling at night. He likened the sound of the tiger's call to "the slow opening of a creaking door."

After a few minutes, the flat trail began to ascend, and as we climbed ("this is better than a StairMaster," Alexis said), the vegetation began to change. The woodlands around the trail started to thin out. The thick greenery gave way to scrubby tea trees and then disappeared completely. It was a curious landscape. Outcrops of white rock peeped over hummocks of low-lying grasses and sedges that ranged in color from light brown to yellow-green to pale, fizzy blue.

We were hiking through a type of grassland known as a buttongrass plain. On the map, there were plains like this on the peaks of hills all around us. Buttongrass plains are strange ecosystems with acidic soils, muddy and boggy during rainy periods and intensely flammable during droughts. And though they don't look like they can support much life, they're populated by creatures like burrowing crayfish, ground parrots, tiger snakes, and quolls. The main vegetative feature we saw was the buttongrass itself, a tan sedge that grew in tussocks with long shoots that sprouted out and ended in round brown seed heads. Filled with tannin, the buttongrass plain smelled pleasingly antiseptic.

According to the experts, this was good tiger habitat—open country surrounded by forest. For thousands of years, as soon as it got dark, Tasmania's herbivores would come out of the forest and out of their burrows to dine on grass and plant shoots. And the tiger, which was built for open-habitat hunting, would come out, too. Then it would begin to chase its prey—a medium-speed, trotting chase—until the pademelon (Mangy!) or potoroo was too tired or frightened to keep going. Then the tiger would pounce and administer a crushing, piercing bite to the back of the skull or neck.

When we finally reached the top of the hill, we looked out in the remaining light. We had a 360-degree view from our grassy perch and were surrounded by rolling hills covered with forest. A low-lying mist in the distance blurred the edges of the horizon. To the south was the Tarkine, one of the most intact temperate rain forests in the world. (We thought about what the owner of the Backpacker's Barn had said on the first day we arrived in Tasmania: *No humans should go into the Tarkine. Humans are dirty, dirty, dirty animals.*)

In the Milkshakes, there was not a single animal stirring. But the grassland was covered with scat, suggesting there was plenty of prey. We decided to make the most of the lingering daylight. Maybe we would find some evidence.

We took out our scat guide, but it was strangely silent on the issue of tiger droppings, given that the author, Barbara Triggs, went pretty far against conventional thinking when she wrote that the tiger "is probably extinct on the mainland, but there may still be a small number in forest areas in Tasmania." *Probably* extinct on the mainland? (The most recent fossil bones of Tasmanian tigers from mainland Australia were at least 3,000 years old.) Despite her optimism, Triggs didn't include a photo of tiger scat or even a description. That's probably because none existed. When the old trappers were snaring Tasmanian tigers for the bounty, they never bothered to put a piece of scat away for future generations.

We began to comb the ground for tiger shit and encouraged Alexis to assist us. We figured asking the millionaires on the team would be out of the question.

"What am I supposed to be looking for?" he asked.

We didn't know. "Something that looks tiger-ish?" We consulted the book again. "Triggs says that, in general, the scat of carnivorous marsupials has an unpleasant odor."

"Great."

The scats came in a bewildering array of shapes, shades, and sizes. Most were clusters of dried brown pellets in groups of four or five—which we had learned to recognize as wallaby and pademelon droppings. Some were remarkably tiny, probably the output of the broad-toothed mouse. There were also crusty, ovoid pellets containing animal fur, perhaps deposited by a predatory bird. And there were long, thin whitish scats that may have been squeezed out by a tiger snake. But nothing we found looked large enough or smelled bad enough to suggest a tiger had been walking through. Soon it was too dark to keep looking.

We took stock of the scene around us. There was no sign of habitation anywhere out to the horizon. No lights coming up from houses or towns. No headlights streaming down unseen roadways. As the nearly full moon cast its icy light over the far-reaching landscape, it reflected brightly off the reedy trunks of white-barked eucalyptus trees. They looked like tall, thin ghosts rising from the dark ground.

"This landscape encourages you to think that anything's possible. Don't you think?" Alexis said.

We started listening, straining our ears to pick up even the slightest vibration. But all we heard was the wind rustling through the buttongrass. And the sound of Alexis flicking his lighter.

Everyone was silent. As the night wore on, we began to feel like UFO buffs sitting in the desert beneath giant radio telescopes, listening for sounds from the stars: *Is anybody there?* We looked up at the Milky Way, and in the sky we saw Orion the Hunter. The constellation was upside down from the way we were used to seeing it. Mars glowed, low on the horizon.

In the silvery darkness, everything—the grasses, the trees, the sky— had turned monochromatic. We thought about the famous flickering black-and-white film of the last Tasmanian tiger and in our minds superimposed them over this scene.

If there was a tiger moving through the gloom somewhere below us, we wondered if we would be able to pick it out. Its sandy-colored body would blend in with the pale grassland and its stripes might look like shadows cast by the moon. Striping is said to be the most ancient form of camouflage. Yet in photographs, the fifteen or so deep black stripes on the tiger's back are what leap out at you. But maybe that's because the only

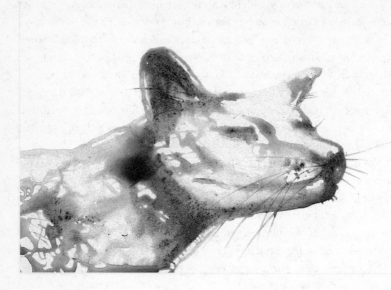

pictures of tigers were taken in zoos, outside their natural habitats. Maybe in a place like this, tigers were invisible.

After what seemed like hours of silence (but was actually exactly twenty-three minutes), a voice suddenly rose from the darkness.

"I wasn't really into those beets on the sandwiches," Chris said. "That's one thing I'm not going to do when I get home."

"Beets are actually really good for salads," Dorothy responded.

"I know. They're just a little sweet on a sandwich."

We found ourselves unable to resist weighing in. "Yeah, maybe they should try sprouts now and then. And what's with the butter?"

Oh, well. Silence is to New Yorkers as roadkill is to Tasmanian devils. It has to be dragged away and devoured.

We heard the sound of a coughing bark behind us, but it was just Alexis clearing his throat. He began using his flashlight to scan the land-scape for wildlife. Nothing.

After a while, Chris decided to head back to camp. His light slowly slalomed down the hill until it disappeared.

We took turns illuminating the buttongrass plains, hoping to catch some sort of animal on the prowl. But it was like a ghost prairie. No predators. No prey. No owls. No night birds. Not the slightest sight of life. The only sound was a rinky orchestra of dung beetles, creaking away in the background.

As we clicked the flashlights on and off, lighting up a barren rock, a dry tussock of grass, a lone twisted tree, we thought about the phenomenon of tiger sightings.

About one official tiger sighting is lodged every month with the Tasmanian Parks and Wildlife Service. They even have a special form—and we had gotten ourselves a blank copy. At the top, it stated, "Every observation, no matter how trivial it may seem, might prove to be important in the search for the thylacine. All information will be received in strict confidence."

We pulled the sighting report form out of one of our notebooks and started to fill it out—just in case.

But when we came to the question "activity at time of sighting," we had to stop. What exactly *were* we doing? We thought about it for a second and then wrote, "sitting on a dark hilltop, listening for the Tasmanian tiger with our pot-smoking artist friend."

It didn't sound good. Even if we saw one, no one would believe us.

It was only midnight when we finally cracked.

"I think the marsupial party is elsewhere tonight," said Alexis.

"Yeah, let's go down." We clicked off our flashlights.

From far below us—at the start of the trail? on a highway?—we saw a series of flashing lights.

"What's that light?" Alexis whispered. It flashed again. "What the fuck *is* that?"

"Do you think it's Chris?" we suggested.

"It can't be. He's nowhere near there."

We weren't sure where Chris was. Probably back at the camp, drinking wine, and clinking glasses with Mangy. But our bearings were screwed up and Alexis's paranoia jangled our nerves.

At night the trail seemed different, complicated and winding. As we illuminated the small space in front of our feet, we drifted into the realm of fantasy. Back in New York, we had imagined countless scenarios in which we encountered the tiger. And we shared one that seemed particularly appropriate for this occasion.

We were camping out in a remote forest, rain dripping down from tower-

ing eucalyptus trees. It was 3:00 A.M. We woke up to the sound of snuffling inside the dark tent. We turned on a battery-powered lantern only to see a live Tasmanian tiger hovering over Alexis's prone body. For a moment, we were thrilled, giddy. Then we saw that the creature was dining on Alexis's heart. (In the original fantasy, the tiger was eating Alexis's innards, but we changed it to his heart after James Malley told us that the tiger was a blood feeder.) *In the shadowy light, we saw the tiger's powerful stripes rippling against its sandy coat. Then we saw its doglike head and gaping jaw lunging for us, teeth first. Our last words, whispered hoarsely into a conveniently turned-on tape recorder were, "It's alive. It's ALIVE!"* (Sometimes, instead of saying "It's alive," we just screamed *"STRI-I-I-IPES!"*)

"How come I always die first in your fantasies?" Alexis asked.

"How come I always have to walk in front of you when we're hiking?" Dorothy said.

"Honey, you know I'm afraid of snakes."

When we got back to the campsite, it was completely silent. Chris was tucked into his tent, and Mangy was nowhere to be seen.

We put on some extra layers against the cold, hopped into our sleeping bags, and got ready for a night on the hard ground—with only the fronds of tree ferns for cushioning. It was cozy to be bundled up, beneath exotic trees, with a friendly pademelon probably sleeping in the forest nearby. But in the middle of the night, we heard some very strange sounds. Around 3:00 A.M.—from the deepest of sleeps—we were roused by bloodcurdling, ululating animal screams. *AHHHHHHhhhhhwaaaghhh. AHHHHHHhhhhwaaaaaaaghhh.* Someone, something, wanted to make its presence known. The cries, which seemed to come from high above us, were followed by a return to total silence. Maybe black cockatoos flying overhead . . .

Early the next morning, we retraced our steps and took a walk through the rain forest trail next to our camp. To our surprise we saw a pademelon, effortlessly leaping three feet into the air and onto a fallen log. This species was perfectly designed to move through dense forest. Small enough to squeeze through thick foliage and agile enough to bound through the understory. We felt like we were getting a peek at the pademelon's true lair— and imagined a Tasmanian tiger chasing it through here.

When we returned to the camp, Chris was making breakfast and Mangy had already arrived. He seemed to have adapted himself to human scheduling—at least mealtimes. And this time, he had brought a friend, a female pademelon with a tiny joey peeking out of her pouch. The joey's head was barely the size of a tennis ball and topped with big, perky ears. "Table for three," Mangy seemed to be saying. "And we'll need a booster seat."

16. 1-300-fox-out

We were at a gas station on the outskirts of Launceston, Tasmania's second largest city. While we pumped petrol into the Pajero, we heard raucous monkeylike calls from above. Sitting atop a telephone wire was a squat, long-beaked bird. It let loose with another set of whooping cries.

"Laughing kookaburra," said Alexis excitedly.

This large kingfisher is one of Australia's most celebrated animals—

almost as famous as the kangaroo and koala—and the subject of the beloved "Laugh Kookaburra" song ("kookaburra sits in the old gum tree/merry, merry king of the bush is he").

Alexis retrieved his *Field Guide to Tasmanian Birds* and paged through it until he found the kookaburra entry. He looked perplexed. "Uh-oh, you guys. Laughing kookaburras are not native to Tasmania. They were introduced from mainland Australia." He began to look slightly angry and gazed up at the kookaburra malevolently. "You fat, motherfucking pigeon."

The sight of Alexis shaking his fist at a bird made us slightly nervous. Dorothy was gone. She was on her journey back to Manhattan. There was no buffer to protect us from the temperamental artist. Chris, while still in Tasmania, had also abandoned us. Apparently spending the night listening for a probably long-dead animal on a deserted hillside wasn't the eco-adventure he had been hoping for. Team Thylacine was down to three.

After our night in the Milkshakes, we decided to stalk what we thought would be more likely quarry: *Vulpes vulpes,* the red fox, a creature that was sure to stir Alexis's blood.

The red fox is not native to Tasmania or any part of Australia. In the 1860s and 1870s, the fox was introduced to the mainland by British settlers. They imported wild foxes along with other familiar species such as the house sparrow and starling, to make Australia seem more like Mother England. But unlike house sparrows and starlings, which were brought in for what passed as aesthetic reasons, the foxes were brought in for sport. They were introduced so that the settlers could engage in an age-old tradition—the hunting of foxes with horses and hounds. In the end, the scheme worked beyond anyone's expectations. By 1930, foxes had spread across the mainland, occupying virtually every type of habitat. But there was a problem: the foxes were the ones that did most of the hunting.

In the annals of animal introductions, the fox is as bad as it gets. The Australian government classifies the fox as a threat to the survival of numerous endangered and vulnerable animals. Foxes will kill any creature smaller than themselves. They have been involved in six animal extinctions over the past 150 years, and are currently threatening the survival of ten other Australian species, including mammals, birds, even a species of tortoise.

Somehow (over nearly two centuries of European settlement), Tasmania was spared the fox. And as a result, all kinds of animals that are extinct or very rare on the Australian mainland thrive there. Tasmania has served as a Noah's ark for creatures such as Tasmanian pademelons and several smaller creatures in the macropod superfamily (potoroos, Tasmanian bettongs), as well as two "native cats" better known as the spotted-tailed quoll and the Eastern quoll. But Tasmania's fox-free status—the ark—had recently sprung a leak.

On the outskirts of Launceston, we met with Chris Parker, the field supervisor for the Fox Free Tasmania Taskforce. Chris was a big man, six feet three inches, with a sunburned face and light curly hair. He wore a gray polo shirt with the task force's insignia, a fox bursting out of a map of the island and being crossed out by the "x" in the word "fox."

He ushered us into the task force's Operations Room and showed us a wall-sized map of Tasmania. It was studded with green, blue, yellow, and red pins. "Each of these represents a fox sighting," he said. "Yellow ones are unlikely, green ones are possible, blue ones are excellent, and the red ones are dead foxes. We've had two dead." The two red pins were just south of Launceston.

The fox task force is a branch of the Tasmanian Parks and Wildlife Service, but it looked more like the offices of Interpol or Quantico. Posters of rusty red, bushy-tailed canids were plastered on the walls, describing their habits and asking citizens to be on the lookout for suspicious characters: "Watch for foxes." Sightings could be phoned in to the task force hotline—1-300-FOX-OUT—twenty-four hours a day.

Before being appointed to the task force, Chris had performed a variety of jobs for the Parks Service, including relocating fur seals that were raiding fishing traps. His size and his ease in the ocean (he grew up surfing in Tasmania's treacherous waters) made him a perfect match for the job. But now he mostly stayed in the office, coordinating anti-fox operations and sending officers out to investigate sightings. Chris handed us a manual, *Managing Vertebrate Pests: Foxes*. The cover pictured two fugitive foxes, one gazing into the camera with the defiance of a serial killer and the other gripping an unidentified marsupial in its jaws. Inside, there was a lurid photo of a blood-soaked lamb, the handiwork of a fox.

On a whiteboard covered with numerous rough drawings, someone had been illustrating a lecture on the fox's gait, footprints, and claws. Beneath it on a table was a polished white fox skull, and next to that were several vials containing long, thin pieces of scat. They were waiting to be analyzed, Chris said. "So far, we've found four scats that have been from foxes."

Chris grew up in Devonport, the city where the *Spirit of Tasmania* ferry docks, bringing in as many as 650 vehicles per day and 1,400 passengers. It's not far from Burnie, the port town on the northwest coast where the thin line between Tasmania and foxes first became apparent. In 1998, a worker at the Burnie dock saw a red fox jump off a container ship that was arriving from Melbourne's Webb Dock. As it happens, Webb Dock is home to one of the densest fox populations in the world. It's almost as if an army of foxes was massing on the border, just waiting for a chance to invade. In the Burnie incident, a mainland fox had apparently stowed away, hopping on at Webb Dock and hopping off in Tasmania. A frenzied chase ensued. Vulpine footprints were found in the sand at a nearby beach. But the fox was never caught. There was talk about tightening up Tasmania's borders and quarantine regulations. And wildlife experts like Chris began to gnaw their fingernails.

Then in 2001, a flurry of red fox sightings was reported near Longford, a small country town in Tasmania's Midlands just south of Launceston. A vacationing couple from England recognized the sound of two foxes calling to each other. A farmer said his chook house was attacked by a fox; he nearly cornered it but it slipped away. Then a respected naturalist had a close-range sighting in the same vicinity. The Tasmanian government became so concerned that expert foxhunters and their hounds were brought in from the mainland. It was thought these professional hunters would quickly track down the fugitives, and the hunters were accompanied by armed Tasmanians ready to shoot the fox on sight. Locally, the hunt stirred up high spirits. There were wagers on when the fox would be caught. Conspiracy theories flew through the community about how the foxes got there in the first place. And one local pub owner began serving up Boag's beer with a fox stole around his neck.

Unfortunately, the dogs from the mainland proved useless in the Tasmanian landscape. They weren't used to seeing so much wildlife and were easily distracted. "They certainly flushed out a lot of wallaby," said Chris. "They had never seen wallaby in numbers quite like that before and all of a sudden they're bouncing around everywhere and it's like, 'Gee, look at this!' "

When the foxhunters and their hounds left, some Tasmanians began to wonder if the fox had existed at all. Infrared cameras set up by the Parks and Wildlife Service to catch foxes in flagrante turned up only photos of native creatures and crabby-looking feral cats. It was all starting to remind people on the island of Tasmanian tiger sightings and the subsequent searches that came to naught.

But the fox story didn't end there. Soon after the foxhounds went home, a pair of mystery men sent a photograph of themselves (heads lowered to conceal their faces) to Tasmania's leading newspaper; the photo showed them holding a dead fox and standing underneath a signpost for the town of Longford. They told the newspaper they didn't want to reveal their identities because they had been hunting without a permit on private property and were afraid of being prosecuted. Parks and Wildlife officials pleaded with the two men through the media to turn in the carcass, assuring them there would be no consequences. After a series of cloak-and-dagger phone calls, the hunters agreed to give the authorities the fox's skin—and true to their word, they sent it in to the parks service through the mail. It arrived unpreserved, putrid, and stinking of decay.

Around the same time, another hunter brought in the dead body of a fox. He said he had shot it in Symmons Plain near Longford. When scientists analyzed the stomach contents of this second dead fox, they found it had eaten small Tasmanian animals—most notably a type of mouse that's only found on the island. The physical evidence was mounting.

Shortly thereafter, DNA analysis of both the fox skin and the dead body showed the two foxes were close relatives and that they came from southern Victoria on the mainland—from a rural population. They hadn't come from the urban population at Melbourne's Webb Dock. So how had they gotten into Tasmania?

The Parks and Wildlife Service came to the conclusion that the foxes had been smuggled in. And some people even began throwing around the word "eco-terrorism." One of the rumors circulating around Longford was that a member of the community had illegally imported and hand-raised two litters of fox pups and released them for the purpose of hunting them. There was a police investigation—but no one was ever identified, charged, or arrested. Even if the alleged eco-vandals had been caught, the courts couldn't have done much about it. The statute of lim-itations on illegal wildlife importation—six months—had already run out.

"As far as we can tell," Chris said, "twelve cubs were intentionally re-leased in the Longford area. Many Tasmanians go to the mainland to go foxhunting. They see those foxes, and they think it's just good fun shoot-ing them. They don't think of the fact that they don't see any other ani-mals there."

If the perpetrators had wanted to introduce foxhunting in Tasmania, they got their wish. The hunt was on.

Stopping the foxes has become a national priority. Losing the thylacine was bad enough. Now Tasmania was looking at a possible cascade of mammal extinctions.

The Parks and Wildlife Service set up the fox task force, bringing in marksmen, dog handlers, trackers, publicists, computer experts, statisti-cians, and geneticists. The task force's sole purpose was to hunt down and kill the foxes before they bred.

In its first year, the task force documented 450 fox sightings all across the island. They ranked them using the same screening process used to rate Tasmanian tiger sightings. How close was the witness to the animal? Had the witness ever seen a picture of a fox? Had the witness been drink-ing? The sightings ranged in quality from very poor to accurate. Using the best sightings, the task force identified hot spots and focused their eradi-cation efforts in those areas. Such efforts included conducting nightly armed foxhunts and burying thousands and thousands of poison baits in the hope that the curious foxes would dig them up, eat them, and die.

One of the problems the task force faces is that foxes are highly elusive. According to biologists, as many as six foxes can be living on every square kilometer of land in an area before they're even detected. "Because of the amount of wilderness and gorse, the Tasmanian countryside is a very good habitat for them to hide in," said Chris. It's also full of food. "We have so many small animals—little bettongs, bandicoots, rabbits, rats, ground-dwelling parrots, rufous wallabies, possums—it's just a banquet for foxes."

If the Fox Free Tasmania Taskforce is not successful, the foxes' grow-ing population would not even be apparent for ten or fifteen years. "Then ground parrots and things like the Eastern barred bandicoot—because they're not at high numbers to start with—they would disappear very quickly . . . If the foxes are breeding, we're going to lose the battle. I suppose time will be the judge of it all."

So far—after hundreds of all-nighters—the task force hadn't caught any foxes. They weren't even sure if they had seen any. It was like they were chasing a red fog.

But the good news was that they did have some kills under their belts. Chris pointed to the big map and to a six-mile stretch of road along the Midlands Highway between Campbelltown and Conara Junction. It was jammed with yellow, blue, and green pins. Some of these "fox" sightings were not very good. People were seeing "foxes" with fluffy white tails and catlike heads. And that muddied the waters for the task force. "What we do in an area with a lot of sightings—if there's any sort of confusion between cats and foxes—we'll take the cats out."

"You take them out?" we said.

"We shoot them." So far, the task force had shot a total of 136 cats.

Alexis's eyes widened. Maybe the Vroom Museum had a future after all.

We wondered. *If people sometimes confused cats with foxes . . .* We asked if we could look over a few sighting reports. Chris showed us an inch-thick folder, and we flipped through it. Quite a few reports described the fox accurately, or nearly so. The words "sly" and "skulking" were frequently used. After reading through about twenty sightings, we found one that seemed suggestive. A couple driving home from their golf club on Tasmania's east coast had reported seeing the following to a task force officer: "Gingery/sandy animal, dog-like, bigger than cat. No eye shine, unusual, 'bouncing' gait. Animal moved toward them on opposite road edge. Then moved into roadside bush."

We looked up. "Is it possible people ever mistake thylacines for foxes?" we asked.

Chris gave us the hairy eyeball.

"Ahhhhh . . ." Clearly, he was stalling, trying to think of a way to be polite. But then he just gave up. "If you want to believe in thylacines, you'll believe in fairies."

"Don't a lot of people here believe it?"

"A lot of people *want* to believe. That's the whole thing, yeah? It was an animal that wasn't scared of humans—and that was probably its biggest downfall. There's plenty of documented evidence of people walking along trails and turning around and there'd be a thylacine coming along behind them. Or they'd walk through a camp in the night. Why does this animal stop doing *that*? Basically, it disappeared. Extinction."

"What do you think of the cloning project?" Alexis asked.

"Interesting," Chris said. He could see why the cloning scientists would want to bring the thylacine back. "It's like any extinct animal. It's a tragedy to think that humans wiped out something." He paused to reflect. "That's exactly what stopping foxes in Tasmania is all about, stopping further extinctions. Because if foxes get established, that's what will happen."

"Then you'll really need to send in the clones," said Alexis. "You'll have to clone every mammal in Tasmania."

17. THE RED FOG

That evening we met Ken Wright, one of several fox eradication officers employed by the Tasmanian government. He was in his mid-forties and had the deeply tanned, sunburned face of an outdoorsman, just beginning to be slashed with crow's-feet. His outfit included khaki slacks, a white shirt rolled up at the sleeves, wire-rimmed glasses, and a brown Akubra hat—the emblem of outback Australia—that matched the color of his short, wiry brown beard. If he'd had a bronze star pinned to his shirt, instead of a Parks and Wildlife patch that pictured a snarling Tasmanian devil, we might have taken Ken for the ghost of Wyatt Earp. His slender, intelligent face exuded a quiet authority.

Ken had picked us up at our motel in Launceston, and we drove south on the Midlands Highway, entering a flat terrain of farm fields lined with hedgerows. Low forested hills hung in the distance. The Midlands was the most British-influenced section of Tasmania, with some of the towns resembling English country villages. But once you got out onto the farmland, it was more like the Wild West.

Ken was taking us foxhunting, something he did virtually every night. As we sped past the hedgerows, the sky turned from pale pink to purple. We all sat quiet, admiring the vast landscape.

"So this is an unusual job," Alexis said finally. "Did you ever think you'd be working as a professional foxhunter in Tasmania?"

"Bloody no."

Ken had worked for twenty-five years shearing sheep in South Australia, Queensland, Victoria, and Tasmania. "That's about as Australian a job as you can get," he said.

Some days, he would shear 160 sheep, one every ninety seconds or so. It was backbreaking work, but he liked country life, raising dogs, hunting, riding. As a sideline back in the 1970s, he had hunted foxes on the mainland and sold their pelts to the fur industry for making stoles, jackets, trimmings. That was when fur was still popular. "Course it's not trendy to wear fur anymore," Ken said. "So the whole industry of selling fox skins basically collapsed. When the skins were worth money, foxes were controlled a lot better."

From an early age, Ken had learned there were all kinds of ways to hunt a fox. The most common method was spotlighting, nabbing a fox in a beam of light and shooting him with a high-powered rifle. Sometimes he would use dogs—terriers in particular—who sniffed out foxes and drove them out of their dens or along creek lines toward waiting guns.

"We'd also whistle them in the morning."

"You just whistle and they'll come?" asked Alexis.

"Yeah, you whistle like a rabbit caught in a trap. And you make it plaintive." He showed us a whistle he kept under the dash. The fox thinks he's headed toward a conveniently injured rabbit—a tasty meal. What he gets instead is a bullet in the head.

"It doesn't always work," Ken went on. "You get an experienced fox, an older fox, he may have been whistled at before and shot at, so he turns tail and runs."

As Ken drove down the highway, he pointed off into the countryside at what was believed to be the epicenter of the fox outbreak. "Just over there about five kilometers, that's where we think the litters of fox cubs were raised and released." In the last year, there had been dozens of sightings in and around this stretch of highway.

Ken said our destination was a sheep and cattle property near the town of Powranna in the Northern Midlands. This area is the heart and soul of Tasmanian sheep farming—home to about 750,000 sheep in a community with a human population of about twelve thousand. Most of the farmers in the district were letting the fox task force search their land.

"Farmers are quite worried about the whole thing," Ken said. "In some parts of the mainland, foxes can take up to 30 percent of your lamb growth every year. That's just huge, that's money down the drain as far as the farmer's concerned."

"Have foxes killed any lambs around here?"

"We've had a few lambs come in that have looked very fox-suspect. Farmers have called us, and we've gone out and had a look. We've seen lambs with their noses eaten off and their tongues eaten out, a typical fox kill. Sometimes they'll chew a little bit of ear, and that's all they'll eat off that one lamb. And they'll just keep doing it.

"But it's not just the farmers," he continued. "Anyone with feelings about wildlife conservation would be worried as well. If the foxes get established here, we'd probably lose every species under five kilos. There are so many native animals in that five-kilo-and-under range that you don't find anywhere else—not anywhere else in the world except Tasmania. Australia's got a terrible record for mammals becoming extinct in the last two hundred years. But in Tasmania, there's only one that's supposed to be gone—the Tasmanian tiger. Now we're looking at twelve, fifteen, twenty species that could go."

"Things aren't looking good for Mangy," Alexis said.

Clearly, foxes were the bad guys in Tasmania. Yet, we found it strange to be rooting for the hunters. In films that depicted horseback-riding aristocrats chasing after packs of bloodhounds, we had always rooted for the fox. This whole anti-fox thing was requiring a reversal of thinking.

Ken slowed down and drove up a dirt road, stopping in front of a wire gate. We got out and surveyed the scene, grassy fields separated by hedgerows. This was just the kind of terrain where we could imagine a foxhunt.

"So, what do you think of foxhunting, you know, the kind with horses and hounds?" we asked.

Ken lit up a cigarette. "Actually, I'm the master of the Northern Hunt Club."

"That's so sexy," said Alexis.

The waning light obscured Ken's reaction.

"Is that on the mainland?" we asked.

"No."

"It's in Tasmania?"

"Yeah."

"Oh." We didn't get it. How could they have a foxhunt in a place without foxes?

"Have you ever heard of aniseed oil?" Ken asked.

"I've had it rubbed on me," Alexis said.

Ken took a deep puff on his cigarette. He explained that at his hunt club, the dogs chased after a lure that had been drenched in aniseed oil. This aromatic lure stood in for the fox. Except for that, the club carried on the old English traditions, with riders dressing in jodhpurs and pinks and sharing glasses of port at the end of the hunt.

A pickup truck drove up to the wire gate, and a man dressed identically to Ken got out. Ken introduced him as John McConnell, another member of the task force. He had red apple cheeks and a jolly demeanor. John put his arm around Ken, so that their Akubras were touching. "We're the best blokes," he said.

These were the kinds of guys you would want to have around if the laws of society broke down. Nice and friendly, but able to pick off a looter at two hundred yards.

John brought out the task force's fox rifle. It had a black plastic stock and shiny stainless steel barrel. Our previous experience with firearms had been limited to cap guns and G.I. Joe's miniature arsenal.

"It's a Ruger .223 caliber," John explained. "It was made in America, actually." He whistled cheerily as he put it together and loaded it with bullets. "I was born and bred on a sheep farm," he went on, noting our fascination with the rifle. "So we grew up with foxes being around all the time and of course as a young kid, not only were they a pest, but very good money in the skin industry. When you weren't doing odd jobs and working on shearing sheds, any spare time you had, you went foxhunting." He shrugged. "Most country kids grow up with hunting."

By this time, night had fallen and it was full dark. John handed the rifle off to Ken, opened the hood of the truck, and hooked up a cable to the pickup's battery. It powered a handheld spotlight. Then John hopped into the bed of the truck.

"Tally ho," he said.

As Ken set the pickup in motion, he rested the rifle across his thighs. In the back of the truck, John moved the spotlight slowly back and forth, illuminating dry fields covered with pasture grass. The beam of light was filled with dust and flying insects. We smelled hay and cow manure.

We passed a shearing shed and stockyards. The paddocks were separated by wire fences and dotted with stands of wattle trees and eucalyptuses. As we drove slowly through the dark paddocks, with the spotlight sweeping the landscape, we heard the occasional *moo* of a cow rising out of the darkness and the shrill call of plovers crying *keee, keee, keee*. A long-eared hare jumped out in front of us, leaving a trail of dust in its wake.

"We're looking for eye shine and movement," Ken said as we drove slowly through the paddocks. "You look for everything, anything."

Up ahead, a pair of luminous orbs shone out from the darkness.

"What's that?" we asked excitedly.

"It's a sheep," said Ken.

"Oh."

A few seconds later, we heard a telltale *baaaaaahhhhh* and passed a ghost-white sheep surrounded by pale brown tussocks of grass. Its eyes flashed a wet globby green. We thought about when sheep were first brought to Tasmania in the early nineteenth century. On bright moonlit nights, their eyes must have looked like neon signs to Tasmanian tigers, blinking "EAT HERE."

"You can get an idea of what animal you're looking at, just by the color and nature of the eye shine," Ken said. "Sheep and deer eye shine is quite greenish, sometimes a yellowy green, and sometimes it appears blue. Brushtail possums have soft reddish eyes. Rabbits have amber eye shine.

And wallaby, you get a little bit of eye shine, but not much—usually you'll see movement first."

"And the fox?"

"With the fox, eye shine is the biggest and first indicator. It's not so much the color as the brightness. The color tends to change depending on the angle or atmospheric conditions. Sometimes a fox's eyes appear reddish, but mostly they're a really bright gold or silver color." He paused to consider the shifty qualities of the fox. "You actually look for a bit of eye separation as well," he added. "A cat gives you a fairly bright reflection, but it looks like it has only one eye. With the fox you can actually see the eye separation."

Ken peered into night. As the spotlight swept the fields, we tried to use our newfound eye knowledge. Hopping rabbits and sauntering brushtail possums were all over the place—flashing us with amber eyes, red eyes. Groups of sheep flashed green and blue. It was like the stars had fallen onto the grassy farm fields.

A rabbit dashed across the headlights. For a moment, we were mesmerized by its golden gaze.

"Rabbits, of course, are nonnative," Ken said. "You know the story of rabbits being brought to Australia?"

"Yeah, what a disaster," Alexis said.

Tasmania's fox problem was only the most recent ecological catastrophe resulting from animal importations into Australia. Foxes and rabbits have a very close relationship, too. Both were introduced into the wilds of mainland Australia by English settlers for the purpose of hunting—the first foxes following on the hind legs of the first rabbits by only a few years. The first twenty-four rabbits were brought to Victoria in 1859. A typical female rabbit can have six litters a year, producing about thirty offspring. With reproductive capabilities like that, those original twenty-four rabbits permutated into an army. By the early 1900s, the continent was overrun. They nibbled grazing lands bare, destroyed the fragile landscape with their burrowing, and displaced native burrowers like the hare wallaby, bilby, and bandicoot. Eventually, mass rabbit hunts were organized. A two-thousand-mile-long fence was built to stop the rabbits from spreading. But the long-eared interlopers simply kept breeding—and dug under.

When foxes arrived in Australia, they could scarcely have found themselves in a more hospitable situation. Rabbits are their favorite food. But hungry foxes did not stop the rapidly breeding rabbits. Quite the contrary. The dastardly bunnies just hopped into new territories and provided food for more and more foxes. And when a fox can't find a rabbit, it will eat a marsupial instead. Together, foxes and rabbits have been called the "deadly duo"—bringing death and extinction to midsized marsupials all over Australia.

Ultimately, the rabbits were somewhat contained. Rabbit viruses were introduced in the 1950s and the rabbit population dropped precipitously. But the rabbit still has a bad reputation. Environmentalists are particularly irked by the story of the Easter Bunny. The notion of a "good" bunny out doing good deeds is anathema. So there is a movement to replace the Easter Bunny with the Easter Bilby, a similarly long-eared but native creature, which now only survives in places rabbits, foxes, and feral cats can't reach. Thousands of pounds of Easter Bilby chocolates are sold every year, and Australian environmentalists hope to one day eradicate chocolate bunnies all across their great land.

Knowing all this, we drew some satisfaction from the fact that both Ken and John were wearing Akubras—made from pure rabbit felt. The superabundance of rabbits was not lost on early Australian milliners, and rabbits are turned into one of the most iconic of all Australian clothing items.

We were scanning the ground beneath a line of wattle trees when we heard John yell from above. "Moggie!"

Ken stopped the pickup, and we felt a crackle of excitement. John was shining the spotlight into a tip, a pit filled with rubbish and farm debris, surrounded by brush. A Cyclopean figure glared back at us, its one eye glowing like a white-hot coal.

We weren't sure what a Moggie was, but it sounded sinister, and we were on the verge of asking just what we were facing when we recognized the animal pinned in John's spotlight. It was a small, striped quadruped: an orange tabby cat. It looked like it had just walked out of a pet shop.

"Moggie?"

Ken opened his door, picked up the rifle, and flipped down the stand onto the hood of the pickup. Then he leaned down and looked through the sight, his finger on the trigger.

"It's a nickname for a cat," he said.

Ken, we knew, had shot foxes from 1,200 feet in Victoria. We were scarcely one hundred feet from the tabby. Moggie, we figured, didn't have much of a chance. Alexis began to look a little pale, and we felt a sudden chill.

We had known cats were on the menu for the evening. But when confronted with this imminent feline assassination, a new idea struggled to the surface of our consciousness: *Were we crazy? What were we doing out hunting a kitty-cat?*

We knew ridding the world of this fluffy beast was for the greater good . . . and yet, when it came down to it . . . shouldn't someone call the fire department and help Moggie get home? We had been culturally programmed to serve and protect *Felis catus.*

A debate began raging in our minds: It was being held on the stage of the Kaufman Theater at the American Museum of Natural History. Speaking against the cats was Mangy. He'd cleaned himself up and was dressed in a suit. A plastic name tag pinned to his jacket read "Director, Vroom Museum." He was standing before a blackboard, using his tail as a pointer and going over the following list. "Repeat after me," he lectured.

Cats are spree killers.

They kill for sport.

They shit on dead wallabies.

They make mincemeat out of cute little macropods.

On the opposite side of the stage was Beatrice. She was narrating a PowerPoint presentation. It was a personal appeal.

Since the time of the ancient Egyptians, cats have been partnered with the human race . . . An audience of house cats—Manx, Siamese, Persian, and Rex—murmured and nodded their heads in approval.

We braced for the blast. But Ken never got a chance to squeeze the trigger. Moggie darted off into a tangle of brush.

The rifle's stainless steel barrel glinted mutely in the moonlight. "He didn't go far," Ken predicted. The spotlight darted through the darkness—as if it were chasing an escaped felon through a prison yard.

"So," we asked nervously, "have you killed a lot of cats?"

"Yeah," he said. "They're not very elusive." He saw us eyeing the gun. "Have a look," he offered.

We took turns peering through the rifle's telescopic sight. Moggie's lair leapt into the foreground. It seemed as if we could see a single blade of grass glowing in the spotlight from fifty feet away.

Ken continued. "What's happening down here is that we're getting sightings of things that aren't foxes coming in as foxes. We'll go out and spotlight and see a big ginger cat running around. We shoot that cat and the sightings stop. So, it gets rid of the background noise—the sightings that are just nonsense basically. Cats are such destructive pests as well. And it keeps us in good practice. If we see a fox, we want to be confident that, when we pick up that rifle, we're going to be able to shoot it."

"So," we began rather tentatively, "have either of you ever had a cat for a pet?"

"Heaps of 'em!" John said enthusiastically. "They're fantastic—if they're able to stay home and be looked after. Unfortunately, in the wrong habitat, they can do a lot of damage. The cat is such a great hunter—it's got that instinct to stalk and hunt. They're great survivors. That's why they cause so much trouble in the environment."

Ken started up the pickup again, and we began cruising slowly around the perimeter of the tip. We were stalking the cat. "Here puss, puss, puss," Ken murmured. An orange blur streaked through the brush and vanished behind a log. Ken stopped and set up the rifle again. It was another tense moment. We were still struggling with our inner cat ladies. Ken began to make kissing noises, "psssssss, pssssst, pssssssst," to lure the cat out into the open. "Sometimes it works," he said. His eye was glued to the sight as John swept the trees with the spot. We waited about five minutes, but Moggie stayed hidden.

"Is Moggie typical of the size of the cats you shoot?" we asked. "He seemed kind of small for a feral cat."

"They're normally about two or three kilos. The biggest cat we shot was nine and a half kilos." Twenty-one pounds. "For a cat, that's a fair lump—and all muscle."

Alexis, who had not said a word since Ken first drew a bead on Moggie, finally perked up. "That's no flabby tabby," he said.

We asked Alexis who he was rooting for, the shooters or Moggie.

"What can I say?" he said. "I don't think I could have handled it if they blew that cat away."

When it came to feline eradication, Alexis could talk the talk but he couldn't walk the walk.

We returned to the prime target, scanning fields and paddocks for signs of foxy activity.

"What are our chances of actually seeing a fox?"

"Tonight?" Ken said, scanning the paddocks. "Less than one percent . . . Personally I've seen four that could have been a fox. But they just wouldn't give us a chance to shoot them. So we can't confirm that."

Ken, John, and all the members of the task force were anxious for such confirmation, to bring in the body of a dead fox. Despite the evidence that at least one fox had dined on Tasmanian animals, the public and some government officials were growing impatient.

The situation was frustrating. Between the two of them, Ken and John had shot thousands of foxes on the mainland. They had the skills—tracking, luring, hunting, shooting. But the incipient population of foxes in Tasmania was proving elusive.

"We're going to be incredibly lucky if we actually get one," John said. "It is really the needle in the haystack. At least on the mainland, foxes have territories—there's pressure. You know where their dens are. But *here,* the world's their own. They're gypsies. They've got no territories. It's a free and easy life with plenty of tucker."

John shone his spotlight on two furry brushtail possums—one big and one small—shimmying up a small tree with feathery leaves and wispy, drooping branches. The smaller possum looked a little nervous. "It's a mother with a joey," said Ken. In the spotlight, their eyes gave off a dull Mars-like glow. "When the young ones leave the pouch, they usually ride on their mother's back for a few weeks."

"That's a wattle tree they're in," John said. "They used to tan the skins of wallaby and possum with wattle bark." At one time, Tasmania had a large trade in possum skins. Tasmanian brushtails have thicker, darker fur than their mainland counterparts, and their pelts were highly prized. As late as the 1970s, as many as 200,000 possum pelts a year were exported.

Tasmania's native possums were doing quite well in the absence of a significant fur trade. "They've gone berserk," said Ken.

In the headlights, we surprised a group of brushtail possums that had overrun a small barn. At least three of the furry creatures were scrambling on the hay-covered floor feeding on a spilled sack of calf weaner pellets. A small brushtail with a beautiful black coat was running back and forth, balancing on a rusting wagon wheel. One reddish possum was sitting in a stooped position on top of a wooden gate—its thick furry tail hanging in front of it. It didn't seem to be scared by our arrival, and with its sprightly long ears sticking up, it appeared rakish and relaxed, like a ranch hand on a break. The scene looked like a goofball postcard and would have been complete if the animals were wearing Akubras and sucking on stalks of hay. *"Greetings from the possum paddock, Tasmania,"* or *"Howdy, Possum!"*

Brushtails were cute and abundant. But at an average weight of 3.3 kilograms (about seven pounds), they were also fox food. If foxes took hold, possums most likely wouldn't be eradicated, but they wouldn't be seen on the ground very often. The survivors would all be hiding in trees.

Ken drove on, and John's spotlight revealed two more animals next to a stand of wattles. They were kangaroo-like, but very small and slightly hunched over, standing about twelve inches tall on their hind legs. Their noses were elongated, more like a rat's than a kangaroo's. Ken stopped the pickup and turned off the engine. We watched them for a moment, then the dark-furred creatures hopped off into the safety of a large gorse bush. As they retreated, the spotlight illuminated white spots on the ends of their long, skinny tails.

"Potoroos," said John from above. "They're also called tip tails."

"That's perfect fox tucker," said Ken.

"Foxes would just have them for lunch," John agreed. "Feral cats would, too." Potoroos weighed about 1.3 kilos (just under three pounds), making them ideal, easy prey.

The long-nosed potoroo was considered a secure species in Tasmania (at least it was until the foxes showed up). On the mainland, however, they were much rarer and listed as vulnerable, having disappeared from many areas due to habitat destruction as well as predation by foxes and feral cats. Tasmania was their last real refuge, and biologists agreed it would be unlikely that Tasmania's potoroos would survive a fox invasion. And, as with any extinction, their disappearance could have implications beyond their own species.

Unlike Bennett's wallabies and Tasmanian pademelons, which are grazers, the potoroo dines extensively on native truffles, which grow beneath the ground. Much like the truffle dogs and truffle pigs that sniff out France's coveted Périgord truffles, the potoroos rely on their long, powerful noses to descry the scent of Tasmanian truffles, the different species of which have been described as smelling like bubblegum, peanut

butter, gasoline, and rotting onions. They use the long, sharp claws on their front paws to dig them up.

The truffles are a type of mycorrhizal fungus, and they have a symbiotic relationship with trees. A truffle draws on a tree's roots for sugar and minerals, but it gives back to the tree a super-growing boost. In a study completed in mainland Australia, trees paired with truffle symbionts grew as much as ten times faster than trees that were deprived of their truffle partners. Truffles are like forest fertilizer. And potoroos are inadvertently like forest farmers, spreading the spores of truffles when they eat and excrete them. It's a delicate balance—a classic ecosystem, with one hand washing another and another in a nearly invisible chain.

So if the foxes eat up all the potoroos, it's not only going to have an impact on the animals; it will change Tasmania's entire ecosystem as well. Interestingly, there is one other Tasmanian animal that eats even more fungus than the long-nosed potoroo—the Tasmanian bettong. Already extinct on the mainland, this little creature is fox bait, too.

Potoroos, in general, are adept at hiding, even creating small tunnels through the grass that they travel through surreptitiously. But it is unlikely they would be able to hide from a large population of foxes.

"Those potoroos don't have a burrow to hide in or anything. There's nowhere they can go to get away from the fox," said John. They couldn't climb trees like the possum.

Even though our encounter with the potoroos was brief, we found them delightful. Like many of Tasmania's native mammals, they were eccentric and had an *Alice in Wonderland* quality. The thought of an intentionally introduced predator shredding through their numbers was maddening.

Ken and John decided to call it quits on the farm. Like all the other fox hunts on the island so far, ours had been unsuccessful. Ken drove us back to Launceston. On the way, we continued to scan the road and surrounding fields for quadrupeds, striped, red, fluffy, and otherwise. But we saw nothing on four legs. Ken told us his night was just beginning. He would be checking out another reputed fox haunt and then, in the early hours of the morning, go whistling for foxes. From the outskirts of town, we watched as Ken's vehicle disappeared into the Tasmanian night.

"These guys are my heroes," said Alexis, staring down the dark road. "They're on the front lines of the war to protect biodiversity."

And they were fighting an invisible enemy. We hoped the Red Fog didn't win.

"Oh, there seem to be naked people with us today." Two elderly women were pointing at Alexis, who lay on a lawn with his shirt off and his shorts hiked up.

We had been invited to the Field Day at the Launceston Field Naturalists Club. It was a combination picnic and flora-and-fauna hunt on the club's grounds in Myrtle Bank, about twenty-five miles northeast of Launceston. The drive over had been hellacious. The outdoor temperature gauge in the Pajero read 30 degrees Centigrade—which in Fahrenheit translated as "insanely hot." If we had cracked the egg of a Tasmanian native hen, we could have cooked it on the blacktop. To make things worse, Tasmania was being hit by wildfires—and the air was tinged with the smell of smoke. Several of the club's members were skipping the day's activities in order to protect their homes from the licking flames.

We found the man who had invited us to the event under the shade of a big spreading eucalyptus tree. His name was Jim Nelson, and he was an expatriate American who had been living in Tasmania for the past three decades. Todd Walsh, our escort into the watery world of the giant lobster, had suggested we get in touch with him.

"What's his specialty?" we had asked Todd.

"Ahh . . . everything. He knows every blade of grass in the bloody bush."

Jim was tall, sunburned, and rangy. For the last couple of years, he had been doing research on burrowing crayfish. "Todd may study the largest crayfish," he said in a deep booming voice that sounded remarkably like William Hurt. "But I study one of the world's most highly evolved ones."

Jim opened the trunk of his car. It held a small library of files containing scientific papers, natural history books, and specimens. He removed a vial containing a crayfish embalmed in alcohol, and we noticed Jim had huge hands. If a crayfish latched its claws on to one of his mitts, he probably wouldn't even feel it.

"This crayfish is actually the one that's on the club's land here and it's an endangered species. It's called *Engaeus orramakunna,* the Mount Arthur burrowing crayfish. It makes its living from burrowing down to the water table rather than living in free water. Consequently, it's changed its morphology to accommodate that sort of burrowing. So when you look at it, it's quite absurdly proportioned. It's got this tiny little tail and this great big bulldozer front end. Its carapace is laterally compressed and its claws are held vertically, so it can squeeze through really tight spaces. It's quite amazing for a water animal to make all these adaptations to live in soil."

Jim was wearing a black T-shirt with illustrations showing *E. orramakunna* in three different poses. Alexis asked if he could photograph Jim and his crayfish—and an odd sort of fashion shoot unfolded. Jim removed the crayfish from the vial, and they discussed whether the crayfish's tail should be tucked under its body or stretched out. They settled on tucked under, and Jim modeled with the crayfish in his palm.

"Faaaahbulous," Alexis said. Click. "So where are you from originally, Jim?"

"The Midwest. I was born in Nebraska, but I did most of my growing up in Illinois on the Fox River, not far from Chicago."

"Why did you move to Tasmania?" Click. "For the crayfish?"

"Um, well I was escaping Richard Nixon."

"Post-Watergate depression?" Click.

"Well, Watergate really blew up after I came here. Richard Nixon was a real, you know . . . I was pretty discouraged with America. Most of my friends that went to Vietnam came back in body bags . . . so I was looking for something else. I had done a degree in psychology and biology and decided that there really wasn't any future for me there. I got involved in ceramics, and I came to Australia to study with a master potter. When I visited Tasmania, I found the lush green more agreeable than the dry mainland. Then I set up my own pottery in 1973, so I've been doing that ever since."

Click. "So how did you start studying crayfish?"

"Well, originally with that giant one that Todd is interested in. Growing up, I was always interested in crayfish. There was something about them that fascinated me. Not so much from a scientific point of view but from an aesthetic one—"

"They're gorgeous." Click.

Jim pointed at the specimen in his palm. "*Engaeus* is the genus of course and *orramakunna* is the aboriginal word for the name of the area. Tasmania's really a hot spot for burrowing crayfish. There's fifteen species of the *Engaeus* and fourteen species of another genus of burrowing crayfish that occur in our buttongrass plains."

Alexis wrapped up his shoot. We told Jim we had spent the night in a buttongrass plain and had been surprised not to see any animals—not even a crayfish.

"Well, it can be really variable by the night. Was it a full moon? Most animals—little mammals in particular—don't much like moonlit nights. They're too visible to owls. They like at least a half-moon."

Jim invited us into the club's study center. It was built out of mud bricks and wood. There were bunks, a kitchen, and a small, well-thumbed library. Many of the books, Jim informed us, had been written by members of the Field Naturalists Club. In fact, as a collective the club had published a book, *A Guide to Flowers and Plants of Tasmania,* now in its third edition, and it was the bible to the island's flora. They had used the proceeds to build this clubhouse.

The club's official emblem was an illustration of a Tasmanian tiger perched on a rock overlooking a valley. The emblem was pictured on name tags pinned to club members' shirts and burned into the wood of a long table in the middle of the clubhouse. It was a regal-looking thylacine. With its head lifted nobly, it was the kind of heroic figure that inspired optimism. We wondered if any of these naturalists thought the tiger was still alive.

We asked Jim what he thought about the thylacine.

"I don't think it's out there anymore." Our hopes sank again. Jim thought the thylacine's large size and the fact that there hadn't been a body found or a photograph taken in nearly seventy years made its survival highly unlikely. "The kind of sightings that people make . . . well, people see something and they want to see something else. So I don't trust all the sightings. Having said that, there have been a couple of really good ones. And there's a zoologist, who's long retired by now—Bob Green—he's still of the opinion that they're out there somewhere."

While the field naturalists ate lunch and chatted, we wandered around eavesdropping, hoping to overhear some sagacious conversation about the tiger. There were experts on everything else: orchids ("there are more than 190 orchid species in Tasmania, including 50 that are endemic"), eucalyptus trees ("twenty-nine species in Tasmania, seventeen of which are endemic"). There were people who had millipedes and worms named after them. When a brown spider the size of a baseball peeped out from behind the clubhouse's rafters, it was welcomed like an old friend dropping by for tea. "That's a huntsman," a club member informed us.

We met a chipper woman wearing a crisp red-and-white-striped Oxford shirt, with short gray hair. Her name was Alison Green (no relation to Bob), and she had been the curator of invertebrates at the Tasmanian Museum for twenty-three years.

"What's your specialty?" we asked.

"Slaters."

"Oh . . ." We weren't *quite* sure what those were.

"Native slaters, not the ones that are introduced."

"Hmmm . . . how many species are there?"

"I think we're up to about sixty-odd species for Tasmania, about half of those have been described and named and the other half are still new and waiting to be described and named."

"Where can you find them?"

"They occur in all sorts of territories—in rain forest, in eucalypt forests, on beaches, and in caves. We've got three species introduced from Europe which are in everybody's gardens."

"What are those called?"

She supplied us with three obscure scientific names.

"Do you have a favorite?"

"Not really. I've got one which I named after my professor. It lives in the rain forest. It's quite an attractive little beast. It rolls up."

We motioned for Alexis to come over. "Alexis, meet Alison, she's a slater expert."

"That's amazing. Do you think we'll see any slaters today?"

"I certainly hope so." She excused herself and said she would see us on the nature trail.

"Alexis, what are slaters?" we whispered.

"I have no fucking clue."

Next we met a young man named Danny Soccol. He was about thirty, a recent graduate of the biology program at the University of Tasmania in Launceston.

Danny had special interests in botany and bush tucker, and he sometimes volunteered to collect invertebrates—spiders, worms—for scientific projects. He actually had a worm named after him, *Diporochaete soccoli*. "I was one of the people who helped with the research. I was digging them out all over Tassie, in rain forests, dry sclerophyll. But it's just a small native worm." He laughed self-effacingly.

"Don't be embarrassed," said Alexis. "We're jealous."

The field naturalists were going exploring on the land surrounding their clubhouse, 150 acres of rain forest, wet and dry eucalypt forest, and open grassland. We followed them down a path of trees neatly labeled with signs. Alison pointed out a *Eucalyptus regnans*. We strained our necks looking up the gray-and-brown trunk and halfway up were hit with vertigo. *Eucalyptus regnans*—more commonly known as a swamp gum—is the largest species of tree in the Southern Hemisphere.

Danny and Jim stopped in front of another specimen, a green bushy shrub with long, leathery, bladelike leaves.

"This is a Tasmanian sugar bush," Jim said.

"Is that an endemic?"

"Yes, it only grows here."

He and Danny tore off a few leaves.

"If you chew them, they taste sweet. It's excellent bush tucker."

We put the leaves in our mouths and gave them a chew. At first, they didn't taste like anything.

"You have to work on it a little bit. It takes a while for the sugar to come out."

We continued chewing. After a moment, the leaves transmitted a slight tingling sensation.

"Mmmm," Alexis said tentatively. The club members looked at us expectantly.

Slowly, we perceived a fiery wave breaking over the soft parts of our mouths. Our gums and cheeks began to burn. Our tongues went numb.

As the green wildfire engulfed our lips, we spit out the leaves and looked at the "sugar bush." There had been a little label in front of the plant all the time. It said "Tasmanian mountain pepper."

"It really has a nice bite," Jim said, laughing.

"And it's very good on pepper steak," Danny added.

We'd been punked! And by a bunch of botanizers. Who knew flower lovers engaged in hazing?

Danny stopped in front of another plant. We looked at it warily.

"Is this another type of bush tucker?"

"No, it's stinkwood . . . I'm giving this one away."

He crushed a few leaves. We took the tiniest of whiffs and were slammed with a wave of nausea.

We had just become honorary members of the club.

We walked down through eucalyptus forest and into a damp, muddy gully with a small stream running through it. In this lush environment, prehistoric tree ferns grew like vertical gardens, their trunks covered in flowering plants, mosses, liverworts, and smaller species of ferns. John

Simmons, the club's president, pointed up at a tree fern whose base was growing from the branch of a sassafras tree about thirty feet up. He explained that the sassafras tree might have originally grown on the tree fern, but over the years, the tree put down roots and lifted the fern into the air.

Some of the tree ferns' moss-covered trunks had bizarrely contorted shapes. One was bent like a snake poised to strike; half of its trunk lay on the ground before it swooped upward. "They'll fall or be knocked over and start growing again. You can even chop a man fern off in the middle and it will reroot or sprout," John told us, "which is why some of them are so twisty."

Tree ferns, commonly called man ferns in Tasmania, are long-lived and very slow to develop, growing only two inches in height each year. John believed that several of the tree ferns in the gully were upwards of six hundred years old.

These tree ferns, *Dicksonia antarctica,* were ancient, possibly existing as a species for as long as 90 million years. And they were all over Tasmania. Yet, in the last ten years, their future had become less secure. Overseas, the tree ferns had become popular garden plants—worth $400 per yard, a height not achieved until a tree fern was thirty or forty years old—and there was an astonishing amount of poaching, with many of the stolen ferns ending up in English gardens.

Danny turned to show us a filmy fern, a nearly translucent green frond, growing off the trunk of a tree fern. Just as he was telling us that the filmy fern was only one cell thick, a land leech dropped onto his hand. We crowded around to look. It moved like a villainous black inchworm across his skin.

Ahhh, we thought, *finally we meet our nemesis.*

Without going through a true metamorphosis, the leech exhibited disturbing shape-shifting properties. Perched on Danny's hand, it looked like a little periscope, twisting back and forth, its head curled in an upside-down U, searching the high seas for blood and a soft place to start chewing. It elongated its body like a living rubber band and morphed its head into a needle-sharp probe.

"Is it feeding on you?" we asked Danny hopefully.

"No, he's looking for a spot. They take quite a while to latch on—a couple of minutes."

"That's *Philaemon pungens,* the smaller of Tasmania's two land leech species," Alison interjected. Both land leech species had two jaws that worked like rasps with which they chewed through the skin and made a V-shaped incision.

In wet forests like this one, leeches could survive for months, possibly even years, without a meal, living through dry spells and all-out desiccation, until they sensed blood and dropped down on an unsuspecting donor. After a thorough blood meal, they could expand to several times their size.

"Once it attaches, it also has an anticoagulant to keep the blood flowing," said Danny.

"How do you get it off, if it does attach?"

"You can put salt on them or you can burn them off." Danny tossed his leech back into the forest—before it had a chance to start feeding. We remembered the famous, cringe-inducing leech scene from the 1951 movie *The African Queen*. The bloodsuckers cover Humphrey Bogart's body, and he and Katharine Hepburn, their hands quavering in primal fear, have to burn them off with a lit cigarette. "Filthy little devils," Bogart curses.

The field naturalists returned to their pursuits and flipped over a rotting log. Underneath it was a riot of life. Eight-legged creatures, forty-two-legged creatures, and many with no legs at all. Alison found a millipede, but wasn't sure of the genus. Jim picked up a fast-moving centipede. It was greenish gray with a red head, legs, and tail. "It's got jaws," he said.

They heaved over a second log. Alison found a harvestman. "This is an arachnid, but it's different from a spider in that it doesn't have a waist." It was a little beige daddy longlegs.

"Harvestmen don't dissolve their prey like spiders," Jim added. "They have to rip it apart." (Spiders inject their prey with venom, wait for its insides to liquefy, and then suck the insides out like a vanilla milkshake.)

Each of these small creatures had its own story—a fact not often appreciated by laypeople. One thing invertebrate lovers have in common is their dismay that so much attention is given to animals with spines. Vertebrates are wonderful, they would tell you, but limited. For example, how many kinds of humans are there? Just one. *Homo sapiens.* That makes human beings very special, but not at all diverse. If you want to see a different type of human, good luck. But take leeches. There are five hundred different kinds around the world. Or take harvestmen—there are five thousand different kinds and probably many more waiting to be discovered. Ninety-nine percent of all animals are invertebrates.

The reason the spineless get such scant attention is that they're so little. It's size that put the giant squid—the world's largest invertebrate—on the map and at the top of everyone's research agenda. And that's why Tasmania's own giant freshwater lobster is slowly gaining notoriety. If each of the creatures under the log were the size of an echidna or a pademelon or a person, then we might all show a bit more respect. In fact, we'd all be running screaming out of the woods, shit-scared for our lives.

John produced a snail from under the log and held it in the flat of his palm. Everyone gathered around. "We haven't seen one of these for years," he said excitedly. It was a Northeast forest snail (*Anoglypta launcestonensis*), one of Tasmania's 116 species of land snails. Like so many Tasmanian animals, this slow-moving creature lived nowhere else in the world—and it occupied its own island within an island, a forty-two-mile by thirty-mile area surrounding the Field Naturalists clubhouse. Its habitat is the underside of rotting logs where it is believed to eat detritus and fungi.

Although the snail was keeping its body hidden, we got a good look at its curious shell, which had a sideways look to it as if the snail was wearing a beret. The shell's outer side was brown, rough, and grainy. John turned it over, exposing a smooth, swirling black underside with a bright lime-colored stripe following the contour of the spiral.

Like the thylacine, this little animal had once been a missing species. In 1970, "they sent parties up into the Northeast to find one, because it hadn't been seen for eighty years," John said. The snail was located, oozing about its old haunts, but this rediscovery eventually launched a controversy.

In an issue of the *Tentacle*, the newsletter of the mollusk division of the IUCN—The World Conservation Union, Tasmanian zoologist and snail expert Kevin Bonham wrote that the Northeast forest snail "arouses strong emotions even among scientists because of its beauty and taxonomic distinctiveness."

In 1995, the snail was listed as a vulnerable species under the Threatened Species Protection Act. Tasmanian conservationists began using the snail's protected status as a shield against the clear-cutting of old-growth forests in the Northeast and held numerous "Save the Snail" rallies. However, in 1996, Bonham determined that the snail's population was secure (much larger than previously thought) and two years later advocated that it be delisted. Conservationists were livid, and an ugly battle, with name-calling, ensued. As the delisting seemed to coincide with new logging proposals, Bonham was accused of being a collaborator with the forestry department—this despite the fact that he was simultaneously advocating that three other snail species be added to the threatened species list.

Alexis snapped a photo of *A. launcestonensis*. "It's an honor to meet such a celebrity," he said.

When we emerged from the shelter of the fern gully, Danny led us over to a big sandy lump on the ground. "Have you heard of jack jumpers?" he asked. "They're very aggressive ants. Very common in Tasmania."

When a jack jumper nest is disturbed, the ants race up from the ground and jump about in an attack frenzy. In their rage to defend their nest, they can leap as far as four inches, eight times their body length. To demonstrate, Danny poked a stick into the ant nest and then kicked it several times. The result was volcanic. Ants with bright orange jaws came hurtling out like chunks of hot lava.

We weren't sure what a respectful distance was. "They hurt, but they're not poisonous, right?"

"Oh, yes, if you're allergic," Alison informed us. "The allergic reaction is almost cumulative."

"They've got big nippers on the front end," said Jim, "and everybody thinks they're getting bitten, but they're actually holding on with those nippers, and doing the actual damage with the other end, stinging like a bee. It's quite an ancient group of ants. Most of the ancient ants sting. The modern ants bite." Over the last twenty years, at least three Tasmanians had died of anaphylaxis after being stung by jack jumpers.

After our walk while cooling off in the shade of a wooden gazebo, we started to question the field naturalists about thylacines. Had anyone ever seen one? Alison mentioned that her father had spotted a tiger when he was a schoolboy in the 1920s near a golf course in Tasmania's Northwest. "But that was a long time ago," she said, "before they died out."

Then Danny—hassler of ants and leading club prankster—took us aside. "I want to tell you a story," he said. He didn't seem keen on anyone overhearing. About eight years before, he said, he had gone for a hike near Golconda, north of Mount Arthur . . . "It was dawn and we were coming along a track that had been put in by a bulldozer, and we went down to a clearing. I saw a Bennett's wallaby running through the bush and it looked pretty frightened. Then I saw this other animal come past and it stood there and yawned. It was front-on and quite large, dog-sized with a big jaw and a woolly front. When it walked off, it didn't move like a dog. It was much more . . . athletic. Because of the time of the day and the shadows, I didn't get to see the stripes. But it had an arrogant look in its eye, like it was telling me, 'I'm king of the castle.' Slim chance it was a dog. I was a bit freaked out. The hackles went up on my neck."

In Australia and Tasmania, "taking the piss" is a national pastime. It means "taking the piss out of someone," knocking them down a peg, joking, making fun of people. After the sugar bush incident, we were feeling particularly leery.

Danny seemed distressed when we asked if he was kidding. "This is not a joke. I don't tease about biology." Besides, he added, why would he? "People who report seeing tigers—people think they're crazy."

He said he hadn't had a camera with him, but he did return later to see if he could find any evidence. "I found a scat, but I never got it tested. There were no tracks. The area was quite hard. I've gone back since then, but haven't seen one. The problem is that houses have been going up in that area. So I reckon that thylacines wouldn't be there anymore."

"How sure would you say you were that what you saw was a thylacine?"

"Ninety, ninety-five percent. I'd want to see it one more time to be sure. I do think thylacines are out there, small populations of them."

We told him we had spent a night listening for the thylacine in the Milkshakes—but hadn't seen or heard anything, except for some mysterious flashing lights.

"Ahhhh . . . min min lights," he said.

"What are those?"

"They're like spirit lights. The aboriginal people won't even talk about them."

As he reached the end of his explanation, we realized the skies were getting darker. There had been a shift in the wind and the smoke from the wildfires was blowing in our direction.

"Maybe the fires are headed our way," Jim said. The botanizing party started to break up, and we drove off through the eucalyptus-perfumed haze, pondering Danny's strange report.

Back at the low-budget motor lodge where we were ensconced in Launceston, Alexis convinced us to join him in a "bowl." We decided to take a puff each—and instantly regretted it. This was not the pot from our high school days. The effect was immediate, like getting whacked with a shovel. Over the years, *Cannabis sativa* had been crossbred to get stronger and stronger. The geniuses that made this weed should be hired to clone the thylacine. They could probably get the job done in weeks.

Alexis seemed to be filled with bliss after breathing in the potent smoke, but we were flooded with dread. Our tongues became dry and swollen. Swallowing became a frightening act. Paranoid ideas floated through our heads.

"Do you think the people we've met are taking a piss on us?"

"That's taking *the* piss," said Alexis.

"You think they're taking our piss? Maybe they're all in cahoots."

In our pot-induced stupor, we imagined the Tasmanians we had met were organized in a vast, interconnected cabal to . . . to *what*?

"Don't you *get* it?" we insisted. "The thylacine exists, but they're hiding it from us. When we get home, they'll reveal to the world the last surviving Tasmanian tigers."

"Okay," said Alexis. Having smoked this stuff every day, he was immune to its disorienting effects.

"Everywhere we've gone was their suggestion. We're like pawns on a chessboard. It's all a game. And while we're sent off on wild-goose chases, they're moving the tigers around from safe house to safe house. Bob Green has something to do with it."

"Who's Bob Green?" asked Alexis.

"The zoologist guy Jim said still *believed*."

"Yeah right. We'll go to his house and he'll answer the door in his bathrobe with a thylacine on a leash."

"Exactly." We started rooting around for a phone book to find Bob Green's address. Maybe we would just go over there and check for ourselves. "Remember that guy Carl at the Backpacker's Barn? He's probably hiding an entire population of tigers in the Tarkine. That's where they're breeding them up . . . Geoff King's in on it. Do you think Geoff King's in on it, Alexis?"

"Definitely."

"Yeah, he played footie with Todd Walsh."

The next day we were feeling like ourselves again. But Alexis insisted that we drive by Bob Green's house. Neither the zoologist nor his pet thylacine were home.

While driving west, we dissected Danny Soccol's sighting. Danny was a trained biologist and able to identify a host of obscure invertebrates. A five-foot-long quadruped should have been a piece of cake, but because he had not seen the animal in good light—and could not check for stripes—even he was not 100 percent sure.

"No stripes, no tiger," Alexis said dismissively.

Still, when we looked out at the green forests and jagged hills, the landscape was infused with an extra charge. Danny's tale had added an element of uncertainty.

We were driving up into the foothills of the Great Western Tiers. This region was another of Tasmania's tiger hot spots—rife with sightings and not far from where James Malley had found his tiger tracks in 1971. Jim Nelson from the Field Naturalists Club had told us that the area harbored some other elusive creatures. There was no doubt they existed, but we would have to go underground to see them. We decided to take a detour from our tiger search.

Mole Creek Karst National Park encompassed 5.2 above-ground square miles. Below its surface were more than two hundred caves, hundreds of miles of passageways, plus subterranean rivers, sinkholes, and blind valleys.

As we got nearer to the caves, we entered a lush forest cut by a stream and filled with spreading tree ferns. The invisible world below us was carved out of 400-million-year-old limestone. Much of the erosion had been caused by meltwaters from the last Ice Age infiltrating the bedrock. The caves were still in the process of being formed. Rainwater from the terrestrial realm leached through the plants on the surface, turned acidic, and drop by drop melted and molded the soft limestone beneath our feet.

Our destination was Marakoopa Cave. There, a ranger named Brooke Cohn would serve as our ambassador to the creatures from below. We met her at the ranger station and observed that she was tall and wiry, with short, curly blond hair. For someone who spent so much time underground, she was remarkably tan and attractive.

Walking toward Marakoopa, Brooke explained there were different zones of life in the cave. Subterranean species were adapted to live at different depths and some lurked right outside the entrance. The cave's entryway was blocked with a steel door to control the flow of people in and out. In front of it, Brooke pointed to one of the creatures inhabiting the cave's outermost zone. "She's all legs."

The creature was a female spider the size of Brooke's hand. From an inch-long body, her legs stuck out three inches on each side. And she was closely guarding her egg sac, a white round ball dangling from a short silk thread in a rocky crevice. "That's a Tasmanian cave spider, an ancient species." Her closest relatives were spiders that lived in South America, dating from the time of Gondwanaland millions of years ago, when all the southern continents were connected.

As we explored the moist folds in the wall of limestone, we realized we were looking at some sort of nursery, as there were at least three egg balls, each guarded by a giant spider. The egg balls were an inch in diameter and dotted with brown tidbits—the mother spiders decorated them with tiny pieces of rotting wood for camouflage. They would guard the egg balls for eight months before their spiderlings hatched.

The male cave spiders, Brooke explained, had significantly smaller bodies. And on their second pair of legs, the males had special hooks that they used to hold the female spider's fangs open during mating. Without the hooks, the males might be eaten before mating successfully occurred—and they often were eaten right after. During the act of mating, a female's fangs dripped with venom.

To find their way in the dark, cave invertebrates are endowed with inordinately long legs and antennae. (The male cave spider's legs can reach seven inches in length.) They can also go a long time without eating—since it's often tough to get a meal in a dark cave where nothing grows except fungus—and as a result they live a long time. Scientists believe the Tasmanian cave spider may live for decades.

Brooke unlocked the door to the cave and a stream of cold air hit us. Because the temperature in the cave is always between 48 and 52 degrees Fahrenheit, a differential builds up on hot days and high-pressure cool air rushes out the cave entrance. The day we visited it was nearly 90 degrees out, and the cave's exhalation was so strong it was hard to pull the door closed. It felt like being run over by an invisible train.

Once we were inside, Brooke flicked on a light that illuminated a cave chamber. It was enormous—the size of a ballroom—with rust brown stalactites hanging down from the rocky ceiling and flowstones creating the illusion of frozen waterfalls. The chamber's far wall was smooth, forming a half-dome-shaped amphitheater, and we heard the roiling sound of an unseen, underground stream beneath us. This chamber, Brooke said, was in the transition zone. Under natural conditions, no light penetrated, though it was slightly influenced by outside temperature and humidity.

"Ready?" she asked.

Brooke switched off the light and we were enveloped in darkness. The sound of the rushing subterranean stream and the wind howling through distant, unseen cave passages grew louder.

"Give yourselves some time," Brooke said from the dark. "Your eyes will adjust."

Overhead, pinpoints of burning blue light began to appear. It was as if, instead of being underground, we were watching stars appearing one by one in the night sky. Or back at the Hayden Planetarium, watching the space show.

"Glowworms," said Alexis.

"Hundreds," Brooke confirmed. "Thousands maybe."

The glowworms were congregating on the rocky ceiling of the natural amphitheater that curved over the underground stream. They were actually not worms, Brooke explained, but the larvae of a tiny fly.

"We've got one species of glowworm in Tassie—they're endemic. They only live in wet caves or terrestrial wet environments—and they're just above us here." The species was *Arachnocampa tasmaniensis,* which means Tasmanian spider grub.

Although not related to spiders any more than they were related to worms, *A. tasmaniensis* had a spider's ability to make sticky silk strands. "They suspend themselves from the undersurface of the cave's ceiling by threads, and it's like they're in a little sleeping bag"—a hollow tube made of silk and mucus—"and from there they drop down multiple threads of silk—very sticky, mucousy fishing lines to catch their prey. That nice dark blue glow—it's them burning their waste products, but it also attracts prey. The brighter the glow, the hungrier they are."

The glowworms' prey is flying insects. The larvae of mayflies, stoneflies, and caddisflies are aquatic and sometimes get swept from terrestrial rivers into underground streams. When these insects emerge from their larval stage and turn into flying adults, they find themselves stuck in the dark. Then, when they see the glowworms' lights, they head right up—and get caught in the sticky fishing lines. The glowworms simply reel them on up.

The glowworms themselves stay in their larval incarnation for up to eighteen months. When they finally turn into flying adults, they have only three or four days left to live. "They don't eat—they don't even have mouthparts. All they do is go out and reproduce," Brooke said. "And they do it carefully, because every one of those glowworms has thirty to fifty threads of silk. And often they get caught in their own fishing lines."

With each passing second—as our pupils dilated—more and more glowworms became visible. There was something creepy about the illusion—these grubs and their sticky little threads so effectively posing as a starry night. The lights were beautiful, intoxicating, and we wondered if people ever became mesmerized by the glowworms—thinking they were sleeping under a starry sky, falling into a cave dream, and never waking up.

Certainly, some animals came in and never came out. "As you can hear, we've got a stream going underneath. That brings other cave fauna in, accidentals," said Brooke. "Often in floods, we get platypus and trout that have been pushed through from about a thousand meters up, from the Great Western Tiers. It's very rare, but they end up down here. And we also get wallabies and wombats that fall through sinkholes. They die. They fall into the water and eventually they decompose—and encourage more insect life in the cave."

After the wind pushed us out the cave door and back into the world of the living, Brooke decided she wanted to show us something else—a wilder cave in a different part of the karst system. As we drove on a narrow, winding road through more wet eucalypt forest, Brooke told us a little more about herself. She was a teacher during the school year—she educated autistic children—and worked as a ranger with the Parks and Wildlife Service during the summer. She lived in a small commune called Platypus Bend. They didn't have electricity and grew their own food. She preferred to live off the grid.

On the drive over, Brooke saw a dead animal in the middle of the road. It was a young devil—badly mashed.

"It's sad, you know. I saw him last night." Her face creased with concern.

"You recognize it?"

"Yeah, you just get a feel for them, their size and markings."

Brooke stopped to move it to the side, and Alexis jumped out, too. The animal's entrails were splayed out across the blacktop, and its nearly liquefied carcass was crawling with flies. Alexis pushed his camera right up next to the body. "Could I get you to pose with that?" he asked. Brooke didn't seem to hear him, but he was able to snap her picture as she used a plastic shopping bag for a glove and moved the body into the brush.

Then we got back on the road. "I'll take you to a wild cave called Snail Space, just to give you a feel for it," she said. We parked by a sign that read "PETS AND FIREARMS NOT PERMITTED," and walked into the woods. The cave's entrance was a vertical slit in the ground, with ferns dripping down over the top and dogwood trees, mosses, and lichens growing all around it. A muddy, two-foot-wide chute led down toward the rocky entryway. One by one, with Alexis in the lead and gripping a small flashlight between his teeth, we slid down the hole.

When we reached the narrow entrance, we put out our hands to brace ourselves against the rock—and felt a tickling sensation. Something was moving. As the hair rose on the backs of our necks, we turned our heads. The rocky wall was heaving with brown insects. Tiny brown eyes, crawling legs, and probing antennae.

"Motherfucker!" we heard Alexis whisper from inside the cave.

"Careful of the cave crickets," Brooke warned.

The cave crickets were only an inch long and didn't have fangs or stingers. They weren't threatening-looking. It's just that there were so many of them, and their antennae were absurdly long—as long as four times the length of their bodies. We experienced a complex emotion: an ancient fear of creepy-crawlies combined with concern that we might squash a rare cave beast.

As we descended through the rocky slot, we tried not to touch or hold anything. It was disconcerting plunging deeper and deeper into darkness, not knowing what might be on either side.

After a few more feet, the rocky slot opened into a small chamber. The four of us barely fit inside—and when Alexis shone his flashlight on the stone walls and ceiling, it illuminated cave spiders and hundreds of crickets.

This area of the cave was called the twilight zone due to the fact that it was not completely dark. When we looked back toward the entryway, we saw a wafer-thin slit of light. That was all that remained of the outside world.

The crickets, Brooke told us, were endemic to the caves of northern Tasmania, usually living near cave entrances in dense colonies. They were considered trogloxenes (*troglo* = cave, *xeno* = strangers), because they sometimes went out. Primarily scavengers, the crickets ate moss growing near the cave entrance and dead fellow invertebrates.

We stepped backward to get a broader view of the chamber and suddenly felt the floor—mud, gravel, and rock—giving way beneath our feet. For a moment, we lost our equilibrium and began falling backward into a deep, lightless hole—filled with God knows what. We grabbed hold of the walls of the rock chamber and, regaining our balance, found ourselves holding hands with what we prayed were cave crickets. From behind, we heard a small rock tumbling down the hole: PLING, PLING, PLING, PLING, PLING, PLING, PLING. Hello? We didn't hear it land. Gingerly, Alexis sidled forward and shined his flashlight down. If there was a bottom we couldn't see it.

"Careful," Brooke said. "There's a drop there."

We had nearly become accidentals, like the unwitting wombats and wallabies that fell down sinkholes and ended up becoming food for famished cave creatures. We looked at the crickets in a new light. They were scavengers, weren't they?

"What's down there?" Alexis asked.

Brooke explained that if you went far enough into the caves, you reached the deep zone where no light penetrated and troglobites lived. In the deep zone, it was humid and the temperature was constant no matter what the season. Troglobites had evolved to live in these odd conditions. They often were pale or without pigment. Sometimes they had no eyes. Since no plants could grow in this lightless environment, being an herbivore wasn't an option. Deep zone creatures had two choices: eating each other or waiting until something fell in that they could scavenge upon.

One of the creatures that was beyond our sight was the cave pseudoscorpion (*Pseudotyrannochthonius typhlus*), a tiny stingerless eight-legged arachnid that over thousands of years of cave life had lost its eyes and pigment. What the pseudoscorpion got in exchange for its eyes and coloration was an enhanced sense of smell, long sensory hairs on its legs with which it could sense the slightest vibration, and a set of rangy-armed pincers for reaching out and grabbing any meat that might fall its way. The pseudoscorpion was a super-endemic, meaning that it only lived in the Mole Creek cave system—and as far as scientists knew, only in a few of those. Like most deep zone creatures, it couldn't survive in the open air. It was listed as rare under Tasmania's Threatened Species Protection Act.

We pondered the pseudoscorpion's genus name: *Pseudotyrannochthonius*. (*Pseudo* = false, *tyranno* = fierce. And *chthonius*?) Chthonius had several lives in Greek mythology. In one story, Chthonius was one of the black steeds that powered Pluto's chariot from the underworld and back. In another, he was a warrior that sprang from the earth and attacked anyone in his path.

When one thought about it, these caves were the perfect retreat for an outlaw species. What if Tasmanian tigers had gone underground when they were being hunted for the bounty? We conjured up a blind, long-whiskered, albino tiger living in Tasmania's unexplored depths. This was the kind of animal Alexis specialized in painting: mutant, cryptic, and improbable . . . We glanced back at the doomsday hole as we climbed out of the cave, covering ourselves in mud.

"Do you have any feelings about the Tasmanian tiger?" Alexis asked Brooke after we had all emerged, blinking into daylight. "Do you think it's still out there?"

She looked pained—the same look she had when she picked the dead devil off the road. "I hope so," she said, not sounding very hopeful. "I hope the tiger's out there somewhere. And if it is, I wouldn't say a word."

20. DRINKING IN THE TIGER BAR

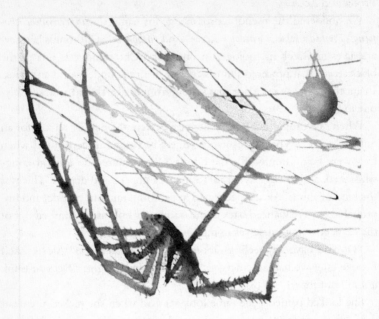

fter our trip down the cave hole, we decided it was time for some refreshment. On the map a place called Mole Creek was the nearest town, so we headed that way. We left the forests and entered a more pastoral landscape: paddocks dotted with sheep, a farm stand selling Tasmanian leatherwood honey, a tabby cat sitting in someone's front yard. We rolled to a stop on Mole Creek's tiny main street.

Alexis climbed out of the Pajero. "You mind if I do some stretching?"

he asked. Before we could answer, he had folded his body over on the sidewalk and begun executing a sequence of yogalike moves. Salutation to the Sun. Downward-facing Dog. Grasshopper Waggling Hindquarters. "You should do this, too," he said, looking at us critically. "You're not getting any younger." He stood up and leaned to the left. "Come on, you guys. *Stretch!*"

We looked around. The street was deserted and we figured what the heck. Creakily, we stretched toward the pavement.

"Thaaat's it. Look! There's money on the ground. Reach for it. *Reach!* You want that money. There you go."

After Alexis put us through our paces, we began looking around and spotted a red-brick building with a Tasmanian tiger painted in the window. Around the tiger, "Tassie Tiger Research Centre" was painted in black letters. We peeked in. It didn't look like much research was going on anymore. Boxes of files and papers were strewn across the floor. Whoever had been looking for the tiger must have given up—or left town fast.

A sign in a neighboring window read "Tiger's Lair Café Bar." We halted just outside of the door. Our pants and boots were still covered with cave mud . . . We brushed ourselves off as best we could.

Alexis strode into the bar—and then froze in his tracks. "I—oh—wow . . ."

We were surrounded. They plastered the walls, loomed over tables, intermingled with bottles of liquor on the bar. It was frightening. A life-sized Tasmanian tiger hovered over the green felt of a pool table, its mouth open in a toothy, papier-mâché snarl. A cuddly tiger toy sat inside a habitat diorama next to a bottle of rum on tap. There were tiger paintings, drawings, cartoons, photographs, newspaper clippings, even tigers set into stained glass.

"It's like the Louvre for tiger freaks," Alexis said in a hushed voice.

We had been in theme bars before. Sports bars. Irish bars. Seventies bars. Goth bars. Transvestite bars. None of them approached the hyper-specificity of the Tiger Bar—or the range of homegrown artistic vision. The imaginations of countless people had been let loose, and creative styles ranged from earnest reverence (oil paintings of noble-looking thylacines poised beside snowcapped mountaintops and gazing across rocky gorges) to wisecracking insouciance (a gang of roguish tigers shooting pool while smoking cigars). One corner of the bar was dedicated to the

Tasmanian tiger in sports. There was a tiger swinging a golf club with its tail sticking out of its pants (titled *Tiger Woods*), a tiger pugilist with boxing gloves (*Tiger Tyson*), a tiger with a cricket bat, a tiger rowing crew.

Walking slowly from image to image, Alexis muttered approvingly as if he were at a Manhattan gallery opening. Then he took out his camera and began carefully documenting each work. It didn't take him long to locate the erotic art. One piece painted directly on the wall above the bar was of a slinky motorcycle chick. She was naked except for a black leather jacket and thigh-high boots, and there was a paw print tattooed on her left butt cheek. We consulted our animal tracks book and discovered that the print was of a tiger's front paw—and anatomically accurate.

"Yeah, baby, give me some of that interspecies luuuhhvv," said Alexis, clicking his camera shutter. "It's getting a little *freaky* in Mole *Creekie*."

We sat down and ordered drinks from the woman tending bar. Even though we were drowning in thylacine memorabilia, we weren't sure what to say. Despite the Planet Thylacine decor, the Tiger Bar wasn't giving off an outsider-friendly vibe.

"Nice pictures," we said to the bartender.

She nodded noncommittally. We noticed that all the bar patrons were women. They looked tough.

"Do you get a lot of people asking about the tiger in here?" we asked.

"Mmhuhm." She didn't elaborate.

Behind the bar, a pile of caps and T-shirts were for sale. They were black with orange lettering and insignia. Beneath the words "Mole Creek Tiger Bar," a mother thylacine and her cub stood next to a tuft of grass. We bought one of each, and the bartender started to warm up.

"Been to the caves?" she asked.

"Yeah." We got the feeling that every ear along the bar was cocked in our direction. "We're actually researching Tasmanian wildlife, particularly . . . um . . . the thylacine and its history—"

She cut us off. "You better talk to Trudy then."

The barkeep pointed to a woman at the other end of the bar. She was somewhat heavyset, with dark, short-cropped hair, and looked to be in her late thirties. We had noticed her before and thought she had been giving us the eye while we looked at the tiger art.

We walked over and introduced ourselves. Trudy was drinking Jim

Beam Kentucky Straight Bourbon Whiskey and Cola. It was a mixed drink that came in a can. For about a minute, there was complete silence. The small crowd at the bar looked at us expectantly.

"So, you're the person to talk to about the tiger around here . . ."

She seemed embarrassed. "Yeah." There was a brief awkward silence. "We like the art."

"It's all right," she said and twisted uncomfortably in her seat.

"Are you affiliated with the research center next door?"

"That's temporarily closed."

"So . . . are you a tiger hunter?"

"Yeah . . . the thylacine . . . yeah . . ."

"Have you ever seen one?"

Trudy laughed nervously. "It's a really hard thing," she said. Then she paused for a long time and took a sip of her drink. "People who *have* seen them—probably people like me—won't actually tell anybody. But they are definitely out there." She paused again. "They're in areas people wouldn't expect."

It was obvious Trudy had a story to tell. We figured if we wanted to hear it, we should attempt to appear more nonchalant. "So are you from around here?" we asked.

Yes, she said. She was from the Mole Creek area. And tigers were in her blood. "My grandfather was one of the old snarers . . . and he used to watch the little fellows for days on end near their den."

She admitted that she had caught the tiger-hunting mania years before while working at a nearby wildlife park, taking care of devils, wombats, and other native animals. The park's former owner, Peter Wright, claimed to have found a tiger footprint near Cradle Mountain and then launched one of the most extensive and well-funded private searches ever conducted—reportedly at a cost of $250,000. In the winter of 1984, he flew supplies into a base camp near Lake Adelaide, about fifteen miles south of the Mole Creek karst caves. Then he set up camera traps in the surrounding bush that were linked by radio to the base camp. Innumerable photographs were developed, but the search turned up no positive evidence of the tiger.

Trudy herself had been actively searching for the tiger since the early 1990s. She pointed at two bulletin boards plastered with newspaper clippings near the bar. Headlines included, "Experts Split on New Tiger Claims," "Extinct or Escape Artist?," and "The Tiger Is Dead: Long Live Our Guilt."

"That's me," she said, pointing at one of the clippings. There was a news photo of Trudy, a few years younger and with longer hair, next to a fellow tiger hunter named Joe Parsons. They were sitting beneath a drawing of a roaring tiger. The accompanying headline read, "Tigers' Secret 'Safe with Us.'" The clipping explained how Trudy and Parsons had opened the Tassie Tiger Research Centre and spent two to three days every week looking for the tiger.

"The way that I do it is I've gone back years—probably thirty, forty, fifty years—where sightings have occurred and then gone back there myself. And I get recent sightings, too, so you can confirm that they're still in the area. I've been plodding along with this for about ten years."

"So have you ever seen a tiger?" we asked again.

She looked at us and gave us a *Mona Lisa* smile.

We decided to try a different tack. "Why do you think there isn't any hard evidence that the tiger survived? Like scat or tracks?"

She thought there probably *was* scientific evidence—but that there was a movement to suppress it.

"The Tasmanian government doesn't want them to be found," she said. "So at the moment you can't take any scat out of Tasmania to prove that it's thylacine, devil, or whatever. There were some guys over from England. They got a lot of scat that they wouldn't let them take out of Tassie."

The story was that a British researcher named Bob Eeles had arrived in Tasmania in June 2001 with the expectation of obtaining scat samples from the Queen Victoria Museum in Launceston. (Over the years, copious amounts of scat had been donated to this museum in the hopes that it would someday be scientifically identified as thylacine excrement.) According to one article, Eeles was expecting to take back "armfuls of poo" to be examined by the "ancient DNA lab" at Oxford. However, the removal of the scat was blocked by museum and government officials, who said the scat was valuable scientific data and they were not permitting it to be taken out of Tasmania—and certainly not back to England. In the words of one defender of the poop, "the days of colonial plundering are gone."

"That's too bad about the scat . . . So what was your best thylacine sighting?" We thought we would try again.

"Personally, or—?"

"Personally."

"I'm not going to say with all these listening." She pointed at the other women clustered around the bar and then turned all the way around on her barstool so that her back was to the other patrons. She spoke quietly.

"It was late last year, in November. No," she corrected herself. "It was in September or October. And it was just one of those things . . . when you see something that you don't believe you've actually seen."

She had been camping out in a tent in the bush near Mole Creek. "It was about three o'clock in the morning. And my dog—a little border collie—started to go a bit silly."

Emerging from behind her car's trailer, she saw a tan-colored animal. And she shone a spotlight on it. "I saw the stripes, and I said 'naahhh, it couldn't be.' So I took the spotlight off it and then put it on again. And it couldn't be anything else. The stripes were so distinctive. It was the first time I'd seen one—after all those years of searching . . . It was nowhere near as big as what I got the impression they were."

"How big?"

"I don't know. Probably eighteen inches."

Eighteen inches? What kind of Lilliputian tiger was that? We found ourselves feeling deflated. Maybe it was a juvenile. Or a big-ass feral tabby cat.

We weren't comfortable directly challenging her story. Instead, as tactfully as we could, we asked if she was teasing us—taking the piss as it were.

She laughed and pointed at an older woman at the bar. "That's the real Trudy over there."

Huh?

Everyone at the bar laughed. "I'm Trudy's mum," the older woman said. "You know Trudy lives out in the bush without electricity."

"With little quolls and devils and things that visit in the night," said Trudy. "And if you want to see it, it will cost you $200."

We politely declined and thanked Trudy for sharing her tiger story. But we were still perplexed. Was she yarning? Or did she really believe she'd seen one? We took one more awed spin around the thylacine art gallery and decided to head out.

Before we left the Tiger Bar, Trudy asked us if we knew anyone in America who would want to fund a tiger search. "It doesn't take much money, but you need the right equipment to prove they're there. I'd like to find a den so that you could get the little fellows and film a documentary from when they're that big to when they disperse. I know it sounds impossible, but it is possible." She seemed in earnest. So we took her phone number and told her that if we ever met anyone with a passion for missing marsupials and money to burn, we would send them her way.

When we got on the road again, we checked the map and decided to drive over to the wildlife park where Trudy said she used to work.

"So what did you think of her story?" we asked Alexis.

"Her embarrassment made me feel she believed she'd really seen one."

"And?"

"It's straight out of central casting—the craggy local who holds the key to the mystery, the earnest reporters."

"And?"

"What do you want me to say? It's like a combination of mythology, cryptozoology, and conspiracy theory. She's off the grid."

The wildlife park wasn't hard to spot. On the edge of the highway, a ten-foot-high wooden sculpture of a Tasmanian devil with pink ears and parted jaws greeted visitors. Next to it, a folksy-looking sign read, "WELCOME TO THE TROWUNNA WILDLIFE PARK, THE STATE'S NO. 1 WILDLIFE PARK. COME UP AND PAT A DEVIL, CUDDLE A WOMBAT, OR FEED SOME OF OUR MANY FREE RANGING ANIMALS."

We walked into the park through a series of gates and found what looked like an outdoor petting zoo. Kangaroos hopped about. A young wombat in a little wooden enclosure came up to the edge of its fence and gave us a friendly look. Eucalyptus trees—stringy barks—grew up between and among the pens. In the center of it all, a young man with multiple piercings and a shirt that seemed to be covered in animal shit was giving a stunningly erudite lecture on Tasmanian devils. He stood inside a small enclosure with four young devils. We knew they were young because their heads weren't big and hulking. Their fur was sleek, shiny, and black. Most of them were snoozing through the talk. Perhaps they had heard it before. A sign posted outside had the words "Devil's Den" carved into it.

As the young man lectured to a group of about twenty people and one attentive devil, a spiny echidna wandered by our feet and a four-foot-high kangaroo hopped over and sniffed Alexis's hand. The kangaroo had light gray fur, a black nose, tall broad ears, and an athletic-looking neck. This was Tasmania's largest macropod species, the Eastern gray or forester kangaroo. We suspected this shrewd-looking kangaroo could box if given a chance. It had been called a boomer by Tasmania's settlers and could tear open a dog if cornered.

When the little crowd around the Devil's Den dispersed, we buttonholed the keeper. His name was Chris Coupland and he gave us the lowdown on Trowunna. "The animal park is a sanctuary on eighteen hectares of remnant dry sclerophyll forest, surrounded by state forest. We rehabilitate and raise animals that are brought to us back into a wild situation." The place was run by Androo ("that's spelled with two o's") Kelly, who was said to be a distant relation of Ned Kelly, Australia's most famous outlaw. When Androo took over the park sixteen years before, he had expanded what had been a kitschy petting zoo into a conservation facility.

"Androo is amazing with animals," Chris said. "He shifted the focus from display to animal rehabilitation, captive breeding, and research." For example, all the wombats in the park had been orphaned, most pulled from their dead mothers' pouches on the side of the road. They were being hand-raised and ultimately would be released into the wild. "Some wombats quite literally release themselves when they're ready, digging themselves under the fence and ranging through the eighteen hectares. From the eighteen hectares, they range into the surrounding forest. It's a soft release program."

In addition to rescuing animals, Trowunna bred them—quolls, devils, and many smaller marsupials—and released the offspring into the wild. With so many threats to Tasmania's wildlife—the fox invasion, speeding cars, animals being shot and poisoned as pests, the lethal disease racing through the devil population, the chopping of Tasmania's forests— captive breeding was now more important than ever in the fight to save species.

"As an example, we've captively bred bettongs for six or seven years now. The bettong's a small macropod that weighs about two kilos. On the mainland, it's called the Eastern bettong, but now unfortunately a lot of people are referring to it as the Tasmanian bettong. Tasmania is the only place it still exists due to the fox. With the foxes in Tasmania now . . . Well, we're stepping up our breeding program." As if to punctuate Chris's remarks, a devil gave off a guttural shriek.

We thought about the Tasmanian tiger. Dozens, possibly hundreds, had been kept in zoos. But they had never been bred in captivity. Chris and his boss Androo were not going to let that happen with the native animals in their care. They didn't want any more animals to disappear into the Styx.

We looked at the four young devils. Two were walking about, sniffing at everything in their path. They looked perky and alert. A big sign behind them warned, "Devils May Bite."

"How did you get to be so comfortable with devils?" we asked.

"This isn't a vicious animal," Chris said. "Their jaws are massively powerful, but devils are actually very timid and shy. All my practical handling experience has been learned off Androo. He's taught me the safe way to handle them and be confident with them." Certainly, he was confident enough to give a devil a friendly pat.

Unfortunately, Chris told us, Androo wasn't around. But we could find his partner, Darlene Mansell, in the café next to the gift shop.

Darlene was having coffee and chatting with some visitors. We introduced ourselves and explained we were doing a project on Tasmanian wildlife. "Oh well, you must meet Androo," she said. "The wealth of information he has, it's really important to hear. I won't let you leave the island without speaking to him." She said we should come back in the morning.

"What do *you* do here?" Alexis asked.

"Presently I'm running the café. But I've been mucking around with Androo up here for about twelve years. We have a ten-year-old son, Rulla, which is the totem of the owl. This place was formerly called the Tasmanian Wildlife Park. Now it's Trowunna, which is actually the aboriginal word for Tasmania. I'm a Tasmanian aboriginal woman."

We found ourselves looking at Darlene more closely. She was attractive, her hair chestnut brown and wavy, her nose broad and strong, her skin tan. We realized we were staring and immediately felt self-conscious. It was an odd feeling meeting an aboriginal person from Tasmania. According to a lot of history books, they were all supposed to be long dead.

Darlene said she got that all the time. She put on a snooty British-sounding accent, "Oh *dahrling*, you're not the *real* thing. What are you carrying on about?" Then she switched back to her own voice, a measured Australian twang. "But we're here. Indeed."

Tasmania is frequently described as a place where colonization led to the total genocide of its native people. A woman named Truganini is usually cited as the last surviving Tasmanian aboriginal. She died in 1876.

"That's a great myth," said Darlene. "She certainly wasn't the last Tasmanian aborigine and she wasn't even the last tribal aborigine. She's used as an iconic symbol for white Australia—and for science."

Darlene's use of the word "science" caught us off guard. Wasn't Trowunna a place that engaged in science? Chris, the animal manager, had an honors degree in zoology. Darlene said she meant that science—supposedly so objective—was actually highly *sub*jective, manipulated to an appalling degree at times by whoever held the reins of power. She said science and its labels had been used to marginalize and denigrate her people.

From the very first days of exploration, Europeans had a great curiosity to see how the aboriginal Tasmanians lived, but very little interest in whether they continued their way of life—or even kept living at all. Aboriginal culture was a source of fascination, and when Europeans first visited the island, they had a strong desire to "study" the Tasmanians.

Captain William Bligh's encounter with the island's aboriginals was not the first, but it was illuminating. He and his crew from the HMS *Bounty* spent three weeks in Tasmania in 1788, resting and refueling after an arduous two months at sea while en route from the Cape of Good Hope to Tahiti. Bligh (who had earlier visited the island with Captain

James Cook) was eager to be the first to make an anthropological study of the Tasmanian people. To Bligh's chagrin, the islanders proved uncooperative, disappearing into the trees whenever he approached. Finally when one of the *Bounty*'s crew made contact, Bligh rushed over hurling trinkets. Alarmed by this ham-handed assault, the Tasmanians ran off. Later, Bligh wrote bitterly in his ship's log that the Tasmanians were "the most wretched and stupid people existing." Or perhaps the residents of Trowunna were quick studies, knowing better than to face down British guns. Incidentally, Bligh's crew visited Tasmania eight months before their famous mutiny.

The Tasmanian aboriginals had more interaction with a French crew a few years later. In 1792, the ships *Recherche* and *Espérance* led by Bruny d'Entrecasteaux landed on the southeast coast of the island. And the meeting was amicable. Unlike Bligh, the French crew wrote that the Tasmanians' eyes "expressed sweetness and kindness" and that they displayed "surprising intelligence." Many gifts of goodwill were exchanged, with the sailors receiving kangaroo skins, shell bracelets, and throwing stones. The French watched Tasmanian women dive for crabs and shellfish, and the men demonstrated their spear-throwing prowess, repeatedly hitting a target at thirty paces. The Tasmanian aboriginals also submitted to all sorts of bizarre measurements being taken. One sailor took thirteen body measurements of a Tasmanian man, including full height, length of forearm from elbow to wrist, width of mouth, length of ears, and length of male member (natural state). In their turn, the Tasmanians couldn't quite believe that there were no women on board and performed their own examinations, frequently checking the sailors' private parts to make sure they were men. This was the last time relations were so friendly.

After the British colonized Tasmania—then still called Van Diemen's Land—in 1803, the relationship between the settlers and aboriginals turned sour within a very short time. The Tasmanian aboriginals were seminomadic. They lived completely off the land, returning each year to shellfishing grounds in one season and to kangaroo-hunting grounds in the next. The settlers began eating up all the aboriginal people's food, killing kangaroos en masse with guns and dogs. And frequently when the aboriginals would return to a coastal spot they had been living in for perhaps thousands of years, they would find it occupied by settlers and soldiers. These encounters led to bloodshed and exposed aboriginals to

European diseases to which they had no immunity. At first the colonial government maintained a policy of détente with the native people. But by the 1820s, the situation had completely deteriorated. In 1828, aboriginals were banned from entering settlement areas and some settlers interpreted the ban as a shoot-on-sight policy. In 1830, the colonial government staged an exercise known as the Black Line. Colonists, convicts, and soldiers marched across the settled parts of Tasmania in a long line in an attempt to capture any and all aboriginals in their path. Though only two aboriginal people were captured during the seven-week-long sweep, the Black Line effectively drove the aboriginals permanently from their ancestral homes around the colonial settlements.

It was in response to these hostilities that George Augustus Robinson began to round up Tasmania's aboriginals at the behest of the government. Robinson, who was a housebuilder from London before he turned missionary, thought he could save the aboriginals by moving them to concentration camps in the Bass Strait and converting them to Christianity. An aboriginal woman named Truganini assisted him. Truganini was born in 1812, nine years after settlement, and her clan was decimated by colonization. Her father had been shot by settlers. Her sister had been kidnapped by sealers and later killed. With Truganini as translator, Robinson went around to the furthest reaches of the island, convincing aboriginals (sometimes at gunpoint) to follow him to a better place. Where he took them were isolated islands in the Bass Strait. There, in camps cut off from their way of life, the aboriginal people died at a rapid rate from disease, poor nutrition, and squalid living conditions. In her last years, Truganini became the symbolic last survivor. And when she died in 1876, her bones were taken by the Royal Society of Tasmania, strung up, and eventually put on display like an animal's. They remained on public view until 1947. They were supposed to be the icon of a lost race.

Darlene called the last aboriginal story a convenient fiction. Truganini's bones, which were displayed for "scientific" reasons, were nothing but a trophy, wrapped up in a phony aura of regret. When the Europeans had eliminated the Tasmanian "aboriginal problem" and taken over all the aboriginal lands, they could pretend the aboriginals were no longer there.

"Science will say that I can't be a black woman, because I'm not black-skinned. I can't be an aboriginal woman, because I can't speak lingo. Science will tell you that we're just descendants or half-castes. That's what I was brought up being called, little half-caste girl."

Darlene was born on Flinders Island in the Bass Strait. "That was where George Augustus Robinson removed a lot of my old people." Most of the aboriginals taken by Robinson to Flinders perished, and the last survivors, including Truganini, were ultimately moved to Oyster Cove, not far from Hobart, where they continued to die off. But they weren't the only aboriginal people on Flinders or the other Bass Strait islands. At the beginning of the nineteenth century, sealers from America and Britain had begun harvesting fur seals in the strait. The sealers kidnapped and lured aboriginal women to the Bass Strait islands to be their wives and companions, and to work harvesting the fur seals. The children of these unions stayed on the islands, and when the seals were hunted to the vanishing point, they began harvesting muttonbirds for their livelihoods.

Darlene's father had been chief of the Mansell clan, the Moonbird people. "That's my cultural totem, the muttonbird, the shearwater. Our community goes once every year for about eight weeks to harvest the birds. I was brought up on them."

Darlene had some muttonbirds salted in brine in the café's kitchen. And she brought one out. She rubbed her finger over the wings of the preserved bird and we each had a lick. It was oily and tasted like salt, fish, the ocean. These were the same birds we had seen flying in a determined line past Geoff King's coastal property.

"When you look at the journey of the moonbird and where he goes, he goes in a figure eight. He travels from Tasmania and he goes up through Japan, where he's harvested by the Ainu people. Then he goes from there up to the Arctic, down Canada, and then he pulls into the native community up there. Then he comes across the Pacific and comes to New Zealand to the Maoris and they also harvest the muttonbird. The moonbird is significant to a lot of indigenous cultures because of the journey he takes."

On the muttonbird migration, the birds travel nine thousand miles in each direction, crossing the Pacific Ocean and traveling to the high latitudes of the Northern Hemisphere and the northernmost part of the Pacific. In search of an endless summer, the muttonbirds average 220 miles a day on their flight. Each year in September, the birds return to Tasmania en masse—usually all on the same day.

The muttonbirds were one of the last threads connecting the aboriginal people to their past. "We lost a great deal through the colonization process," Darlene said. "In that process language was taken." And their culture was nearly decimated.

We knew the tiger had been an important animal to aboriginal people. Was there any chance the tiger survived, or was that lost, too? We asked Darlene what she thought.

"I'd like to think the tigers are still out there. A lot of people tell me they are. But I don't know. I've been up in the skies and looked down at this little island, and I don't think there's too much where there hasn't been a human imprint." She sighed. "Tigers *are* really symbolic in aboriginal culture in terms of dreamings and dreamtime. Our old people related stories of animals and their symbols, like the quolls with their spots and dots, or tigers with their stripes."

But such tales are hard to come by. War, murder, disease, and dislocation had destroyed the thread of stories that had been passed down for more than ten thousand years on this island at the edge of the world.

"There are strands of old myths and stories that survive. But we've had a lot taken from us. It's like trying to find the missing pieces to a jigsaw puzzle."

In the aboriginal languages of Tasmania—it's believed there were about a dozen of them—the Tasmanian tiger was known as *corinna, lorrina, kannunah*. At least those were the names recorded by early settlers. Today, the people of aboriginal descent who survive in Tasmania are often forced to turn to European recorders of history to access their own languages and stories.

How *did* the tiger get his stripes? In the book *Touch the Morning* by the Tasmanian writer Jackson Cotton, a series of stories tell the origin of Tasmania, how the aboriginals came to live there, how the devil got its snarling voice. The tales are said to be collected from aboriginal people by the author's ancestors, a Quaker family that had been in Tasmania during the early years of colonization. The story of "Corinna, the Brave One" was told to them by "Mannalargenna, the chief of a Northeast Coast Federation of Tribes."

Palana, the little star, was the son of Moinee. As a boy he loved to wander in the bush and had many happy adventures. One day, however, he had a nasty encounter with Tarner, the big boomer kangaroo.

Tarner was huge and powerful, and in a very short time Palana, even though he was the son of the great Moinee, was in dire trouble. The boomer knocked him sprawling and attacked him with his huge heavy hind feet.

Somehow Palana managed to get up, but when he tried to run away Tarner caught him in his arms and quickly throwing him again to the ground, began to stamp the life out of him.

Palana screamed as loudly as he could, "Help! Help!"

The echoes chased around the bush, rushing from tree to tree, crag to crag.

A nameless hyena pup, enjoying an unequal chase with Lenira, the Bandicoot, heard the cries. He stopped chasing Lenira, who could not believe his good luck, and raced to help.

Fearless, the hyena pup leaped into the fight, ripping and tearing at the big boomer. Tarner picked up the boy, and backing against a rock, squeezed until Palana felt his life almost ebbing. The Great Kangaroo kept the young hyena at bay with his big raking hind feet.

The smart pup quickly dashed up onto the rock and sprang at Tarner, driving his sharp fangs deep into the big animal's throat. Holding the boy with one forearm, Tarner clutched desperately at the brave pup trying to break the deathhold he had on the kangaroo's throat.

But the little hyena was there to stay.

Body tense and eyes closed, he concentrated all his strength in the mighty effort to close his jaws. Slowly he felt the flesh and sinew give under the pressure of his grip, and suddenly his teeth crashed together with a loud snap.

The big boomer staggering and trembling violently, crashed to the ground, taking Palana and the pup with him.

They lay motionless, exhausted and stunned beside their dead enemy.

Some time later a party of blackmen picked up the unconscious pair and carried them back to the camp. The pup recovered first. Soon Palana stirred and looked about him.

There he saw Moinee, the god, his father.

Walking up to Palana, the god smiled down at him and said, "You have done well for one so young, my son. You have come through your baptism of danger bravely and unaffected. In a very short period of time you have passed from childhood and now stand on the threshold of young manhood. So be it."

Straightaway the little boy arose and stood proudly.

He appeared to ignore his father so intent was his gaze on the hyena pup. Moinee read Palana's thoughts and a look of admiration crossed his stern face.

"From today you will make your own decisions," Moinee said, "and you will bestow your own rewards."

But Palana heard not a word.

Walking over to the little hyena, the boy put his arms around the torn and bleeding neck, gently helping the pup as he rose painfully to his feet on tired, wobbly legs.

Looking into the weary yellow eyes, Palana said, "Truly you are the bravest of the brave. Today you fought not as a pup but as the Wurrawana Corinna, the Great Ghost Tiger."

Kneeling down beside the pup, Palana reached down to where his blood had run into the ashes of the fire, and with his fingers, mixed the blood and the ashes into a thick paste.

Then, with this thick brown paste, Palana described a number of dark stripes across the pup's back from the top of his shoulders to the butt of his rigid tail, saying as he did so, "From this day forward, all shall know you as Corinna the Tiger."

The story of the Great Ghost Tiger seemed dimly familiar. We thought about the rock art Les Bursill had shown us on the mainland. The stripes on that four-thousand-year-old thylacine drawing had been made using charcoal from an aboriginal campfire, too.

We continued along the highway until we reached the town of Deloraine, where we decided to spend the night at a "hotel," a bar with accommodations attached. The walls of our room, a triple with three lumpy beds, were cotton candy pink.

At dusk we walked down to the river that flowed through town and onto a bridge built with stone masonry. From underneath, we heard cooing and the flapping of wings. Pigeons flew into view. "You can never escape the usual suspects," said Alexis.

The river—called the Meander—presented a beautiful scene. The sunset was a flamelike mix of orange and yellow and the trees lining the banks were reflected on the slow-moving, placid water. The few houses on the river were Georgian and Victorian in style. The setting evoked a tranquil river town in England—an effect that was slightly tempered by the sound of local youths drag racing on a road that paralleled the far bank.

Down at the river's edge, we gazed at the colors of the sunset on the water. Alexis took out his pipe and lit it. As he began to inhale, we heard a burbling noise. At first we thought he had put a bong attachment on his pipe, but then we traced the sound to the middle of the river. A dark form was blowing bubbles just under the surface.

We squinted, trying to identify the creature. In the waning light, we saw that the stream of bubbles was coming out of a ducklike bill attached to some sort of furry animal. The only thing that could have surprised us more was a shark fin breaking the surface.

"One platypussums," said Alexis in a singsong voice.

The bubble trail moved toward us. Then with a splash, the platypus dived underwater. Reeds rustled along the bank by our feet, and the platypus disappeared.

"I think it just went into its burrow," Alexis said. We envisioned the platypus curled up in a muddy tube in the riverbank somewhere below where we were standing.

It seemed impossible that a platypus would be so acclimated to human activities. What was one of the strangest animals in the world doing swimming alongside a Tasmanian village with a pub not two hundred steps away and keeping company with a bunch of pigeons?

We waited a few minutes, but the platypus didn't emerge from its riverbank home. As we followed the Meander upriver, however, we soon observed the telltale bubbles of another platypus. It was repeatedly diving and re-emerging, so we were able to see tantalizing bits of its unusual body. A beaverlike tail . . . *splash splash* . . . a webbed foot topped with long claws . . . *plop, splash* . . . a bill . . . *bubble bubble* . . . a smooth head with no apparent ears . . . *splash*.

"They're unconvincing as an animal even in real life," said Alexis.

It was true. The platypus was an animal that continued to stupefy people with its bizarre combination of parts. We had to sympathize with someone like David Collins, who was the first European to publish an account of a live platypus. In his description, he played down the duckbill, either because he did not know what to make of it or perhaps fearing he wouldn't be believed. First, he labeled the platypus as an "amphibious animal, of the mole species." Then he described the platypus's feet in great detail (webbing between the toes, claws) and only at the end did he mention the curious fact that the "mole" had a duckbill—perhaps hoping that readers would accept this idea once they knew a few believable details about the creature.

According to *Touch the Morning*, Tasmanian aboriginal legend said the platypus was originally two animals, a burrowing mammal and a duck. Together, these two creatures double-teamed young frogs, chasing them into a riverbank burrow and eating them. As punishment, they were torn apart and mashed together again into one half-and-half beast minus the duck's feathers and the mammal's hind legs.

When the first platypus specimens from Australia were sent back to England in 1798, people thought they *were* two unrelated animals sewn together. A faked-up mermaid (which was commonly fabricated from monkey remains and fishtails) was more understandable. At least mermaids were well-known mythical creatures. But who would believe an otter-and-duck combination?

In the end, scientists discovered that the platypus was not only real, but even weirder than was immediately apparent. For one thing, the platypus seemed to be some sort of reptile-mammal hybrid that broke the bounds of the existing classification systems. The platypus had fur like a mammal, but laid eggs like a bird or reptile. It had mammary glands (the hallmark of being a mammal) and nursed its young with milk—but it didn't have nipples. Instead, the platypus produced milk from slits in its abdomen. And like reptiles and birds, it had a cloaca—one hole from which to pee, defecate, have sex, and lay eggs. (Male platypuses did, however, have a separate penis.)

While watching the platypus repeatedly dive and blow bubbles in the Meander, we discussed how this amazing egg-laying mammal was ultimately placed by scientists within the unromantically named classification of monotreme.

There are three classifications of mammals in the world: placentals, marsupials, and monotremes. Placental mammals (like us humans, dogs, cats, rabbits, and lions) are named after the nurturing organ that surrounds the fetus. (We placentals are also called eutherian, which translates as "well-formed beast.") Marsupials (kangaroos, thylacines, devils) are named after *marsupium*—the Latin word for pouch, which sounds nice and comfy. But monotremes (just the platypus and echidna) are named for their "one hole" (*mono* = one, *treme* = hole). This was, Alexis noted, "a massive failure in public relations."

"Someone should promote the platypus's venomous character," he suggested. We didn't think platypuses needed too much more publicity, but it was true that this was an attribute that was not commonly known.

Male platypuses have inch-long retractable spurs on their hind legs (on the inner side of their heels) that are remarkably similar in structure to the fangs of a pit viper. From these curving, hollow spurs, they can—when bothered—inject a powerful cocktail of poisons, four of which are not known to occur anywhere else in nature.

Scientists are unclear when male platypuses use their spurs in the wild—possibly against rival males during mating season. But male platypuses have been known to spur people who pick them up, most commonly platypus researchers. Platypus venom causes pain that is said to be exquisite. No known painkiller can lessen it or make it more bearable. Even giving morphine to victims has no effect, and the venom from a single platypus spur can paralyze a limb for weeks.

"What if you picked one up and it spurred you in the balls?" Alexis said. "That would be the ultimate blunder Down Under."

Maybe for "publicity" purposes, the platypus would be better off focusing on another of its little-known attributes. The platypus's bill conceals an amazing ability—and despite appearances, it is nothing like a duck's. A duckbill is hard, stiff, and inflexible. It's made of keratin, the same substance in fingernails. But a platypus's bill is pliable, covered with skin, and filled with nerve endings that can sense electrical impulses. Strip away the outer layers and the skeleton of a platypus bill looks like a divining rod—and that's exactly what it is. The platypus has a sixth sense.

When a platypus dives underwater, it closes its eyes, nostrils, and ears, and turns on its electro-sense. Sixty thousand receptors in the platypus's bill pinpoint minute electrical signals given off by prey—crayfish, mollusks, tadpoles, and aquatic insect larvae. Using this ability, a platypus spends up to thirteen hours a day foraging, diving as often as eighty times an hour, and capturing and eating half its own weight every single day.

Alexis bent down and put some mud from the Meander's bank in a plastic bag. Then the three of us walked out onto a dock. Another platypus surfaced near a lily pad, sending off ripples that shimmered in the last purplish light of the sunset. Alexis took out his digital camera and attempted to take some photographs, but the platypus kept most of its body underwater. We tried to imagine the scene beneath the surface. With its webbed feet and paddle tail, the platypus must have looked marvelous scooting through the Meander, diving down, probing the dark water for its dinner.

We went back to the hotel and Alexis put a big Y for yes on the platypus page of his field guide to Tasmanian mammals. Then he held up his bag of river mud, and began extolling the virtues of Tasmania's wildlife.

"This is my idea," he said. "The wildlife of this island, as diverse as it is, is almost polite. The mainland has the vulgar, harsh, dangerous wildlife. Everything here is nice and furry, not too camouflaged. It reminds me of Beatrix Potter. It has a very Victorian persona, except everything's upside down. One of their major crops is opium poppies. Things just don't quite fit. The giant lobster, the Tasmanian devil, the burrowing crayfish. What the hell is *that*? The platypus? Come on. The fauna is surrealistic. It's almost inspiring enough to make me an artist."

That was an interesting thought, considering he *was* the expedition artist, and so far, we had noticed, inspiration had yet to strike—though he did have a growing collection of materials for making pigment, including wombat scat, two types of river mud, ocher, charcoal, and various types of dirt.

"So are you going to draw something with that river mud?" we asked.

"Yeah," he said, lying down on his sagging bed. "But not tonight. I'm off duty."

23. QUOLLING ABOUT

The next morning we were waiting outside the Deloraine hotel in the Pajero. Alexis was still inside, placing a phone call to Dorothy back in New York. In our peripheral vision, we saw a middle-aged man in green camouflage fatigues and orange wraparound sunglasses wandering up Deloraine's main street. We didn't pay too much attention until he pressed his nose against the driver's side window.

"Uh, yes?" We reluctantly rolled down the window.

"You're waiting for Andrew?" He nodded in a military sort of way.

"Yes . . ." We were confused. Had the Trowunna Wildlife Park sent someone over to collect us? Darlene had said she wouldn't let us leave the island without speaking to Androo. How had they known where we were staying?

"So," he said. "We'll all be going over to Jackie's Marsh. Which vehicle should we take?"

This was beginning to feel like a carjacking. We eyed the guy nervously. Was it normal in Deloraine to wear full-body camouflage? "Uh . . . who's Jackie?"

Suddenly, our interrogator looked at us warily. "Are you waiting for Andrew Ricketts?" he said sharply.

Were we? What was Androo's last name? Panicking, we strained to re-member . . . *Kelly*. That's it, like the outlaw. We're going to see Androo Kelly. And we weren't waiting for him. We were driving over to see him.

"So what are you here for?" he asked as Alexis emerged from the hotel.

We were so relieved to see Alexis—and to have some backup if neces-sary—that we almost shouted, "Quolls! We're going to see some quolls."

"Ahh," he said mysteriously. *"Dasyurus maculatus."* Then he strolled off down the street.

We told Alexis about the strange grilling. "What do you think his story was? Why did he know the quoll's scientific name?"

Alexis thought about it for a minute. "I think he's Green," he said fi-nally, "unless there's a whole new level of redneck."

Half an hour later, we were back at Trowunna and walking through a mob of free-range marsupials, including a large forester kangaroo that blocked our path in front of the zoo's café. We gave it a wide berth.

We found Androo Kelly mucking out an empty wombat enclosure. "Yeah, Darlene said you might be coming," he said. "It's a bad day. Half my staff is off for this weekend. If you don't mind following me around when I'm doing my chores, we can talk." He bent down to pick up a chunk of wombat scat with his gloved hand.

"Rulla, can you get me a bucket?" A young boy with blond hair emerged with a water pail. "This is Rulla, my son. He's helping me out today."

Androo looked to be in his mid-forties. He was rail-thin, with dark hair, a scrappy beard, and intense gray eyes. In addition to rubber gloves, he wore a long-sleeved T-shirt that pictured Tasmanian devils in three dif-ferent poses. Also, he was on crutches. His left ankle and foot were en-cased in a fiberglass cast.

"What happened to your leg?" Alexis asked.

"Oh, I took a bad step and landed on a rock. Rushing around as usual."

Trowunna was a private wildlife park, and it operated on donations, a handful of small grants, and a backbreaking amount of hard work. Al-though it looked like a folksy petting zoo, appearances could be deceiv-ing. Androo was the world's top expert in the breeding of Tasmanian devils and quolls. "Trowunna is an anomaly," he said. "This facility is the only private operation that's a member of the zoo industry proper as far as captive breeding goes. But what makes it important is that it's in situ, in Tasmania."

Androo hobbled out of the wombat enclosure and hopped toward a small building. The crutches and broken ankle didn't seem to slow him down much. "Rulla, come on, we're going to the kitchen."

Inside, a worker was grating apples and adding them to growing mounds of shredded roughage. "Peter is preparing food for wombats and pademelons. We give them twenty-seven to twenty-nine different fruits and vegetables. This gives them a variety of tastes. So when they go back to the wild, they'll feed on different food sources. It's much better than a mono-diet."

"What do you feed the carnivores?"

"I usually feed the quolls a mixture of chicken, rabbit, and wallaby. The devils get whole or partial carcasses."

Androo crutched into an outdoor Tasmanian devil exhibit. "There are two little devils in here. One got attacked by a dog. The other had denned under a house and the owners trapped it and brought it here." The devils were young and agile, climbing onto a propped-up log. The toes peeping out of Androo's cast looked like they might make a tasty meal for a young devil. But Androo seemed oblivious as he shunted the devils aside to muck out their pen.

"There's a rural myth that devils are dangerous," Androo said, observing our wondering look. "Most devils here at Trowunna will let me pick them up, even while they're eating. The devil by nature is a timid animal. They have a very sophisticated confrontation avoidance system. They *are* aggressive around carcasses, and there are some devils you can't pick up. They'll bite you and go, *Rah, rah, bug off, you*."

Although these two devils had been rescued, a large number of Androo's devils had been born at Trowunna. The wildlife park had a breeding population of more than thirty devils and he was working to build up the numbers, due to the epidemic striking Tasmania's devil population. Although Androo didn't think the disease would push wild devils to the brink—the species had recovered from epidemics before—he was increasing Trowunna's breeding population just in case.

Androo and Rulla went into a pen with five young devils. One devil approached Rulla, hissing and baring his fangs. Rulla's leg wasn't much thicker than a wallaby's tail, and we were momentarily alarmed. But Rulla executed a dance step around a water pan to get out of the way. "Aww, that's just Mr. Kim," Androo said of the bad-tempered devil as if he were referring to a petulant teenager.

"So," we asked uneasily, "how did you become so comfortable with wild animals?"

Androo looked a little wild himself. His hair was tousled and spiky. "Animals were always important to me from a young age," he said. "I grew up in a beautiful environment on the banks of the Huon River. I have memories of when I was three and seeing a potoroo. They have a gleam in their eye and a little smiley look to them, and I used to talk about potoroos as my friends. No one believed me, because no one else saw them. They thought I was talking about a fairy in the garden."

His affinity for wildlife also accounted for the unusual spelling of his name. "About fifteen years ago, I realized there were a lot of other Andrew Kellys about. So, I changed my name to Androo with two *o*'s like the potoroo.

"Potoroos," he added, "are everywhere here at Trowunna. We're a sanctuary for these small animals. That's why we're here. Once they cross outside our fence into that next paddock, it's guns and dogs, feral cats and foxes maybe, poison baits. It's war."

We asked if he thought the thylacine would have benefited from this sort of sanctuary.

"I don't think about the thylacine that much," he said.

Oh.

Obviously, things had changed since the wildlife park changed management. Androo wasn't going to launch an expedition to find the thylacine anytime soon. As far as he was concerned, it was extinct. What needed to be kept alive, he said, was the thylacine's story, so that people would learn from its tragic history and more animals wouldn't be pushed to the brink by human activities.

"I'm concerned that what happened to the thylacine could happen to animals now on the edge. Look at the thylacine's relative, the spotted-tailed quoll. This is the world's third-largest carnivorous marsupial after the thylacine and the devil, and there are long-term threats to it. These animals are being pushed more and more from vulnerable to threatened."

Quolls are such unknown animals in America that our edition of *Web-*

ster's didn't even include their name. Androo said that this ignorance extended to Australia. "The problem with quolls is that a lot of Australians wouldn't know the word 'quoll' or what a quoll is. They might know the saying 'quolling about,' which is like ferreting. But they don't know the animal."

We followed Androo to an open-air enclosure fenced off by chicken wire. Inside, there were ferns, tree stumps, branches, and rocks scattered on the ground. A cockatoo squawked from a nearby tree.

Androo opened the gate to the enclosure, and we saw an unusual creature. Its body was long—about fourteen inches—and its black fur was covered with white spots. "We have two species of quolls in Tasmania, the Eastern and the spotted-tailed. That's an Eastern quoll, black morph." The quoll's small face tapered sharply to a wet, hairless pink nose. Its body sat low to the ground like a ferret's, and its black tail was long and bristly. As soon as we walked in, the spotted beast dashed away in a blur of motion.

The Eastern quoll (the fourth-largest carnivorous marsupial in the world) is believed to be extinct on the mainland. The last one documented was run over by a car in a Sydney suburb in 1963. The Eastern quoll had once ranged throughout southeastern Australia, but competition from foxes and feral cats, forest habitat destruction, and poisoning by farmers had written its epitaph. Tasmania was the only place the Eastern quoll survived.

"Look at its whiskers and sharp little face," said Androo. Though Eastern quolls occasionally stole food from Tasmanian devils and caught mice, small marsupials, and ground birds, they lived primarily on a diet of insects in the wild.

In a neighboring enclosure was another Eastern quoll, this one with an orange-brown coat and white polka dots. It sat quietly next to a rock and didn't dash away when Androo approached. "It's blind," Androo said. "Parks and Wildlife gave me that one. It was hit by a car, but he's doing okay. It's a fawn morph. The majority of Eastern quolls are this color."

We looked at the quoll's round perky ears and sightless almond-shaped eyes. Its short legs were covered in white fur.

Breeding quolls in captivity isn't easy. They only breed once a year, and males and females have to be sequestered soon after mating—because males can become very aggressive. But the process is rewarding. Like devils, Eastern quolls give birth to supernumerary offspring, as many as thirty, although they only have six teats and usually only raise three or four young. Seeing the young ones is a touching experience, Androo said. Quolls are smaller than a grain of rice when they're born and highly undeveloped. Yet, even when they're only a couple of inches in size, still furless and naked, the pouch young already have spots visible on their skin.

Watching the pouch young grow is heartwarming, too. The Eastern quoll's pouch is small relative to a kangaroo's and after about three months, the young outgrow it and are left in a grassy shelter inside a cave, log, or tree hollow. If the mother needs to change dens, she carries the young on her back. The mother doesn't teach the young to hunt. They do it instinctively, so captive-raised Eastern quolls are not disadvantaged when they're introduced into the wild.

Androo moved on to another enclosure, where we saw another species of quoll. It was larger and more powerful-looking. "That's the big tiger quoll, also called the spotted-tailed quoll, a female."

She had a muscular back and longer legs than the Eastern quoll. In the sun, her fur glinted chocolate brown. White spots ran the length of her body and all the way down her long, bushy, impressive tail. She looked intimidating. Her head was round and hulking and her back was humped like a devil's.

"Now that's a predator," said Alexis.

Spotted-tailed quolls dispatched their prey—possums, birds, rabbits, chickens—by ambushing them and delivering a crushing bite to the back of the head or neck. "Quolls are sequatorial," said Androo. "That means they are equally adept at hunting in trees and on the ground."

"They're rarely seen because they're nocturnal," he added. "People usually only see their handiwork—getting into a chicken coop and killing every chicken that moves. Similar to what a fox does." To farmers that made quolls Public Enemy Number 1. And though some farmers live-trapped the quolls and moved them to different locations, or even brought them to Trowunna, many of the barnyard raiders got shot or poisoned. "One year I knew of nineteen spotted-tailed quolls that were killed because they were getting into chicken coops. I'm trying to keep up with the killing. My job's to keep breeding and releasing them. I released thirty-seven quolls last year."

The killing was reminiscent of the thylacine bounty. The spotted-tailed quoll population was crashing on the mainland. Once widespread, these quolls now lived in fragmented populations and had become extinct over parts of their original range. Listed as vulnerable by the Australian government and rare in Tasmania, where there was an estimated population of just three to four thousand animals, spotted-tailed quolls were still being treated as pests. The Parks and Wildlife Service had put out a fact sheet on "living with" quolls, with instructions on how to construct quoll-proof poultry coops. In cases where quolls were persistent, the fact sheet stated, "The Parks and Wildlife Service may issue permits to trap troublesome individuals for relocation. Usually these permits are only issued where someone's livelihood is threatened." The fact sheet went on to say, "Some people do take the law into their own hands and set poisons. However, this is illegal." Apparently, the law didn't have much teeth to it. To Androo's knowledge, no one had ever been prosecuted for illegally killing a rare quoll.

We followed Androo into an indoor quoll house. "In here, we have an old male spotted-tailed quoll," he said. "Devils are old at five. Quolls are old at four."

The old quoll was ginger-colored with white spots. He lay on his stomach on top of a branch with his long thick tail hanging down. His body was much larger than the female's—about three feet long compared to her twenty-five inches—and his head was heftier. When Androo changed the quoll's water, he remained on his perch and bared his long, piercing fangs.

We told Androo about our curious encounter with the man in camouflage and his reeling off of the spotted-tailed quoll's scientific name, *Dasyurus maculatus*.

"I know Andrew Ricketts. He's a good guy. Jackie's Marsh is an area where a lot of alternative people live, stalwarts of the conservation movement—forest restorers and craftspeople. It's where they want to build the Meander Dam."

Ahhhh, this made sense. We had read about the dam project in the local newspapers. The plan was to dam a portion of the Meander River, the river we had seen the platypuses in, so that farmers could irrigate their fields. Environmentalists had been arguing that the dam was a threat to the spotted-tailed quoll, because it would flood 730 acres of the quoll's habitat.

"We've all been involved in the fight against the Meander Dam," Androo said. "It would benefit about twenty farmers. But it would flood a stronghold for the quolls. Someone has been poisoning the dam site. They think if they get rid of the quolls then there's no argument about the dam. Ricketts might be trailing the people who are poisoning the quolls."

So the camouflaged stranger was on the side of *Dasyurus maculatus* after all.

Androo said it was a shame that so few people seemed to appreciate the quoll. "A spotted-tailed quoll is the closest animal we will ever have to a thylacine. They're closely related. The difference is that the quoll is a tree dweller. You hand-rear a little quoll, and there's a stage in the development when you could fool someone into believing it is a thylacine pup. The head structure is identical."

In a neighboring enclosure that was filled with foliage, an agile, golden brown spotted-tailed quoll jumped from branch to branch, using its long tail for balance. When it pushed its face up to the glass to get a look at us, we saw its head straight-on and saw the resemblance to the thylacine.

Androo pointed to the quoll's jaw. "When you look at a quoll's smile line—when they have their jaws closed—they have an extra smirk line. That jawline is what allows them to open their mouths so wide."

The quoll had the same sly grin as the thylacine.

"Do you think you could have bred the thylacine in captivity?" we asked.

"I believe I could have," he said. "But it's a bit late for that, isn't it?"

24. BLOOD AND SLOPS

We felt almost decadent continuing our tiger search after talking to Androo. But seeing a living creature that so resembled the thylacine fueled us on. There were still thylacine-related people to see, places to go. And there was one spot we were itching to explore: a tiny town called Pyengana in Tasmania's Northeast.

According to guidebooks, Pyengana had three claims to fame: a gourmet cheese factory, the second-highest waterfall on the island, and a pub with a beer-drinking pig. But we had also quolled out the fact that Pyengana was the location of a much trumpeted tiger sighting. In 1995, a part-time park ranger reported that, while bird-watching there, he had spotted a thylacine through his binoculars. This sighting was widely reported in the media, and because it had been made by a park ranger, we decided it was worth investigating.

The road to Pyengana proved interesting as well. We had obtained a copy of a report titled "The Tasmanian Tiger—1980" published by the Parks and Wildlife Service. The report analyzed 320 tiger sightings dating from 1936 to 1980 and concluded that the sightings were not randomly distributed. Most tiger sightings weren't near big towns or population centers, but concentrated in areas where the tiger had actually been known to live and that still had good habitat. A large percentage of the sightings were made from vehicles, and one relatively lonely road— the northeast section of the Tasman Highway—had more tiger sightings than any other stretch of pavement. That was the road we were on.

The author of the report, wildlife officer Steven J. Smith, wrote:

An exceptionally large proportion of these sightings have occurred on the Tasman Highway in the North East, particularly in the Sideling and Weldborough areas. In these areas the highway passes through wet sclerophyll forest and rainforest which are continuous with extensive forests on each side of the highway, including habitats which, historically, are known to have been used by the thylacine, and where many bounty payments were made.

Smith concluded that despite the lack of physical evidence that the tiger survived, the clusters of sightings in such pristine habitats gave "some cause for hope." We wondered, twenty-five years later, if it was still true.

By noon, we were driving through the Sideling, a mountainous, winding route named for its snakelike curves. Though Smith had specifically mentioned the Sideling as a tiger hot spot, we were having trouble understanding how that could be. In some sections, the terrain was still gorgeous. The narrow road curved like a meandering black stream through wet green forest, and we could imagine a thylacine leaping up a fern-blanketed embankment or dashing across an isolated bend. But as we drove further, we were confronted with a stark reality. The habitat was being taken out of this place. From one mountain overlook, we had a panoramic view of the Sideling, and rather than the continuous forests that Smith described, the landscape was riddled with bald spots. The areas, which had been logged, looked like patches of burned skin.

From another overlook, we saw nothing but foreign trees. Many were familiar as they, like us, came from North America. Instead of wet eucalyptus forest, there were redwoods, ponderosa pines, and Douglas firs. We wondered what the native animals thought of these exotic species.

A sign erected by Forestry Tasmania read, "Sideling Arboretum . . . The arboretum was planted to allow forest researchers to determine the best softwoods to grow in Tasmanian plantations. Tasmania's radiata pine industry grew from the experiments conducted in this plot." Radiata pines were the plantation trees we had seen encroaching on the edge of Todd Walsh's lobster habitat. They were fast-growing, water-sucking imports from California and had replaced large swaths of native Tasmanian forests.

The sign had been defaced multiple times. At the bottom one graffito read, "Invest in old growth FOREST not weeds, ya bastards!" Another scrawl extended the sign's logo so that it read, "Forestry Tasmania DE-STROYING OUR FORESTS."

We were beginning to wonder what Forestry Tasmania's story was when we rolled into Scottsdale, the area's regional center. There were a few shops and a bank, but most conspicuously there was a stunning, swooping building on the town's edge. It rose like a spaceship out of a browning cow pasture. A sign out front read "Forest EcoCentre."

The building was shaped like a truncated cone, flat on the top and leaning to one side. Its curving exterior walls were made of large panes of milky-colored glass set into a thin grid of pale wood.

Alexis studied it with a critical eye. "On the one hand," he said, "I'm thinking a UFO in a cornfield. But on the other, it looks like a giant tree stump."

We walked inside the building and were confronted with a bizarre forest simulation. A concrete walkway, sparingly lined with ferns and other forest plants, encircled the base of the glass walls. Overhead, an enormous flat-screen monitor aired a tumbling waterfall in the middle of a cool, lush forest. A sign with an arrow directed us to the "Animal Walk," a dark corridor with color posters of a devil, quoll, and potoroo interspersed with potted plants. On another video screen, a documentary scored with sentimental music and birdsong extolled the beauty of *Eucalyptus regnans,* the largest tree species south of the equator.

Outside, the sun beat down on brown grass. There was hardly a tree in sight—unless you counted the lobbed-off tree ferns that had been transplanted into a bed of wood chips.

"I don't get it. Is this where the forestry people have their offices?" Alexis said.

It was. The EcoCentre was actually a building within a building. Forestry Tasmania's offices were hidden from public view in a three-story wooden structure surrounded by the outer glass wall. The EcoCentre was designed to be energy-saving, tilting toward the north to receive maximum sun exposure in winter. During the summer, louvers—controlled by smart-building software—opened and closed to keep the building cool and funnel the warm air back outside. The public space, with its high-tech hardware and software, wrapped around the offices like a doughnut.

It was a postapocalyptic design. An eco-friendly building erected by the same people who were destroying habitats just down the road. They even had an Orwellian slogan: "Forestry Tasmania: Growing Our Future."

Alexis looked like he was going to foam at the mouth.

"Is this their vision of the future?" he said. "Highly controlled simulations of what Tasmania used to look like? It's like *Silent Running.*" (In the movie *Silent Running,* the world's last forests are preserved on a spaceship bio-dome, because they can no longer survive on a ravaged Earth.) Alexis began to peruse the informational sheets scattered around the exhibits. A fact sheet on Tasmania's tall trees explained that Forestry Tasmania protected all trees over eighty-five meters tall (279 feet) and suggested that if visitors wanted to see some of the Northeast's tall trees they should drive to the Evercreech Forest Reserve. The reserve was thirty miles from the EcoCentre as the crow flies and one hundred miles by road.

"What's wrong with the forests nearby?" Alexis said. "Why don't they promote those?"

"Maybe they don't want people to get too attached to them," we suggested.

"It's like they're keeping trees in concentration camps—like they did with the Tasmanian aboriginals," he continued.

We wandered into the EcoCentre's gift shop, where we found stuffed devils and possums. They all had a curious flattened look. "They look like they've been run over by logging trucks," said Alexis. "I think I've seen enough fake forest."

We returned to the relentless, shadeless heat of the real world. Inside the car, the wombat and devil scat had been brought back to life by the baking sun, and the Pajero smelled like the Bronx Zoo. As we drove off, we imagined wiggly stink waves trailing behind us.

Alexis stared out the window and loaded his pipe. "That was depressing," he said. "Human beings never fail to disappoint me."

About thirty miles further down the highway, we saw a sign for the Weldborough Pass Rainforest Walk and stopped. It turned out to be a well-groomed path through a 272-acre patch of temperate rain forest. It was filled with interpretive signs intended to educate children about the rain forest. The signs, put up by the Parks and Wildlife Service, were told from the point of view of "Grandma Myrtle," an ancient rain forest tree. The actual forest was luxuriant and primeval. The understory was dominated by huge tree ferns—sunlight streamed through their ten-foot-long fronds creating patterns on the ground. Reaching up high into the sky were furrowed old myrtle trees, their trunks covered in aquamarine lichens and their roots carpeted with moss.

Grandma Myrtle's home was beautiful, but it was also desperately small. The total acreage translated to less than half of a square mile, and we could have finished the circuit in ten minutes if Alexis hadn't wandered off the path to pee behind a tree fern. No one had ever mapped the territories of thylacines, but one scientist who studied bounty records estimated the home range for a pair of tigers could be anywhere from thirty-four to fifty-four square miles. For a thylacine, this reserve could hardly be called a habitat. And the thylacine's relatives, the spotted-tailed quolls, were particularly reliant on wet, old-growth forests like these. They used fallen logs and tree hollows as hiding places and dens. Male spotted-tails had territories of twelve hundred acres (about two square miles) and could travel twelve miles a night. If you think of a territory as an animal's house, the reserve would just fit into a quoll's broom closet.

And much of the forest outside its boundaries was still fair game for the chainsaws.

From the top of the Weldborough Pass (elevation 1,952 feet), the road plunged into the Pyengana valley, nestled between wooded hills and filled with verdant pastureland. Tasmania is known for English-style landscapes, and this lush valley truly fit the bill. Except for the eucalyptus trees on the hills, Thomas Hardy would have felt quite at home.

By the time the winding road reached the valley floor, Alexis was not only high but entering a post-pot food frenzy. We made a beeline for a sign that read "Pyengana Dairy, Makers of Cloth-bound Cheddar Cheese."

Behind a long, low building, a hundred brown-and-white dairy cows were grazing on emerald green grass. Inside, we found a formal tasting room, where a young woman offered us cubes of cheddar cheese, starting from mild and moving up to sharp.

"God, this is delicious," Alexis said, eyeing some lemon-flavored biscuits on a shelf. "Should we get cookies? Let's get cookies."

We ended up with a brick of sharp cheddar and a round of soft washed-rind cheese named George after the George River that cut through the valley. Then while leaning against the Pajero and breaking off hunks of cheese, we pulled out a photocopy of a *Sydney Morning Herald* article about Pyengana's 1995 thylacine sighting. The park ranger had told the newspaper that he was 150 percent sure that he had seen a thylacine:

> *What I viewed for two minutes was about half the size of a fully matured German shepherd dog, he had stripes over his body from about half way down, and his tail was curved like a kangaroo's. . . . He sniffed the ground, lifted his head and ran into the bush. He was a scrappy color like a dingo—that horrible sandy color that looks like he needed a bath.*

It sounded pretty convincing.

After gorging on cheese, we drove over to the Pub in the Paddock, which was the only other building in the valley as far as we could see. It looked like a good place to get information. However, just outside the pub, we were sidetracked by the sight of a spectacular pig. The pig—which was the size of a mini-tractor—was standing in a pen, where a sign announced his name was Slops and read "HI! GEEZ I'M DRY. I'D LUV

A BEER." Funny, he didn't look dry. He looked like he had just come back from *The Lost Weekend*.

Next to Slops's muddy pen, two rusting drums were filled with hundreds of empty beer bottles, or stubbies as they're called in Australia. The most popular beer in northern Tasmania, we had learned, was locally made Boag's Draught. But Slops wasn't picky. Sifting through his collection, we found bottles of Cascade Export Stout, Victoria Bitter, James Boag's Premium Light, Mercury Medium Sweet Alcoholic Cider, and Carlton Cold-Filtered Bitter. He snorted at us through the fence. On closer inspection, he didn't look so much like a souse as a friend, grunting congenially and inviting us to share a cold one with him.

"Do you think he wants another beer?"

"If Slops has a drink, I'm going to light up another bowl," said Alexis.

The Pub in the Paddock was a bed-and-breakfast as well as a pub, so we decided to take a room there for the night in order to pursue our tiger investigations. Inside, the barman and four or five customers were deep in conversation. After much hemming and hawing, we finally caught his attention. In spite of the fact that he owned a beer-drinking pig, he was a no-nonsense guy. He asked us to pay for our room in advance—and he informed us that since there was nowhere else to eat in Pyengana, we would be having dinner in his pub at six o'clock.

We were aching to ask about the Pyengana tiger sighting, but there was something about the barman's cool manner that made us reticent to raise the subject.

"Nice pig," we said instead.

This turned out to be an okay topic. The barman informed us that Slops had recently been cutting back on his alcohol consumption. Representatives from the RSPCA had stopped by not long before. They had suggested that drinking Boag's Draught night after night wasn't healthy for a pig. So the barman had begun watering down the contents of Slops's stubbies, creating a pigs-only lite beer. The barman sighed and looked wistful. Gone were the days when Slops could drink seventy-six full-strength beers in an evening.

He seemed to be opening up, and we thought it was a good time to introduce the subject of the tiger.

"So . . . uh . . . we'd heard there was a tiger sighting here a few years ago . . ."

He looked at us coldly for a moment, as if he were examining a speck of dirt on the bar. "Hoax," he said curtly.

The men and women huddling around the bar looked our way. We saw a ripple of recognition in their eyes: *oooooh, tiger nutters*.

The barman looked as if he would have liked to have ended the conversation there.

"But wasn't it a park ranger who saw the tiger?" we asked.

"It was a *hoax*," he repeated. Clearly, something about the story offended his sensibilities. He told us the rest of it reluctantly.

The Pub in the Paddock—and Slops—changed hands frequently. This barman was the fourth owner since the purported tiger sighting. The fellow who owned it in 1995 had evidently paid a part-time forest ranger $500 to say he had seen a tiger by the town's famous high waterfall. "It brought a mess of TV crews and visitors from the mainland. The pub was crowded for three weeks." It had all been a ploy to drum up business—apparently it was still working. The people at the bar seemed to be quietly chuckling.

We decided to buy Slops a beer. At least the pig wasn't a hoax. The barman sold us a watered-down Cascade Premium Lager with two Tasmanian tigers on the label.

As we walked out to Slops's pen, Alexis looked dejected. "I can't believe it was a hoax," he said.

"Aren't all sightings inherently hoaxes if you think the tiger's extinct?"

"I don't know . . . Maybe I was temporarily deluded into thinking there was some hope."

Not sure about the proper method of feeding beer to a pig, we tentatively poked the bottle over the fence. Slops seized the neck between his lips and chugged it in a single gulp.

Alexis went over to the Pajero and grabbed the heavy case containing his art supplies. "I'm going to paint a platypus," he announced.

"You're not inspired to do a thylacine?"

"Not today. I don't want to go near the animal that suddenly seems *never* to have existed." He disappeared into the pub.

We decided to leave him to it—this was the first time he had seemed interested in drawing—and drove six miles out to St. Columba Falls, where the barman said the fake sighting had occurred. Who knew? Maybe the hoax was a hoax.

We left the Pajero in a parking area next to a tour bus—with the image of a thylacine painted on its side. It took us about ten minutes to walk along the path to the falls. They were 295 feet high, with water pouring down on huge slabs of rock. The stream that flowed out of the waterfall burbled alongside banks overgrown with sassafras trees and tree ferns. The scenery reminded us of the Cascade Beer ad. All that was missing was a seductive-looking thylacine emerging from a bank of tree ferns to lap the water.

We stood there for about twenty minutes, willing a Tasmanian tiger to come out from behind the trees. We weren't picky. Relict, ghost, clone, animatronic, even one made from carpet fragments would do. But all we saw were black cockatoos flying over the treetops.

When we got back to the pub, we found Alexis in our room. It was pretty nice, a triple, designed for families and groups traveling together like ourselves—and it had been immaculate when the barman first showed it to us. Though we had been gone for less than two hours, Alexis had completely trashed the place. What had been a prim, bounce-a-coin-off-the-tight-fitting-sheets kind of room was now an artist's atelier cum opium den. The scent of marijuana blended with the acrid odor of chemicals. Dirty paintbrushes, crumpled pieces of paper, and plastic cups filled with dark, oozy liquids were spread around the room. Bloody tissues had been scattered across the floor.

"I lost my shit," Alexis said.

We were stunned. Apparently he had gone off the deep end. "What happened?"

"No, I really lost my shit. Take a look out the window."

The bags of devil and wombat scat had been removed from the Pajero and were now lying on the ground next to a neighboring cow pasture.

"I was drying them on the windowsill—and they fell out."

We turned around and noticed that Alexis's foot was bandaged up.

"Have you been bleeding?"

"A leech got me. I must have picked it up when I went to pee in the forest."

We imagined a hungry leech sensing the hot stream of urine and thinking "mealtime!" before inching over to Alexis's sandals. Alexis turned on his digital camera and showed us photos of the leech embedded in the sole of his bare foot. He had used his mini-blowtorch to heat up the ravenous worm until it disengaged. Then he put the creature—still engorged with his blood—in a clear, lidded paint cup. He had completely documented the experience on camera. At the bottom of the paint container, the leech was still alive, writhing slightly.

Unfortunately, he'd had a little trouble staunching the bleeding. "Yeah, it was really flowing." As the leech was slurping, it had secreted the anticoagulant chemical, hiruden, from its salivary gland to prevent Alexis's blood from clotting.

Despite the chaos in the room, Alexis had produced a striking drawing. He had mushed up mud collected from the Meander River with acrylic matte medium from his art case. The result was a chocolate brown pigment.

"I mixed up four different concentrations, and I started with the lightest density and then progressively went darker. Then it sort of had a life of its own."

It *had* come alive. Alexis had transformed the detritus-flecked mud into a platypus. The duck-billed animal was pictured from above, propelling itself through invisible water and twisting slightly, with its furry brown tail acting as a rudder.

"What about the scat?" we said, glancing out the window.

"Maybe just leave it."

"You don't want to use it for pigment?"

"I don't know if it'll work. It's kind of obvious, don't you think?"

"Uh—" Did other artists use wombat scat in their paintings? Either way, we couldn't leave it there. The publican had already branded us personae non gratae after our tiger question. If he toured the building's perimeter every night before bed, we didn't want him to find Baggies full of unexplained animal shit lying outside our window.

Retrieving the contraband would be a delicate matter.

"Let us handle this," we told Alexis.

We located an unobtrusive side door (so we wouldn't have to go past the prying eyes in the bar), snuck out, hopped over some cow-proof fencing, and retrieved the renegade scat. No one was the wiser.

When we got back to the room, we saw that our thin-skinned friend had painted more than the platypus. He *had* made a drawing of the thylacine. It was in mid-stride, glancing furtively off to the right side of the paper and drying under his bed.

25. BEACHES AND BEASTS

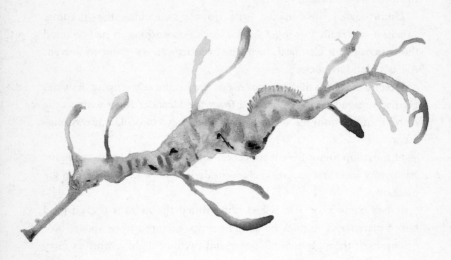

We left the valley with our tails between our legs and headed down to the coast. From Pyengana down to the sea was only thirteen miles, and we soon found ourselves in St. Helens, a funky beach town and fishing port perched on the mouth of George's Bay, where the George River (the one with the cheese named after it) poured into the sea.

In front of us, the vast expanse of the Tasman Sea stretched out toward New Zealand. Before getting to the coast, we had been feeling glum. Things were looking grim for the tiger. But the wide-open ocean inspired us to take a break from our search. We would wash away the hoax with a swim.

Driving north along the coast road, we saw vista after vista of pristine coves and inlets. We stopped at one, Binalong Bay, a semicircle of blue water bordered by a curving stretch of pure white sand. In the distance, a small motorboat was collecting saltwater crayfish from submerged traps attached to buoys. We walked for about a mile along a sandy trail lined with white-barked eucalyptus trees and coastal shrubs, then climbed over slippery rocks, put on our swimming masks, and jumped in. Considering how hot the air temperature was—about 85 degrees—the water in the bay was unexpectedly cold. However, we forgot about the chill when we saw what lay below us.

The granite reef was as alive as any forest. Tall kelps and seaweeds grew from holdfasts on the rocky bottom and swayed with the current. It felt like we were sitting on top of a greenhouse looking down through the glass on unusually active and unruly garden beds. The kelp came in a variety of colors—gray, olive green, black-brown, even pinkish—and in an astonishing array of forms, branching into long streaming "leaves," blooming into saw-toothed needles surrounded by air-filled floats, waving cabbages, rocking conifers, rolling corals, slow-dancing twigs, and nodding ferns. It was mesmerizing.

Underwater, we could see thirty feet in any direction. In the kelp beds, schools of silvery minnows dashed among the flowing strands. Dozens of domed blue jellyfish pulsed through the water. We dove into the cool of the streaming forest, and when Alexis surfaced, he cupped his hands and pushed a seahorse up through a column of water. The seahorse was yellowish green with a long snout, a dragonish mane, a long curled tail, and a prominent gut. We recognized it as the aptly named big-bellied seahorse, which is sometimes kidnapped from its salty home for the aquarium trade and for use in traditional medicines. Lacking the strong-muscled tails that most ocean vertebrates use to propel themselves through the water, seahorses are very weak swimmers and have to curl their tails around kelp strands to prevent the current from dragging them away. After getting its bearings, Alexis's seahorse teetered down to hide itself amongst the kelp again.

When the seahorse finally disappeared, we looked up to see a large stingray—about five feet across—hovering in front of us. Before we had time to panic, it glided off, fluttering and curling its winglike fins. It occurred to us that there were other large creatures out there: sharks, sea turtles, dolphins, seals, and somewhere further out even the giant squid.

Giant squid, also known as *Architeuthis,* are the largest invertebrates in the world. Until the 1860s when the first partial specimen was brought back to land, giant squids were thought to be creatures of myth—sea monsters that haunted sailors' nightmares. Though more than a hundred specimens have since been recovered (either washed up on beaches or caught in fishing nets), to this day no one has ever seen a giant squid alive in its undersea habitat. From dead bodies and other evidence (undigested giant squid beaks as long as six inches have been found in the stomachs of sperm whales), it's known that giant squid can grow to a length of fifty-five feet, possibly longer. Their two long tentacles and eight arms are

lined with round, toothed suckers that they use to grip their prey. Their beaks are used to hack up prey before swallowing, and their eyes (hubcap-sized, growing as large as fifteen inches in diameter) are the largest of any animal in the world. They're preyed on by sperm whales—which themselves reach a length of sixty feet and ninety thousand pounds—and in whale-on-squid battles, the giant squid sometimes leave circular sucker scars on whales' heads.

Some of the first reports of the giant squid's existence came from whaling vessels. We thought about *Moby-Dick*, Herman Melville's mid-nineteenth-century account of a monomaniacal whaling voyage to the

South Seas. In one chapter, the narrator, Ishmael, and the crew of the *Pe-quod* encounter a giant squid while sailing toward the island of Java:

> *A vast pulpy mass, furlongs in length and breadth, of a glancing cream-color, lay floating on the water, innumerable long arms radiating from its centre, and curling and twisting like a nest of anacondas, as if blindly to clutch at any object within reach. No perceptible face or front did it have; no conceivable token of either sensation or instinct; but undulated there on the billows, an unearthly, formless, chance-like apparition of life.*
>
> *As with a low sucking sound it slowly disappeared again, Starbuck still gazing at the agitated waters, where it had sunk, with a wild voice ex-claimed—"Almost rather had I seen Moby Dick and fought him, than to have seen thee, thou white ghost!"*
>
> *"What was it, Sir," said Flask.*
>
> *"The great live squid, which, they say, few whale-ships ever beheld, and returned to their ports to tell of it."*

The first known sighting of a giant squid in the Southern Hemisphere (documented by the French explorer François Péron) was off the shores of Tasmania in 1802. And over the past twenty years, three giant squid have washed up on Tasmania's east coast beaches, suggesting they might frequent waters only a few miles from the island's shore. The most recent stranding was in July 2002 when a female giant squid weighing 550 pounds washed up on Seven Mile Beach, less than ten miles from Hobart, the island's capital. When the squid was examined, biologists found she had sperm packets embedded in her mantle.

Giant squid are believed to have a bizarre and violent method of breeding. The male's penis, which can be more than three feet long, is like a hydraulic nail gun. And rather than directly fertilizing the female squid's eggs, the male injects packets of sperm (as long as eight inches, and about a quarter of an inch in diameter) under high pressure into the female's long arms. The sperm packets are stored in the arms until the female is ready to spawn, or deposit her eggs. How the sperm gets to her eggs isn't known. Scientists have suggested that the sperm packets might migrate through the female squid's body until they reach the area near her oviducts or that the female may tear open her own flesh with her tentacles. It's also possible that the sperm packets are so chemically attracted to the eggs that they burst through her skin to complete the fertilization process. Each method of conception seemed dreamed up by the creators of *Alien*. Solving this biological mystery is just one reason seeing a giant squid in the wild has become an obsession for many scientists. One undersea expedition even strapped a camera to a sperm whale's head in a failed attempt to glimpse *Architeuthis*.

As we were treading water, Alexis looked out toward the ocean and began musing. "The giant squid's the thylacine of the sea—but in reverse—people thought *Architeuthis* was a mythical animal and then it turned out to be real. So the giant squid is still in the process of being discovered. The thylacine's a real animal that's in the process of becoming a myth." He paused, his thoughts turning to more practical matters. "Do you think they still have the ink from the squid that washed up here? It would be great if I could get some giant squid ink to do a drawing." Like other squid, octopi, and cuttlefish, giant squid secrete ink that they expel to cloud the water and confound their enemies. He gazed off determinedly, as if he were mind-melding with a squid and forcing it to wash up on the rocks. "I would give all the wombat scat in the world for one vial of giant squid ink."

Just then we noticed Alexis's lips were beginning to turn blue. "We better get out before a male *Architeuthis* decides to impregnate you," we said.

We swam back to the shore and, as we attempted to haul ourselves up on the boulders, realized our energy was sapped. While the octopus's garden was beguiling us with its charms, we had nearly gotten hypothermia. After using the last of our strength to drag our leaden legs out of the water, we sat there panting in the heat.

That night, we stayed in a town called Swansea. In the 1880s, the farmers from this region—the oldest rural municipality in Tasmania—had been the first to demand an islandwide bounty on the thylacine. At a local history museum, we found a bleak display. Hanging from the wall was a huge, rusting metal apparatus labeled "Tasmanian Tiger Trap." It had massive metal jaws and an evil serrated grin. Beneath the trap was a blowup of an old black-and-white photo of a bearded hunter posed with his gun beside a strung-up Tasmanian tiger. The tiger is hanging upside down, its body stretched out to the fullest extent and its huge head and snout just inches from the floor. The tiger's long tail arcs stiffly behind its back. Dating from 1869, this is the only surviving nineteenth-century photograph of the thylacine. Interestingly, the Tasmanian tiger was never photographed in the wild.

In the morning, we headed for Hobart. As we got closer to the capital, the number of logging trucks coming toward us began to increase, about one every three minutes.

"This really upsets me," Alexis said after about ten huge trucks had left us sucking their wind. "Tasmania's lifeblood is spilling onto the black-top."

Hobart was originally founded as a British penal colony in 1804. But much of its early prosperity derived from the sea. Built near the mouth of the Derwent River and surrounded by channels and bays, Hobart is a port city. And when we crossed the bridge over the spectacular Derwent and found ourselves in the city's center, we were immediately charmed. Along the waterfront was a huge marina, Sullivan's Cove, filled with yachts, fishing boats, and long piers lined with seafood restaurants and fishmongers. The far end of the cove was fronted by a long row of yellow sandstone buildings. Once countinghouses and warehouses, they now housed fashionable bars, restaurants, shops, and art galleries. Up above on a bluff called Battery Point, winding streets were lined with historic homes, many of them originally built by the owners of whaling vessels. In the early days of the colony, whalers went after right whales that literally swarmed in the bays surrounding Hobart. They made fortunes on whale products—blubber from the whales was rendered and used for lamp oil; the whales' baleen was sold for making hoop skirts and corsets. In later years, when the right whales had all been killed (right whales are still an endangered species, not yet having recovered from the mass slaughter that took place over 150 years ago), the Hobart whalers turned to sperm whales, which were harder to catch and lived further out to sea.

The Tasmanian Museum and Art Gallery was located just behind Sullivan's Cove. Growing in size since it was founded as the Royal Society of Tasmania in 1853, the museum complex incorporates the oldest surviving colonial building in Hobart as well as glassy, modern additions. Every year, the museum fields hundreds of inquiries about the thylacine. It's a mecca for thylacine seekers like ourselves. Walking into the galleries was like entering a dream museum, a temple dedicated to our long-lost love. There were taxidermies of thylacines inside glass cases draped in blue velvet. A watercolor of a thylacine dated 1833 by the famous limerick writer Edward Lear. A macabre pincushion fashioned from a thylacine's jawbone. In the natural history galleries, a film loop of the Tasmanian tiger played over and over again on a television monitor. The TV was positioned on top of a crate labeled "Beaumaris Zoo/Fragile/Hobart TAS." Every time the loop replayed, it offered the following information:

> *Last known thylacine died in the Hobart zoo on 7 September, 1936. . . . September that year had very unusual weather. The days were extremely hot and the nights were very cold. Often the animal was left without access to its night sleeping quarters. Thus exposed to the extreme elements, the thylacine passed away that night.*

The black-and-white footage made the tiger come palpably to life. It showed the tiger pacing about, crouching as if to spring, sniffing the edge of the zoo enclosure, devouring what looked like a chicken, looking at the camera with unnerving deep black eyes. How many extinct, or probably extinct, species had been filmed in this way? Not many. Though designed as a sort of eulogy to the thylacine, the exhibit didn't put the problem of the tiger's extinction to rest. The tantalizingly short film simply raised more questions. How had the tiger behaved in the wild? Was this really the last Tasmanian tiger or simply the last tiger to live in a zoo?

A glass case beside the television monitor held a log of bounties paid by the Tasmanian government to tiger hunters. The log wasn't the original but a reproduction produced by the Calligraphy Society of Tasmania. The pages showed £1 bounties paid from January 12 to June 7, 1898, and the localities where the skins were collected. In all, thirty-four dead Tasmanian tigers were turned in during that period, and the names of several places we had visited popped out: Stanley, Wynyard, St. Helens, Mole Creek.

We went to talk to David Pemberton, the museum's senior curator of vertebrate zoology. In his office, a taxidermy of a Tasmanian devil sat on a file cabinet, its mouth opened in a full-fanged snarl. On a counter a platypus taxidermy was set up with the front feet splayed out to show the ducklike webbing.

We wondered what David made of all the people who came seeking answers and the never-ending searches. Was looking for the thylacine like trying to get a glimpse of *Architeuthis* in the wild, difficult but still within the realm of possibility? Or was it more like the search for Bigfoot and the Loch Ness Monster? Creatures that have never been proved to be anything more than imaginary. We weren't quite sure how to pose this question. One more blow to our thylacine dream might prove fatal to our expedition. Fortunately, Alexis jumped right in. "Do you ever hope that the thylacine still exists?"

"Well, we can't escape the fact that the tiger did exist, and it existed here well into the 1950s. It's unlikely that the last one to die in captivity was the last wild thylacine. Then sightings like Naarding's arguably put the animals into the 1970s and 1980s. That's not long ago. And that gives hope. You can still have hope."

David had lived in Tasmania for more than twenty years, first working for the Parks and Wildlife Service and now for the museum. He told us that, like Naarding, he was originally from South Africa.

"Did you know Naarding?"

"Oh yeah, I knew him well. He worked in Tasmania for ten years or more. His sighting is phenomenal. He was either lying or he saw it. There's no way he misidentified it. He counted the stripes and smelled it. I reckon he saw one. That northwest area is phenomenal for tiger sightings. Always has been. Naarding's sighting was just prior to mass forestry activity up there. Where that animal lived is gone now. The habitat is destroyed."

"Is it possible the thylacine could still be out there? Could it have eluded searchers for so long?"

David thought it was conceivable. "They can't even find foxes. And they're living in paddocks up the road."

But the fact that he thought it was conceivable didn't mean that he thought it was likely. The thylacine had faced too many guns, too many snares. "Some people will promote the theory that the thylacine was 'on the way out,' that it had reached the end of its road in terms of evolution and would have died out anyway. But the thylacine had been living here with aboriginals for ten thousand years when the white man arrived. It was not on its way out. The settlers blamed the thylacine for stock loss, and then killed it. You could also argue that collectors were one of the nails in the thylacine's coffin. They were frantically trying to get them for zoos and museums. Probably a thousand animals were taken out of the wild for collections. Then in the 1930s and 1940s we know that poisons like strychnine were being used to kill rabbits and devils. That probably killed thylacines off, too."

Ugh. Human beings *were* dirty, dirty animals.

David said people needed to start thinking of Tasmania's natural world in a more integrated fashion. "The real wilderness starts up in the highlands, goes down through the forests, and goes out to the continental shelf where the giant squid and the sperm whales live. This whole wild wilderness is a continuum."

We thought about the buttongrass plains up in the Milkshakes flowing down to stain the Hebe, flowing down to the Arthur River and out past Geoff's place to the sea. David had said it was okay to have hope—and we were basking in it. But Alexis seemed to have other things on his mind. From the look on his face, we could tell that the moment David mentioned the giant squid, he had been struck with thylacine amnesia.

"Are there *Architeuthis* specimens here in the museum?" Alexis asked.

Indeed there were. Although thylacines were still the favorite *land* animal at the museum, giant squid had their fans, David said. When the 550-pound female giant squid washed up on nearby Seven Mile Beach, her body was transported on ice to the Tasmanian Museum and an announcement was made that the world's biggest calamari would be displayed to the public. The giant squid caused a near stampede and the museum packed in more visitors than on any day in its history.

Alexis was champing at the bit to ask if the museum had any *Architeuthis* ink. When he finally did, David said he would be glad to give Alexis some, but they didn't have any on hand. The museum, he believed, had given its giant squid ink to the Tasmanian calligraphy society. We could see the wheels turning in Alexis's brain. "Calligraphy!??!! *Calligraphy?* They gave their rare giant squid ink to the winners of a perfect penmanship contest?" Alexis looked crestfallen, but he quickly recovered. "What about sperm whales? Do you have anything I could use for that?"

"Blubber is really good," David said. "Sperm whale blubber is incredibly tough. But then it runs like a fluid when it gets warm. It's amazing stuff."

Alexis made an appointment to meet with the museum's art history department, and the next day walked out triumphantly with a tiny bottle of translucent amber liquid. A white waxy lump lay at the bottom. The bottle was marked, "Spermaceti from Stranded Sperm Whales, Strahan, Tasmania, 1998."

"What have you got there, Captain Ahab?"

Alexis explained that this was the next best thing to squid ink. Spermaceti was the oil found in the forehead of the sperm whale—and it was the most lucrative product of the old whaling industry. The most massive of all toothed cetaceans, sperm whales have huge heads like battering rams, and when whalers cut a captured whale's head open it was filled with barrels of a rose-tinted oil called spermaceti. Before electricity was harnessed for lighting and wax substitutes such as paraffin were devised, spermaceti was used to make the world's finest, most clean-burning candles. It was also used in cosmetics, including lubricants and lotions. (Why was it called *sperm*aceti? For some reason, it was once thought the oil, which congeals into white lumps on contact with air, was actually involved with the whale's reproductive system and that the lumps were the whale's sperm. Whale scientists are still not sure what the oil filling the whale's head is for, but it might help these deep-diving whales—they plunge to three thousand feet in the dark abyss where no light penetrates and giant squid are believed to live—maintain enough buoyancy to return to the surface.)

We gazed at Alexis's spermaceti. This was the stuff that once anointed the heads of kings. It may even have been used as an aphrodisiac.

Spermaceti's fine qualities were memorialized in a very curious chapter of *Moby-Dick* in which Ishmael, along with several other seamen, takes on the job of squeezing the lumps out of spermaceti and has a peak experience:

> It was our business to squeeze these lumps back into fluid. A sweet and unctuous duty! . . . as I bathed my hands among those soft, gentle globules . . . as they richly broke to my fingers, and discharged all their opulence, like fully ripe grapes their wine; as I snuffed up that uncontaminated aroma,—literally and truly, like the smell of spring

violets; I declare to you, that for the time I lived as in a
musky meadow. . . . Squeeze! Squeeze! Squeeze! all the
morning long I squeezed that sperm till I myself
almost melted into it; I squeezed that sperm till a
strange sort of insanity came over me; and I found
myself unwittingly squeezing my co-laborers' hands
in it, mistaking their hands for the gentle globules.
Such an abounding, affectionate, friendly, loving
feeling did this avocation beget; that at last I was
continually squeezing their hands, and looking up
into their eyes sentimentally; as much as to say,—Oh!
my dear fellow beings, why should we longer cherish any
social acerbities, or know the slightest ill-humor or envy!
Come; let us squeeze hands all round; nay, let us all squeeze
ourselves into each other; let us squeeze ourselves universally
into the very milk and sperm of kindness.

The way Ishmael described it, squeezing spermaceti with
your friends and co-workers was like being at a party where
everyone's on X. We looked at the waxy lump that had formed
in the vial of oil. We thought about having a group squeeze,
but then settled for unscrewing the lid and tentatively sniffing
the bottle. It smelled like a combination of canned sardines
and wet Labrador. Maybe it was the packaging, but the white
lump of spermaceti reminded us of a kidney stone.

"Have you ever thought of giving up your pot for spermaceti?"

Alexis shook his head. He had other plans for his new stash.
He held up the vial to the light and calculated. "The sperm
whale feeds on the giant squid, right? That means there's got
to be *Architeuthis* in here someplace."

We went down to a seafood restaurant on the waterfront
and ordered fried calamari. Later, Alexis drew a sperm whale
with the tentacle of a giant squid hanging out of its mouth.

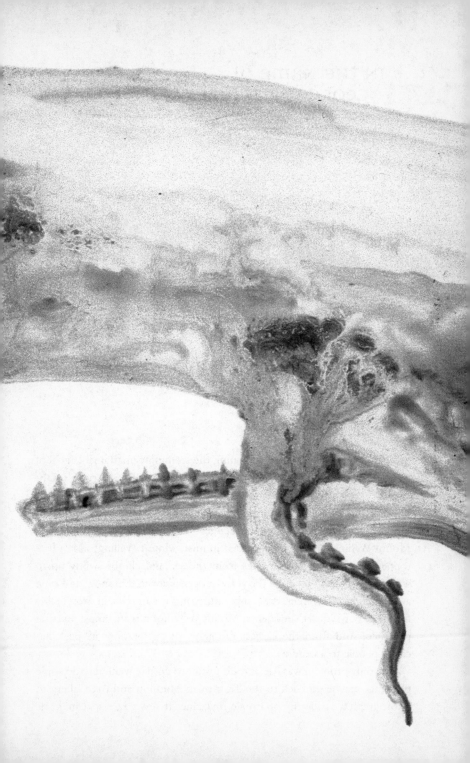

IN THE NAME OF
GEORGE PRIDEAUX HARRIS

One thing that made pursuing the seemingly unattainable goal of
seeing a tiger easier was achieving a series of smaller goals. Observing a Tasmanian devil. Check. Watching a wombat jiggle its
butt. Done. Swimming with platypuses. Sort of. Now that we were in
Hobart, another one of these challenges was immediately in front of us:
Mount Wellington. Often shrouded in mist, Mount Wellington is a flat-
topped, dolerite knob that rises from the sea and climbs swiftly up to
4,166 feet. During much of the year, its peak is covered in snow, and even
at the height of summer, the temperature on the summit can drop below
freezing. For Hobart's residents, Mount Wellington is an almost mystical
presence. And from the earliest moments of exploration, its peak has
called people to ascend it.

The only problem was Alexis didn't want to go. He wanted to do some
painting, maybe go back to the Tasmanian Museum and Art Gallery to
photograph a taxidermy of a male thylacine. It was a rare specimen, he

said, because it displayed the tiger's testicles. Maybe he would go to the bookstore. Bookstore? Had he forgotten that Charles Darwin, the great evolutionist, had climbed Mount Wellington? That at the end of his five-year worldwide journey on the *Beagle,* just a few months after visiting the Galápagos, Darwin had visited Hobart and been unable to resist the call of the mountain?

In the past Alexis had made pilgrimages to three sites associated with Darwin: Darwin's home in London, South Africa's Cape of Good Hope, which the evolutionist had written about in his *Origin of Species,* and the rain forests of Brazil. "Darwin was here in Hobart at this exact same time of year," we coaxed. "Today could be the anniversary of his climb." This was not technically a fib. The precise date of Darwin's ascent was unknown.

We could see Alexis turning the parallels over in his mind. Darwin and Rockman. Rockman and Darwin. "I guess we could go to the museum later," he agreed.

We consulted our copy of *The Voyage of the Beagle.* Although Darwin wrote that the *Beagle* had arrived in "Hobart Town" on February 5, 1836, and remained in port for ten days, the date of his assault on the mountain remained vague:

> *Another day I ascended Mount Wellington; I took with me a guide, for I failed in a first attempt, from the thickness of the wood. Our guide, however, was a stupid fellow, and conducted us to the southern and damp side of the mountain, where the vegetation was very luxuriant; and where the labour of the ascent, from the number of rotten trunks, was almost as great as on a mountain in Tierra del Fuego.*

This was not Darwin at his best. The great evolutionist must have been feeling uncharacteristically crabby that day. Not wanting to suffer as Darwin felt he had or to be labeled stupid fellows, we decided to make life easy on ourselves. Since Mount Wellington was an urban mountain, we thought it would be appropriate to take a taxi partway up to Fern Tree, a small suburb about one thousand feet in elevation, where several trails led to the top. After paying the driver, we bought three bottles of water at a gas station, then found a trailhead on the side of the road and began the hike to the summit.

As soon as we plunged into the forest, we knew we were walking in Darwin's footsteps. In his log, he described the lower section of Mount Wellington this way:

In some of the dampest ravines, tree-ferns flourished in an extraordinary manner; I saw one which must have been at least twenty feet high to the base of the fronds, and was in girth exactly six feet. The fronds forming the most elegant parasols, produced a gloomy shade, like that of the first hour of the night.

The ferns were still there and they were still huge, their spongy trunks twisting up and their fronds drooping like curtains, brushing against our faces. We would never get used to walking in the shade of these prehistoric giants. "I'm always expecting to see a triceratops pop out from behind one," said Alexis.

We walked along winding trails through a fern gully dotted with eucalyptuses for some time. We could have been in any Tasmanian forest. There were no views, no sense of elevation. But then the trail broke free of the trees and began to ascend Mount Wellington's eastern face. Two thousand feet below, we could see the blue Tasman Sea stretching out to the horizon.

As the trail climbed the side of the mountain, the forest thinned and the vegetation became bristly and stunted. Instead of towering, luxuriant ferns, we saw crouching, miserly shrubs. We had entered the subalpine zone, the realm of the Tasmanian snow gum (*Eucalyptus coccifera*). These hardy but cautious trees adapted themselves to circumstances, growing slowly and sometimes attaining only the height of a small bush. Tasmanian snow gums are among the only broad-leaved trees in the world that can survive long freezes without losing their leaves. They held on to their long blue-green foliage through sleet, snow, hail, whatever the mountain dished out.

For a long stretch, the trail was unvaryingly mild, not steep or taxing, just a slow, steady slog up the side of the mountain. Then we reached the Zig Zag Track. It switchbacked dizzyingly toward the summit and seemed to suck our breath away. Though the air was cooler due to the higher elevation, we began pouring sweat. As we climbed up the steep slope, the vegetation continued to shrink. Rather than growing into trees or even shrubs, tiny plants clung desperately to the sheltered crevices between rocks. These alpine plants had adapted to freezing temperatures and high winds on the mountaintop by growing close to the ground. Surrounding us was a boulder field, and the rocks outnumbered the small, spiky plants by ten to one.

We continued to climb, boulder after boulder, and congratulated ourselves on being fit enough to tackle the mountain. Then a Lycra-clad gentleman raced by, kicking up tiny, sharp stones and leaving us in a haze of dolerite dust. He was *running* up. Immediately, we thought, *We should be running, too.* We attempted a couple of jogging steps and then doubled over, gasping for air. Maybe it was time for a rest. We leaned back against a boulder and wheezed.

While looking at the ocean below, we observed that next to us was an impressive rock formation. Titanic, 300-foot-high shafts of gray rock were lined up in rectangular pillars. They were called the Organ Pipes, and it's said that at certain times the wind whistled through the rocks and they moaned like a calliope. We imagined the Organ Pipes playing a symphony based on our hike, a jolly reel followed by a grinding dirge. Then we thought more about Darwin's log.

Perhaps Darwin had been fatigued from his long travels by the time he reached Hobart. Or maybe he was just excited to be in an English-speaking colony under the rule of the British crown. Whatever it was, he failed to notice how unusual Tasmania was. In his short description of his visit, he didn't write about seeing a single native animal and hardly observed anything about the island's singular flora and fauna. He never saw or looked for the thylacine or the devil. He never even mentioned them. But he must have known they were there. Both creatures had been written about in European scientific journals and it is unlikely that the existence of such odd creatures would have escaped his notice.

Our thoughts turned to a British explorer far less well-known than Darwin: George Prideaux Harris, one of the first settlers in Tasmania—and the first person to scientifically describe the Tasmanian tiger and devil.

Harris had been a lawyer in Plymouth, England, who, at the age of twenty-eight, had left his career and home to become part of the expedition to found Australia's second settlement. The expedition was headed by David Collins, who had participated in the founding of Sydney in 1788 (and was the man who first described a living platypus to the European public). Why Harris gave up his law practice is unknown. And why he signed on with the Collins expedition, or what even qualified him for it, is also mysterious. Just weeks before the Collins party departed with two ships bearing nearly three hundred convicts, a garrison of forty-six Royal Marines, and more than fifty free settlers, Harris was named Deputy Surveyor-General of New South Wales (as the entire Australian colony was then called). Though he lacked training as a surveyor, he was a skilled amateur when it came to painting, sketching, drafting, and architectural drawing. He also knew the art of taxidermy. In truth, his real ambition was to make his mark as a naturalist. Since Captain Cook's first voyage to the South Seas, the discovery of new animals—the naming and ordering of the natural world—had become a passion among the British educated classes. To name a species was an achievement of the highest order—and Harris hoped to name many.

As his ship was drawing toward Van Diemen's Land, Harris wrote that there was talk of a large predator living on the island:

> *We know kangaroos to be in great abundance, and if accounts from Port Jackson* [Sydney] *and some persons who have been here can be credited, a quadruped not quite so pleasant to live in the neighborhood of, is also an inhabitant of Van Diemen's Land. Traces of a carnivorous beast have been found in many parts, like a leopard or panther, but I do not hear that any person belonging to the settlement has seen the animal itself.*

When the Collins party landed, it sought out an existing military encampment. A ragtag group of marines and settlers had been sent to Van Diemen's Land the year before to prevent the French, who had also been exploring the region, from establishing their own colony there. The marines had set up their small garrison in Risdon about fifteen miles from the mouth of the Derwent River. But when the Collins party arrived, it was apparent how unpromising the Risdon site was. It had poor soil, brackish water, and little game. Collins asked Harris to investigate possible spots further downriver for relocating. In his explorations, Harris and another officer hit upon the site of what is now Hobart. As they prepared to set up the foundations of the town, Harris wrote to his brother in England that the location of Hobart was "the most beautiful & romantic Country I ever beheld."

Such enthusiasm was one of the things that set Harris apart. Most settlers looked outward to the sea—for ships from home, for supplies from Sydney, for whaling vessels. Harris had not forgotten England, but he was also eager to look inward, to embrace Van Diemen's Land. For someone bred an English gentleman and who had lived his life in large towns, he was remarkably at ease in wild country, perhaps more at ease than anywhere else. Confronted with a new land, he was inherently alive to the natural abundance around him. Others were not so inspired. In fact, many found the antipodean landscape perverse.

As one early explorer wrote, "This land is cursed . . . the animals hop, not run, the birds run, not fly, and the swans are black, not white."

Some settlers just couldn't get over the black swans. The European swan's whiteness supposedly represented purity and elegance. By contrast, Australia's black swans were perceived as devilish, suspicious, and unnatural. But Harris didn't see it that way. In a letter (his first written from Van Diemen's Land), he described "Black Swans in such astonishing numbers. . . . Mr. Mountgarret (the Surgeon) assured me that towards the head of the River, he had seen fifty thousand Swans in a flock—It is a great thing for us to have such a Supply of fresh meat, for they are excellent food, as white & good as any I ever eat in England."

He had a similar reaction to Tasmania's trees. While other settlers were bemoaning the uselessness of eucalyptuses (their timber wasn't good for building ships), Harris was enthralled by them:

The hills and sides of Table Mountain [Mount Wellington] *are covered with immense trees which all the year round are in verdure—some of the trees are of an incredible size. In an excursion I made a few weeks since towards the Mountains, I saw one tree the bottom of which was hollow & on the inside measured from side to side 14 feet 8 inches—& on the outside 44 feet round. It grew perfectly strait for full 160 feet before a single branch grew from it & was altogether the most stately tree I ever beheld.*

The tree he described was a *Eucalyptus regnans*, the botanical marvel of the Southern Hemisphere.

Something more of Harris's happy nature can be gleaned from his detailing the members of his "domestic establishment" in an early letter to his mother. His cat, he informed her, was named Sir John Harris. His dogs had been named Lagger, Spanker, Weasel, Sultan, Van Diemen, and Dingo. And when he later wrote of his marriage to a young woman from England who had come over on the same ship, he was ecstatic:

> *My dearest mother I have to beg pardon of you for doing something without your leave, but for the life of me I could not help it . . .* married? *Yes, my dearest Mother & what is more enjoy* the most perfect happiness. *My sweet little Girl is one of the most ameanable Disposition I ever met with— and her affectionate attachment to me is such as must render my life devoted to her happiness in return.*

About a year and a half after arriving in Van Diemen's Land, he wrote to his brother that he planned to complete a multivolume work of zoological drawings, but was hampered by a lack of supplies. His desperate need for paper was a constant theme in his letters home. He wrote his brother that he wasn't able to purchase paper for "love or money." And he repeatedly asked for paper, pens, pencils, watercolors, and pigments. One supply of paper his brother shipped all the way from England was stolen in the middle of the night. At one time Harris wrote that he could only send one brief letter home, because there wasn't another scrap of paper to be had in the colony.

Somehow, though, Harris gathered enough materials to begin the work of making watercolors and sketches of animals. What made this all the more remarkable were the rough conditions he was working under. Hobart was not exactly a civilized town. Hobart and the colony of Van Diemen's Land were under the authority of a military garrison that in turn was in charge of hundreds of convicts. Convict offenses ranged from forgery and petty theft to harder stuff. And the system was that rather than being jailed, most were "assigned" to work in exchange for being housed and clothed. On the one hand, the convict population was often treated brutally and unfairly. Punishments were cruel and the military officers exploited convict women and the wives and daughters of male convicts who had crossed the sea with them. On the other, some escaped convicts had murdered aboriginal people and free settlers.

Physical living conditions were miserable. Harris and his wife lived in a one-room shack with a dirt floor. He described it as the size of a nutshell. Moreover, 1806 was a famine year. The crops had failed miserably. There was no flour, therefore no bread. The town's residents lived off kangaroo meat or starved.

Yet 1806 was also the year Harris managed to find enough paper and ink to send his descriptions of the Tasmanian tiger and Tasmanian devil to Sir Joseph Banks, the president of the Royal Society and the leading patron of British science. Having accompanied Captain Cook on his first voyage to Tahiti, Australia, and the South Seas and brought back thirty thousand specimens in 1770, Banks had become an instant celebrity and gone on to become one of the most influential men in England.

In writing to Banks, Harris exhibited a deeply respectful style:

> *I take the liberty of transmitting to you drawings & descriptions from the life of two animals of the Genus Didelphus, natives of this Country, which I believe are in every respect new, at least I have [not] seen any descriptions of either.*
>
> *As I believe it is not uncommon for accounts of newly discovered animals to be communicated to the Royal & Linnean Societies if you Sir, judge those sent worthy that Honor I shall be amply repaid for my labours.*

Harris gave the tiger the scientific name *Didelphis cynocephala* (dog-headed possum) and called the devil *Didelphis ursina* (bear possum), *Didelphis* being a catchall name at that time for marsupial quadrupeds. He sent Banks sketches of each. Though Harris had personally kept a pair of devils in a barrel to observe their behavior, his devil sketch was rather poor. The devil's legs were portrayed as spindly rather than muscular, the head and facial features dainty rather than hulking. His tiger drawing though flawed was better, even though it was based on a dying animal. According to Harris, "That from which this description and the drawing accompanying it were taken, was caught in a trap baited with kangaroo flesh. It remained alive but a few hours, having received some internal hurt in securing it."

The tiger's deep black eyes were emphasized, as was the long, wicket mouth and the big, doggy head. The front legs rippled with power. Strangely, when it came to the stripes, Harris presented them as thin and wispy.

Along with the tiger sketch, Harris sent a detailed description. The specimen he captured was five feet ten inches from nose to the end of the tail. The head, he noted, was very large, "bearing a near resemblance to the wolf or hyena." In the colony, Harris noted, the animal was called a zebra wolf or zebra opossum. And when he dissected the animal following its death, he found the half-digested remains of a "porcupine ant-eater" (an echidna) in its stomach. As far as the tiger's behavior in the wild, he could only conjecture:

The history of this new and singular quadruped is at present but little known. Only two specimens (both males) have yet been taken. It inhabits amongst caverns and rocks in the deep and almost impenetrable glens in the neighborhood of the highest mountainous parts of Van Diemen's Land, where it probably preys on the brush Kangaroo and various small animals that abound in those places.

In contrast with the elusive and mysterious zebra opossum, the devil was easily found and studied. Harris elaborated on its habits with relish:

These animals were very common on our first settling at Hobart Town, and were particularly destructive to poultry, &c. They, however, furnished the convicts with a fresh meal, and the taste was said to be not unlike veal. . . . A male and female, which I kept for a couple of months chained together in an empty cask, were continually fighting; their quarrels began as soon as it was dark (as they slept all day), and continued throughout the night almost without intermission. . . . The female generally conquered.

Harris must have sent these scientific descriptions by the fastest ship available, because in less than eight months, they were being read by Sir Joseph Banks before the Linnean Society in London. Unfortunately, it's not known whether Harris ever got word of this honor. Today, it's hard to imagine how cut off Harris was from home. It had taken nearly three years for the first packet of letters to reach him from his family back in England.

After musing for several minutes about Harris and the thylacine, we decided it was time to get going. We marshaled our energy for the last leg of the hike and reached the summit, our lungs aching. "We conquer this mountain in the name of George Prideaux Harris," we huffed.

"And Darwin," Alexis added.

We sat on top of some big boulders and looked down on Hobart and the harbor. The sky was clear and we could see for fifty miles. On the lower slopes, eucalyptuses grew on the mountain, beyond that there were white strands of beaches and intricately carved coastline. Below the city stretched out—white homes and buildings hugging the shores of the brilliantly blue Derwent River and Storm Bay beyond. Down in the city, we could make out the indent of Sullivan's Cove and its dollhouse piers along with tiny sailboats plying the water.

It was stunning: a compact, tidy city nestled between mountain, peninsula, and sea. Using a map we identified some of the landforms down below. Eaglehawk Neck. D'Entrecasteaux Channel. Port Arthur. Each place had a story to tell. This little settlement had been through a lot. But on the summit, there was one story that preoccupied us.

By the reckonings of history, Harris was not a winner in life. In 1808—the same year that his descriptions of the Tasmanian tiger and devil were published in the *Transactions* of the Linnean Society of London—he protested the flogging of a convict woman on the public parade in Hobart. We could see the site of the old parade from where we were sitting atop Mount Wellington, just behind Sullivan's Cove near what is now Hobart's Town Hall. Harris, who had never seen or heard of a woman being subjected to flogging, ran to see what the commotion was and found the woman in a fainting fit. Outraged, he asked Edward Lord—a lieutenant of the Royal Marines who was acting as the head of the settlement in the temporary absence of David Collins—under what authority he had ordered the punishment. Lord told Harris to shut his mouth, and when Harris persisted, Lord had Harris arrested at gunpoint by the marines. Harris was subsequently placed under house arrest and accused of insubordinate conduct. He remained under house arrest for about six months. Although the charges were finally dropped and the matter resolved, the stress and long confinement took a severe physical and psychological toll. In 1810, in failing health, Harris died after a short illness at the age of thirty-six.

Harris never had a chance to finish his work on the zoology of Van Diemen's Land, and the scientific name he ascribed to the tiger didn't stick for long. The year he died, it was decided by Geoffroy Saint-Hilaire, the famous French biologist, that *Didelphis* didn't really describe the genus properly, and the name *Dasyurus cynocephalus* was applied, *Dasyurus* being the new descriptor for carnivorous marsupials. In 1824, the Dutch naturalist Conrad Jacob Temminck proposed a new scientific name for the tiger that would have honored Harris: *Thylacinus harrisii*. But while *Thylacinus* stuck, the *harrisii* part was rejected. (The scientific name of the devil was altered, too. But in this case, Harris's contributions to natural history weren't forgotten. In 1837, the Tasmanian devil's scientific name was changed to *Sarcophilis harrisii*, Harris's Lover of Dead Flesh.)

Edward Lord, incidentally, went on to live a long and prosperous life. He became one of, if not the, largest stockholders in Van Diemen's Land. In 1817, a Tasmanian tiger measuring six feet four inches was killed on Lord's property, purportedly after killing some of his sheep. This incident was the first published report of a tiger attacking livestock—and it was the beginning of the end for Harris's tiger.

At the top of Mount Wellington, there was an informational sign. It stated that great tracts of the original eucalyptus forest on the lower slopes had been cut down by 1870. The "immense" trees, the "stately" trees, the trees "of incredible size" that Harris had written about were long gone.

We wondered if Harris had more paper, would he have finished his work on Tasmanian zoology? Would he have become a famous man? There was something ironic about the fact that the eucalyptus trees he loved so much were now being clear-cut for manufacturing paper.

Alexis glowered down the mountainside toward Hobart. "If that fucker Edward Lord was still alive, I'd hurl his ass off this mountain." Then he said, "I can't wait to get back and do some work."

How *were* we going to get back? We briefly considered walking down the Zig Zag Track. Then we looked at one another and stuck out our thumbs. A winding road snaked all the way down the mountain, and we hitched a ride in the back of a van. It dropped us off in Battery Point, and from there we walked back to our motel. We had found what was literally the last room in the entire city, everything being booked up due to a popular annual boat festival. It was conveniently located above Hobart's only twenty-four-hour liquor store.

Back in our room, Alexis took out his case of art supplies. Clearly the urge to create had possessed him. He removed the paint cup containing the leech that had sucked his blood on the Weldborough Pass. "Well, well . . . what do we have here?" he said. It was payback time.

"So I want to turn this leech into pigment," he told us.

We agreed to help mash it up. Using the butt of a Bic pen as a pestle, we began grinding the nasty little animal to bits.

"Die, *you* . . ."

"I think it's already dead," Alexis informed us.

He looked down at the little black flecks of leech muck at the bottom of the paint cup. There didn't seem to be any blood in there. The leech must have digested it. "I don't think that's enough material to make pigment with," he said. "Maybe I should add some more of my own blood. Do we have anything sharp?"

We didn't question whether adding human blood to the pigment was really necessary. In fact, we had read that ancient aboriginal artists had used blood as a binder for making their rock art pigments. *And* we had read that Michael Howe, a Van Diemen's Land convict-turned-bushranger who headed up a band of outlaws that raided farms and rustled sheep from 1814 to 1818, had been so desperate to record his nightmares that he made parchment out of kangaroo skin and wrote his dreams down in blood. *That* was keeping it real. We began searching the room and found a set of needles in our first-aid kit.

"How about this?" We showed him a big needle and then sterilized it with his mini-blowtorch.

Alexis jabbed his index finger with the tip of the needle. "Ow! This is duller than a two-by-four."

"We'll do it. Just turn your head away."

"No! Please, I need my hands. Haven't we got anything sharper?"

We pulled out a thinner, sharper needle from the first-aid kit.

"Why didn't you use that one in the first place?" he complained.

"Hold it, we've got to sterilize this—and your hand, too." We flamed the needle with the blowtorch and wiped his fingers with an alcohol swab.

Alexis took the needle and slowly pierced the tip of his finger about a quarter-inch deep. "Fuck," he muttered.

He turned his hand upside down over the container that held the mashed-up leech and began milking his injured finger like a cow's udder. Nothing came out.

"Am I dead? Where's all my blood?"

"Maybe you're a vampire."

"All right . . . let me do this again." He shoved the needle into his fingertip and emitted a kamikaze scream. A drop of bright red liquid emerged and he quickly squeezed it into the paint cup. Altogether he squeezed out three or four small drops.

"That's going to have to be enough," he said. He stirred the mixture, creating a brownish paste, and then added a splash of acrylic medium from a small bottle. "If I need more, I'll just add some instant coffee."

Then he took out brushes and paper and swirled the invertebrate slime, blood, and coffee into a twisting, gaping-mouthed leech—about one hundred times its actual size.

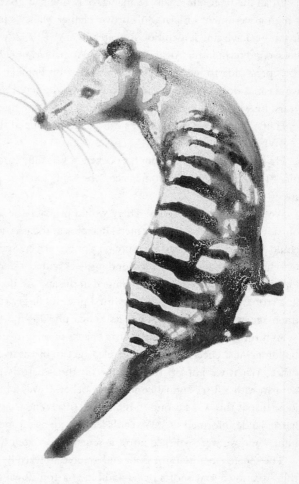

The next morning, we were still a bit groggy from the one-two punch of climbing Mount Wellington and bloodletting Alexis. And we were late for an appointment, one that had been difficult to arrange. We struggled to find something decent to wear in our packs, and managed to dig out a few unrumpled clothes. To our chagrin, we discovered we only had hiking boots with us—not that the lack of formal wear should have come as any surprise. We smoothed down our hair as best we could, then raced down to Hobart's waterfront and a cluster of small office buildings.

Of all the tiger hunters in Tasmania, only one had gone on to become a high government official. Bob Brown, James Malley's partner in crime from the Thylacine Expedition Research Team of 1972, was now serving his second term in the Australian Senate. We had arranged with the senator's press aide to interview him at his office on Franklin Wharf. And as we dashed down Hobart's steep streets, we wondered if, after all these years, he would still be interested in talking about the tiger.

Half a block from the senator's office, Alexis stopped short.

"What *is* it?" we asked.

He pulled his pot pipe from his pocket. It was fully loaded for his next hit. "I should leave this someplace," he said, looking around on the street.

We started to get nervous. There would probably be a security check outside the senator's office—a metal detector at the very least. But where could Alexis hide his stash? We were on a public street. Suddenly, Alexis—who had been scanning the surroundings—executed a startling layup. He loped toward a small street tree, jumped in the air, and deposited the pipe in a crook between two branches with a graceful finger roll. "Let's hope the magpies don't snatch it," he said as he came down.

As it turned out, there were no bag checks or security guards inside the building—just cheerful, helpful people eager to direct us to the senator's office. When we got off the elevator on the senator's floor, we saw a woman with a furry animal in her coat pocket. It was a brushtail possum joey. Just as this was starting to remind us of a scene from Dr. Dolittle, a harried aide informed us, "We can't let him give you more than half an hour," and we were whisked into the senator's private office.

The senator met us at the door and greeted us warmly. He was tall and thin, wearing a gray sports jacket and blue button-down shirt. His gaunt handsomeness suggested a fifty-something Jimmy Stewart. His office was decorated with a map of Tasmania, botanical drawings of endemic flowers such as Milligan's mountain heath, and a photograph of him with his partner standing beside a lichen-covered rock. In the window, a triangular yellow sticker read, "NO WAR—THE GREENS." Bob was one of only three Green Party members in the entire Australian Parliament. He was also the party's unofficial leader. Over the years, he had become an environmental crusader and an outspoken advocate for human rights.

If we had imagined the senator would no longer be interested in the tiger—that he would find the subject trivial or dated—we were widely off the mark. He was still compelled by it, and his memories of his thylacine search, which had taken place more than thirty years before, were crystal-clear. Something about that time period, he said, had galvanized him—made him what he is today.

Bob had originally come to Tasmania to see Lake Pedder before it was flooded. (Lake Pedder was the world's largest glacial lake, a two-square-mile shallow body of water in southwestern Tasmania bordered by a pink quartzite beach. When Bob arrived, it was slated to be inundated by a se-ries of dams that would generate hydroelectric power. Intense opposition to the dam had led to the formation of Tasmania's Green Party.)

Trained as a doctor on the mainland, Bob had taken a job practicing medicine in Launceston in 1972, and it wasn't long before he bumped into James Malley and Jeremy Griffith. James and Jeremy were already searching for the tiger and Bob was intrigued.

"Those two guys were bright-eyed. They had talked to a lot of people who had seen it, and they *knew* the tiger was there. It was just a matter of tracking it down. As a kid I had read about the Tasmanian tiger and I was always fascinated by it and the sightings. And yet, I was the skeptic. When I first came to Tasmania, I thought the animal was most likely extinct. But you couldn't yet make that decision."

At that point, the tiger had not been officially declared extinct—and the possibility that it survived had not been fully explored. Bob cited the example of the takahe, a flightless bird from New Zealand that had been presumed extinct for fifty years and then was rediscovered in 1949. "The takahe's as big as a turkey," he said. The rediscovery of such a large crea-ture raised the possibility that the thylacine, despite its large size, might also have survived undetected in a remote area. Considering how signifi-cant the tiger was—so much a part of Tasmania's history and sense of place—it was not an animal to be given up on lightly. At least Bob felt it was important to have a systematic look—and that was what he, James, and Jeremy set out to do.

With his own money—what he had left after taking out ads in every newspaper condemning the flooding of Lake Pedder—Bob set up an office and telephone hotline for the thylacine expedition team. When they received a report of a tiger sighting, they would proceed to the area, look for tracks, and interview witnesses.

One of Bob's jobs was to help set the camera traps that Jeremy had designed to capture a photo of the thylacine. This involved placing live chickens in treehouse pens and coming back periodically to feed them. "For the time, it was a sophisticated little system. If an animal tried to get at the chook, a line would be tripped and the camera would go off." Like other camera traps before and after, these produced snapshots of possums, wombats, and quolls—but no tigers.

Some of their investigations sent them on far-flung, life-threatening journeys into the bush. "Jeremy was totally driven," said Bob. "But mind you, so was James. I went into the Tarkine with James looking for tigers, and we crossed the Little Rapid River, and when we came back it was in flood. The river was fifty meters wide and flowing very fast. James couldn't swim. I said, 'We have to camp here for a few days.' But James was going to cross and that was it. I got a rope to the other side and he walked across. James was a big man. If he had fallen in, he would have drowned."

They also drove thousands of miles back and forth across the island, interviewing eyewitnesses. This was where the work became discouraging. So many of the reports turned out to be cases of mistaken identity. One of the most promising dispatches came from a remote west coast beach. A young man had reported seeing a tiger while duck hunting. "He said it was getting dark, and suddenly there was a tiger standing on a dune looking at him from just twenty paces away. He had a gun with him and was against shooting it. We got there three days later, and there was great excitement. Men were fishing there for flounder, and James talked to the men. One of them had been to the museum in Hobart and was the most reliable witness among the lot. He said it was a tiger. There was a half-raised print on the dune. Then a couple of hours later, a guy came up the beach on a tractor. Loping up behind him was an Irish wolfhound. Everybody went quiet. I said, 'Did you have that wolfhound tied up two nights ago?' With quite a lot of embarrassment, he said, 'I—I—I, yes, I did.' I didn't believe him at all. . . . It was extraordinary. That dog was the last thing you would expect to see on the west coast of Tasmania. But there it was in front of all of us."

Ultimately, however, it was a sighting Bob made himself that permanently altered his perception—and Jeremy's as well. Bob was driving home one night through a wooded area and saw a startling vision in the headlights. "Here was this *animal*. I immediately went back to get Jeremy, and I said, 'You've *got* to see this.' We went right to the spot, and the animal was still there. I got it in the headlights, and it was extraordinary. It had pointy ears and a long snout. It had a thick rump and a kangaroo-like tail and four chocolate-colored stripes across its fawn-colored back." Bob paused as we leaned in expectantly.

"And this is the thing. It was a greyhound dog that had the pattern and coloring of a thylacine."

Eyewitness sightings, it seemed, were not very reliable. "We looked at 250 sightings and at the end of the day only four of those could not be explained by something else: a wombat, a dog, a feral cat."

Upon investigation, even some historical sightings came under question. The tiger team interviewed veteran tiger hunters, including Arthur Fleming, the retired police inspector who, while working for the Tasmanian Animals and Birds Protection Board, had found tiger tracks in the southwest wilderness during the late 1930s. As a result, he continued to search for the tiger over many years. Bob visited Fleming to ask him about a series of sheep mutilations that were blamed on tigers in a farming community in 1957. Sheep had been found with their throats slashed, their bodies intact but cleaned of blood as if the blood had been slurped up. These vampirelike attacks were believed to be the work of a tiger and were long used as evidence that the tiger survived at least into the 1950s.

"Inspector Fleming gave us the full story," said Bob. "Yes, there were a number of tiger sightings. So they put out a big steel box cage and baited it with liver. One morning they approached the box and there was a big animal in it. When they got to it, it was an Alsatian dog. They dispatched the Alsatian, and the sheep killing stopped. It was so typical. That component of the story was never conveyed by the media. It's always the excitement of the chase, never the evidence."

The noose seemed to be closing around the thylacine's neck. At the time of the thylacine expedition search, plenty of trappers and others who had killed tigers for the bounty were still alive. While Bob, Jeremy, James, and others like them were finding it impossible to get even a whiff of a tiger, the older hunters described the tiger as easy to catch.

"I interviewed a lovely old man in Buckland. He had a big tree stump [on his property] and there were iron spikes right around it. Each one of those spikes represented the skull of a tiger that was kept on it. At his back fence were two big holes dug in the ground. They put tabletops over the holes and the tabletops had a steel axis across the middle. A tiger coming down the fence line would tread on one side of the table and it would tip. The tiger would drop into the pit and the table would close over it. In the morning they would take the tigers out. He told me they got forty tigers from a fence line that was half a mile long. That tells you how prevalent tigers were and how rapidly they were destroyed."

We were surprised that the senator had called the killer of forty thylacines a "lovely old man." His anger was directed not at individuals, but at the misguided policies behind the state-sponsored persecution of the thylacine.

"Nobody wants to talk about the deliberate extirpation of the tiger," he said. Had we known, he asked, how close the vote had been that created the government-sponsored thylacine bounty?

Local livestock organizations, such as the Van Diemen's Land Company, had been putting up their own bounties through much of the nineteenth century. But it wasn't until 1886 that the Tasmanian government put up an island-wide bounty—effectively turning the killing of tigers into a business.

Sheep farmers on the East Coast had lobbied Tasmania's legislature for three years in a row to pass a government bounty. A petition they submitted in 1885 read:

The Native Tigers and other destructive animals are making such serious inroads on our flocks that many of us fear we shall have to abandon the Crown Lands occupied by us and give up sheep farming altogether, unless some means can be devised for combating this evil.

In the debate over this issue, sheep owners made outrageous, overblown claims that thylacines were ravaging their flocks. The bill's key supporter was John Lyne, a British-born sheep owner from Swansea, who claimed as many as fifty thousand sheep were being killed a year in his district. (Critics have noted that there were not that many sheep in the entire east coast region.) Opponents of the bill suggested the sheep farmers do more to protect their own flocks. Far more frequently than thylacine attacks, sheep were lost to disease, poor care, bad weather, and rustlers. But in the final vote, the bill was narrowly passed, by twelve to eleven. The government of Tasmania would pay £1 for the skin of a dead adult tiger. Bounty hunters could keep the skins after they had been properly marked by government officials and then earn another few shillings from their sale to the fur trade.

"From then on, every area of Tasmania was under the hunt," Bob said. "If you look at that bounty book, each entry is a hunted-down tiger, a dead set of pups."

In 1888, the first year the bounty was in effect, 81 thylacines were presented for the £1 payment. In 1889, 118 tiger skins were turned in. For the next sixteen years, the numbers varied from a low of 90 in 1890 to a high of 153 in 1900. Then in 1906, the numbers began to drop: 58 in 1906, 42 in 1907, 17 in 1908, 2 in 1909, zero in 1910, zero in 1911, zero in 1912.

By this point the animal was rare and worth considerably more than £1 to zoos. In 1914, Professor T. Thomas Flynn, a prominent zoologist at the University of Tasmania and the father of screen idol Errol Flynn, wrote that the thylacine

> is extremely rare, and on that account fetches a very high price in the market. . . . It is, however, rather to be regretted that such an interesting relic of a primitive type should be allowed to altogether become extinct, and the present writer, with others, has consistently advocated the establishment of some safe retreat, such as an island, where these animals should be allowed to live without having the opportunity to cause damage.

Errol Flynn referred to his scientist father as a "tall hunk of scholarship." Be that as it may, nothing was actually done to protect the thylacine. And thylacines continued to be exported to zoos, ultimately commanding prices as high as £150.

"I think it's one of the most frustrating stories of the twentieth century," Bob said. Saving, or even just seeing, the thylacine seemed so close, so within reach. "Yet it was snatched by greed, £1 greed."

We knew what Bob meant. It was hard to let go of the tiger, to let it just drift off into the Styx.

In the end, Bob never saw a living thylacine, though he did see the last of Lake Pedder before it disappeared beneath the floodwaters. And when the Tasmanian Hydro-Electric Commission decided in 1979 to dam the Franklin and Gordon rivers, two spectacularly wild waterways in Tasmania's Southwest, Bob got involved. He rafted the Franklin River, organized an enormous blockade of the dam site, and spent nineteen days in jail after six hundred protesters were arrested. Ultimately, the protests led to the area surrounding the rivers being named a Wilderness World Heritage Area by the United Nations. In 1983, Australia's federal government intervened and the dam was stopped by a narrow decision of the Australian Supreme Court. The Franklin and Gordon rivers were saved. That same year, Bob became the first Green candidate elected to Tasmania's state Parliament where he served as an MP for ten years. Then, after a three-year break, he was elected senator from Tasmania to the Australian Parliament. He remains one of the most vocal advocates for protecting Tasmania's natural heritage and environment.

"We've got such a great wild intact island compared to the rest of the world," he said. "Yet we're looking at the greatest slaughter of Tasmanian ecosystems in history. This year 150,000 logging trucks each carrying thirty tons of our forests will go to the wood chip mills to export what's left of the great Tasmanian forest to the Japanese paper mills. The utilitarian view is still there. If you can get £1 for the tiger, do so. If you can get wood chips from an ancient tree, cut it down."

Bob handed us a copy of a small book he had written about a wilderness area just an hour and a half's drive from Hobart called the Styx Forest. It was home to the tallest trees anywhere in the Southern Hemisphere. Yet it was being subjected to heavy, industrial logging.

"It's called the Styx?" we said. "How did it get that name?"

No one knew exactly, Bob said. The river through the valley had been marked as the Styx on maps as early as 1826. Whoever named it had a "fear of shadows" and a little knowledge of Greek mythology.

But the Styx had more than just big trees. This area was one of the last known homes of the Tasmanian tiger. "The last six thylacines trapped in the wild came out of the headwaters of the Styx, Tyenna, and Florentine rivers," Bob said. The wild mountains from which these rivers flowed down had been a refuge for tigers. "A trapper named Elias Churchill caught them there in the early 1930s. And that included the last one that died at the zoo not far from here."

One of the last places where Tasmanian tigers were known to have lived was being clear-cut. Talk about adding insult to injury.

We glanced at the clock. Our time with the senator had long run out. His aides kept popping their heads in the door and glaring at us. Bob ignored them.

"I have something to show you," he said. The senator opened one of the drawers in his desk and found a photo of a captive Tasmanian tiger. The picture was slightly grainy and a significant portion overexposed. But it didn't matter. The total number of photos of live thylacines was limited. There were none from the nineteenth century, and only a handful from the early part of the twentieth. This was one we had never seen. On the back, the scene was identified: "Battery Point Zoo, 1913." It had been taken in Hobart. The photo showed a thylacine behind a makeshift chicken wire enclosure putting its nose up to the obscured face of a man squatting outside. The tiger looked powerful, the muscles in its hind legs rippled. It had twelve broad stripes across its back and cast a near perfect shadow. "I bought this at a local market two years ago," Bob said.

Once again, the picture raised more questions than it answered. "Where was it captured in the wild?" Bob wondered. "Was this animal sent to a zoo overseas?" Although the senator's search had officially ended decades before, he was still collecting and sifting evidence.

28. fLaiLing in the styx

A few days later, still mulling over the fate of the tiger, we headed west out of Hobart with Suzi Pipes, a campaigner for the Tasmanian Wilderness Society. She was driving us to the Styx valley—the one Bob had told us about—in her Nissan Bluebird station wagon. And while relieved to let someone else take the wheel for a while, we were not entirely comfortable with her laissez-faire motoring style. She seemed to think the road was a distraction.

Suzi was about five feet two inches tall, with a short blond bob. She was bonding with Alexis over the topic of pets. He had shown her the boudoir photo of his cat, Beatrice.

"I really miss my puss'ems," he said.

"I know how you feel," said Suzi. "I already miss my rats."

Suzi kept Norway rats as pets. They roamed freely through her house. Recently they had staked out territory in her bedroom and were biting holes in her bedsheets. While telling this story, she was looking over her shoulder at Alexis in the back seat. Meanwhile, we were trying to alert her that we were rapidly approaching a car stopped in our lane.

"Uh, Suzi . . . there's a car . . . watch out!"

She turned around and slammed on the brakes just in time. "Sorry," she said cheerfully. Next to the stopped car, a man and a woman were crouching on the highway and examining the pouch of a dead wallaby, presumably looking for a joey that might have survived the crash. Little did they know how close they had come to becoming roadkill themselves.

As she slowed down to observe them, Suzi told us she had always wanted to look after an orphaned marsupial. "If you're caring for a joey, you can take them to work with you. You can take them to the cinema. You're allowed." We wondered whether young Ruby, the wallaby who hopped through our motel room in Arthur River, would have enjoyed going to the movies. Perhaps Ruby would have appreciated marsupial exploitation films like *Kangaroo Jack* and *Howling III: The Marsupials*.

The Wilderness Society, Suzi told us, was heading the crusade to preserve Tasmania's old-growth forests. The Styx Valley was home to some of the tallest trees in the world. Yet half the valley was designated as "production forest," which meant that large swaths of old-growth trees were being chopped down.

Suzi drove off the highway onto an unpaved logging road, and we crossed a wooden bridge over the Styx River. We paused to consider the implications of crossing a real river with a mythological name and watched the dark water curve off into shadows beneath ancient trees. The bridge's supports were made with whole, unfinished logs of astonishing size. The thylacines that had once drunk from this river had truly lived among giants.

Our first stop in the valley was the Big Tree Reserve. Ironically, we had to pass by ugly clear-cuts and tree plantations to get there. The reserve is home to what has been dubbed "The Big Tree," a *Eucalyptus regnans* that is eighty-six meters (282 feet) tall. We walked along a gravel trail lined with informational signs that had been laid down through the forest.

When we reached the Big Tree, we looked up and thought, Living things aren't supposed to get this big. At its base, the Big Tree was forty-three feet around. It would have taken an army of tree huggers to embrace it. Next to it Alexis looked like a termite standing underneath a chair leg. It was impossible to get the tree in perspective. It was eighty feet taller than the Statue of Liberty. We leaned back, arching our spines as far as they would bend. The Big Tree shot up like an Apollo rocket and exploded into a burst of green fireworks high in the sky.

"It looks so sparse," we said. The Big Tree was all trunk for more than half its height, and the first branches didn't appear until 180 feet up.

"That's because the canopy is so far away," Suzi said. "If you climbed up to where the leaves are, it would be like a jungle."

Eucalyptus regnans means the "reigning" eucalyptus tree. Currently, the only trees in the world taller than *Eucalyptus regnans* are California's coastal redwoods. The redwood champion, the Mendocino Tree, reaches a height of 367.5 feet. But according to the *Guinness Book of World Records,* the tallest tree in modern history was actually a *Eucalyptus regnans.* In 1885, loggers on the Australian mainland purportedly felled a *Eucalyptus regnans* that measured 470 feet.

Next to the Big Tree, a sign put up by Forestry Tasmania read:

Look up! . . . Due to the natural processes of ageing, the Big Tree is shrinking. Look how the top of the tree is slowly dying back. Storms and strong winds have blown off the upper parts of the crown.

A chart showed that in the 1950s, the Big Tree was ninety-eight meters (321 feet) tall. Now at eighty-six meters, the Big Tree is just above the eighty-five meters that Forestry Tasmania had designated as the minimum height of a tree worthy of saving. Not eighty-four meters, not eighty-three. Once this tree "shrank" below the cutoff mark, we suspected it would be headed for the chopper—no matter if it was four hundred years old and growing when the explorer Abel Tasman had first sighted Tasmania.

Suzi and the Wilderness Society wanted to prevent that from happening. They proposed turning 37,000 acres of the Styx valley into a national park. It would be called "the Valley of the Giants." Then these old-growth forests would be preserved in perpetuity. But Forestry Tasmania had other ideas.

We looked for a sign that might give us some facts about *Eucalyptus regnans* trees. What did the flowers look like? How much oxygen did each tree produce? Instead, we found this one:

A single 70 meter [230 foot] tall tree can produce more than a hundred tonnes of usable timber. Carefully graded and converted, this will make enough thinly sliced decorative veneers to panel the walls of a four story hotel plus enough solid wood to make a full set of household furniture, table chairs beds and cupboards plus enough saw and timber for the framing and roof trusses of an average family house plus and after all that enough pulp wood to photocopy the complete works of Shakespeare more than 3000 times over.

It was good to know that the wonders of the world could be of use instead of just sitting there looking pretty. We imagined a sign posted next to Michelangelo's *David* on the industrial applications of marble:

> *The by-products derived from taking a sledgehammer to just one of Michelangelo's great works can produce enough tiling to panel the bathroom in every suite at the Ritz-Carlton. And after all that, enough scrap marble will be left over to make 800 six-inch-high souvenir reproductions of* David *for sale at our gift shop. Don't forget to stop and shop.*

From the Big Tree Reserve, it was a surprisingly short drive to where Suzi took us next.

"This was Olivia Newton-John's coupe," she said. For a brief moment, we imagined Olivia dancing in black leather pants, hugging a big mossy eucalyptus, and singing "You're the one that I want. Oooh-ooooh-ooh, honey!" The pop singer had filmed a TV spot in the coupe (the name given to areas designated for logging) to advocate its preservation. Since then, the loggers had gotten physical with her forest. The area had been cleared and burned, and it was covered in huge stumps that looked like rotted, black teeth.

Alexis sucked in his breath. "Look at the size of those."

We walked across charred ground, past chunks of smashed-up, ash-covered wood toward one of the biggest stumps. It was taller than we were. What remained of its bark was black and crumbling. We grabbed on to handholds and hauled ourselves on top of it. Twenty-five people could have stood up there with us. From this perch, we could see the Maydena Range—about a mile off. It was thickly covered with *Eucalyptus regnans* and myrtles. A single slash ran through it for running hydroelectric wires, but otherwise it was twenty thousand acres of uncut, old-growth forest.

"It's got no roads. No tracks," said Suzi. "If you go over there you need a compass. That's the heart of our proposed national park."

As we stood there, we contemplated the enormousness of the stump and the size of the tree it had once been part of. We hoped it had been used for Shakespeare and not toilet paper.

Actually, Suzi said, some of the wood hadn't been used at all. "With the old-growth, they're often more interested in the land than the trees," she said. Once the virgin forest was cleared, Forestry Tasmania could turn the land into a tree plantation. Behind the clear-cut was a plantation of young trees not native to Tasmania, growing in neat soldierlike rows.

Suzi said that to prepare the land for replanting, the clear-cuts were burned at extremely hot temperatures. Helicopters flew over the stumps and dropped packets of petroleum gel that exploded on impact. They worked like napalm. After the scorched ground had been reseeded, forestry workers laid out poison baits to stop native animals from browsing on the plantation trees. Weirdly, the poison—called 1080—was put in carrots dyed the color blue. When possums, wombats, pademelons, and wallabies came to graze on the young shoots, they also dined on the blue carrots—and ended up dying slow, painful deaths from the poisoning.

The use of 1080 poison in Tasmania was highly controversial—pet dogs sometimes scavenged on dead animals that had eaten the blue carrots and then died in horrible convulsions. And animal lovers didn't like to see so many native creatures knocked off for the purpose of enriching corporate tree farmers. Suzi positively shuddered as she described it.

Suzi drove on to another coupe, this one old-growth forest that had been marked for the chainsaw. She parked on a logging road, and pointed out a small trail that Wilderness Society volunteers had blazed through the woods and marked with little flags. It led through moss and tree ferns to an unusual double-trunked eucalyptus tree. At the base, it was fifty-six feet around. About fifty feet up, the trunk separated into two trees. Because the slope was so steep, one of the double tree's massive roots actually shot through the air, forming a bridge we could walk under, before embedding itself into the soil.

Suzi was trying to come up with a catchy name for the double-trunked tree to get people to rally around saving the forest. We racked our brains to think of something Classic that would fit in with the theme of the Styx. The Pillars of Hercules? Jupiter's Salad Tongs?

"I don't mean to be crude," said Alexis, pointing toward the double tree. "But how much would you get for a tree this size?"

Yeah, we thought. Picassos and Pollocks sold for millions of dollars. How much was this forest worth?

When all that remained of Jupiter's Salad Tongs was a dead stump,

Suzi replied, the government—the people of Tasmania who owned the land—would receive $1,200 to $1,400. About a quarter of a cent per resident.

It was sobering. We started to head back down the trail, following the flags, but soon became disoriented. We couldn't find the next trail marker—or the one behind us either. Somehow we had gotten off the trail. We turned to Suzi, assuming she would have a plan—but she looked baffled. "This is why I don't usually do these kinds of bush walks," she said.

You don't?

"Well," Alexis said, surveying the steep terrain. "It's all downhill from here."

We commenced an off-trail bush bash. The forest floor was thick with stalks. Several times as we pitched downward, our way was blocked by the roots of giant trees and the twisting trunks of ancient ferns. As we picked our way down, we began to name some of the obstacles. A rocky hole, hidden by a cover of leaves, became Zeus's Folly. A fallen log was dubbed Sisyphus Didn't Know the Half of It. And the forest itself became the Ferny Labyrinth of the Minotaur. After dishing out the proper amount of woody recalcitrance, the forest spit us out a quarter mile down the road from where Suzi's station wagon was parked.

After this little adventure, Suzi suggested we cool off in the river. Fortunately, the forest immediately bordering the Styx River was protected by law. No logging was permitted within 130 feet of the banks. So far, that rule had been obeyed at least in this part of the valley.

Suzi led us down a path through pure rain forest that was junglelike with myrtles, tree ferns, and spikes of native laurel with green drooping leaves. Along the riverbank, sunlight poured through a gap in the canopy. The Styx was only about twenty-five feet wide and dark reddish brown, stained by runoff from the buttongrass plains higher up.

When we dipped our feet into the water, our toes went numb. The Styx was frigid. Backing away, we resigned ourselves to standing on the bank and admiring the tree ferns. Suzi dropped into the river without testing it and then began mocking us from the opposite shore. "I go swimming here every time I come, no matter what season. Come on!"

"No rat lover is going to show me up," Alexis muttered. He grimaced as he hit the water, then doggy-paddled over to the far bank, lifted himself out, and shivered in the sun. We plunged in, too. The swiftness of the current caught us off guard. We struggled to get hold of a moss-covered snag so as not to be swept downstream.

Fending off the chill, we took in the surrounding rain forest. The far bank was a riot of life. There were round-leaved myrtle trees, possibly as old as five hundred years; tree ferns with spongy brown trunks hosting countless species—epiphytes, lichens, fungi, finger ferns, filmy ferns— that wore their dying brown fronds like beards; and dead wet logs covered with bright green mosses. Suzi said this rain forest was the work of a thousand years. Yet it was also continually being renewed, always young.

We ducked our faces into the water. All we could see was brown murk. The icy temperature was unbearable. We quickly leapt out and attempted to defrost.

Suzi filled up a plastic bottle with river water. It was the color of Lipton's iced tea and had tiny bits of detritus suspended in it. She offered us a drink.

"No thanks."

She looked offended.

"It won't make you sick. The Styx River is pure here."

We took tentative sips of the tea-colored liquid. It tasted fine.

"Here's to immortality," said Alexis.

We hoped no platypuses had been crapping upstream.

We were still dripping wet when Suzi turned the station wagon off the main route through the valley into a gravel offshoot. It was called Skeleton Road and had been built for logging, but the forestry folks had run into a snag. A wedge-tailed eagle's nest had been discovered in one of the trees intended for felling about two hundred feet from the road. These eagles, which had wingspans of seven feet, were an endangered species in Tasmania. There were only 130 pairs of breeding "wedgies" left on the island. Their nests were huge conglomerations of sticks, usually added to over many years and constructed in the highest eucalyptus tree available. Nests could weigh more than eight hundred pounds.

Under the Forest Practices Code, Forestry Tasmania was required to leave a buffer zone of about twenty-two acres between any eagle's nest and logging operations so that the wedgies would not be scared away. Currently, the nest was not occupied, but the forest had been given a temporary reprieve in case the eagles decided to come back. Meanwhile, the Wilderness Society had been using the protected forest surrounding the nest to promote the Styx to the world.

Suzi took us to see the Chapel Tree. It was an eighty-three-meter-(272-feet-) tall eucalyptus, standing on an enormous base measuring eighteen meters (fifty-nine feet) around. Its buttressed roots were huge, the size of trees themselves, and they looked like the talons of a Brobdingnagian eagle gripping the forest floor. The entire base of the tree was covered in vegetation: a blanket of moss, hard water ferns. Myrtle saplings were actually growing from the Chapel Tree's trunk.

Suzi pointed out a narrow, triangular opening in the tree's side. It was about seven feet high, and when we walked through, it led into a large hollow. On one occasion, she said, twenty-eight people had crammed inside. The tree hollow was like a cave, dark and smelling of fungus. We shone a flashlight over our heads, but the light was too dim to see how high the hollow went. Liquid dripped down from above. "That smells like bat piss," Suzi said.

Despite appearances, the hollow was not unhealthy to the tree. When *Eucalyptus regnans* trees reach the age of about 120, hollows start to form at the base, or butt, from rot, fungi, bacterial activity, and wood-eating insects. Water and nutrients are carried to the treetop through the xylem inside the outer trunk, so the rotting heartwood isn't terribly consequential to the life of the tree. However, loggers don't care for the hollowed-out butts because they can't sell the wood, and when they cut a tree like this one, they usually discard the butt and burn it. The hollows were useful to wildlife though—in fact, they were critical to forest life.

"This is an apartment block for animals," Suzi said from the hollow's darkest recess. Because there was so much decay going on inside—microbial action made things warmer—the tree hollow was actually "heated" in winter. Bats, black cockatoos, sugar gliders, and owls all took refuge there. We wondered if a family of thylacines had ever used the Chapel Tree as their den.

Suzi said that Catholic priests, Buddhist monks from Tibet, aboriginal spiritual leaders, and representatives of the Ainu people had all visited the Chapel Tree and prayed for the forest. We decided to have a moment of silence ourselves.

As we meditated, we thought how apt the name Styx was for this for-

est—particularly this one around Skeleton Road. The forest was trapped in limbo—designated for the ax, but in a state of reprieve. How long before the choppers came and took this forest to the other side?

"O Great Pan," we prayed, "save yourself!" Unfortunately, forest gods were notoriously unreliable.

"The government has the ability to act," Suzi said. "If the government had acted a hundred years ago, we would still have the thylacine. It's the same thing with our old-growth forests."

On our way out of the Styx valley we saw a few last scenes of devastation: a steep forested slope that had been cable-logged, more clear-cuts, and denuded land with invading trees growing in rows.

What made this all the more excruciating was that just to the west was the border of Tasmania's Southwest National Park. Somehow in drawing the boundaries for the national park, the largest trees in the Southern Hemisphere had been left immediately outside the lines.

Back in Hobart, we had dinner at a fish place called Mures. We sat outside on the docks and Alexis jabbed his fork menacingly at a seagull that approached too close. A festive umbrella shaded our table and when we looked up we saw the face of the Tasmanian tiger. The umbrella was sponsored by the Cascade Brewery, and the stylized tiger was their logo. Thylacines were everywhere in Tasmania—and nowhere.

Our last hope for the tiger was a gentleman named Col Bailey. He was sometimes described as a "true believer" and had been searching for the thylacine for nearly forty years. When we called him at his home in Maydena, a town in the Tyenna valley near where the last known wild thylacine was captured in the 1930s, he instructed us to meet him at a crossroads outside of Mount Field National Park—just a few miles north of the Styx.

In the morning we headed back out toward the wilderness, following the main road along the Derwent River, then joining up with the more remote Gordon River Road. When we arrived at the agreed-upon location, Col was waiting for us by a bridge over a babbling stream. Considering how hot it was, he seemed overdressed. On top of a long-sleeved shirt, he wore a thermal vest as if he were preparing for weather only he had been informed about. His eyes were screened by thick polarizing sunglasses. And his graying sideburns peeked out from beneath a cap with the face of a neon green thylacine on it. Something about his manner made him look like a retired FBI agent. But the green thylacine made us think crypto-cop.

He waved us over to a wooden picnic table and gave us his card. It read, "Col Bailey, thylacine consultant, author, researcher." On it was a black-and-white photo of Col holding a pair of binoculars and appearing to stare at two thylacines in the background.

As we studied the card, he said, "I know without a doubt, 100 percent certain, that the tiger still exists. Just leave it at that."

We sat across from Col, and he laid down a manila envelope on the table. We readied ourselves for some new evidence. "I really enjoyed reading your prospectus," he said. He opened the envelope, and took out a neat stack of paper. It was a copy of our proposal for this very book with a full-color reproduction of one of Alexis's thylacine paintings on the cover.

Our eyes popped open. How had he gotten a copy of that?

"You're probably wondering where I got a copy of this."

"Well . . . yes."

He smiled a tiny smile. "I can't reveal my sources."

As Col slowly paged through the proposal, we felt a surge of embarrassment. How had we described him? Did we call him a colorful Tasmanian character? Had we used the word "kooky"? Actually, we had introduced him as follows:

> Bailey is a full-time tiger hunter, who lives in Maydena outside of Tasmania's Mount Field National Park. He is certain that Tasmanian tigers survive in the wild—although he has yet to prove it. As the director of the Tasmanian Tiger Research and Data Centre, he has documented and investigated a total of 3,200 eyewitness accounts.

"Where did you get this 3,200 number?" Col asked.

"Wasn't it on your Web site?" we said.

Col maintained a Web site where people could send in their sighting reports and contact him for information. And he got plenty of hits. As one of Tasmania's most visible tiger hunters, Col received constant media inquiries. He had appeared in several documentaries about the thylacine and been interviewed by hundreds of reporters. The media frenzy was not limited to Australia either. "Tons of Yanks hound me. The Japanese hound me. I get inquiries from Sweden, Germany, Italy, France. No Russians or Chinese yet. Sometimes I want to run away and hide."

At home Col had carton after carton filled with newspaper clippings about the tiger—some of which he had written himself. He laughed. "I've been married for forty-four years, and I've been researching the Tassie tiger for nearly as long. My wife says, 'Better you're messing about with the tiger and not with another woman.' "

"How did you originally get interested in the thylacine?"

"I saw a tiger in 1967."

"Where?"

"I was canoeing along the Coorong."

The Coorong? The Coorong coastline was on the Australian mainland where the thylacine had been extinct for thousands of years. At least that's what we'd been told.

Col knew the mainland location of his thylacine sighting might tend to undermine its credibility in certain circles.

"You may think that's strange to see a tiger over there, but I believe it was a tiger to this day. I spoke to a lot of people in southeastern South Australia that claimed to have seen the same animal." In fact, the mainland had as many thylacine sightings as Tasmania did.

Col's 1967 sighting had a strong impact on his life. Not long afterward, he began flying down to Tasmania to interview Tasmanians about the tiger. For three decades Col tracked down trappers and bushies and people who claimed to have seen the animal. When he got tired of flying back and forth, he moved to Tyenna and started publishing oral histories about the tiger in the local newspaper, the *Derwent Valley Gazette*. Eventually, in 2001, Col published these stories in a book called *Tiger Tales*.

The publication of *Tiger Tales* shook even more informants out of the woodwork. "When I had my book out, a fellow rang me from Keith [a town] along the Coorong. He said, 'Hey, I saw the same animal that you did a year later but I never told a living soul until now.' " Further evidence emerged when Col gave a lecture at the Mount Field park center. A man from the audience came up to him and said that his grandfather used to transport thylacines from Tasmania to the mainland on fishing boats and sell them to private zoos. This provided Col with a logical explanation for his sighting on the Coorong. "These tigers could have been released on the mainland," he said. "Or they could have got out and bred up."

As for Tasmania itself, Col was certain the tiger was still out there. "I get reports, thirty to forty a year, from all areas of the state, from the Northeast, the Northwest, the Central South highlands, and the west coast. They can't all be the same tiger. There have to be viable breeding colonies."

Col had recently investigated a promising sighting from the northern part of the island. A man and his wife were driving on a dirt track across their property in the early hours of the morning. As they were crossing a creek bed, they saw a thylacine walk across the track and up the bank. The man turned his four-wheel drive around and shone the lights on the animal. Both he and his wife got a good look and agreed it was a Tasmanian tiger. When they got home, they told their family about the sighting and their daughter-in-law said she had seen the same animal six months earlier in the same place. "These people are in typical thylacine country," said Col. "Not heavily bushed. Light understory. Tigers were caught there during the early days of the bounty. I've been up there looking, but it's a lot of area to cover."

"Where is that exactly?" we asked.

"Now, that's top secret." He smiled.

We asked Col what he thought of other thylacine hunters. Did they share information?

"We're all a little jealous of each other," he admitted. "We don't get together often." We imagined Col, James Malley, and Trudy Richards hunched over a map of the island, divvying up their turf.

We told Col about our own expedition to the Milkshakes. It was no surprise to him that we hadn't run into *Thylacinus cynocephalus*. He informed us that we had made a critical error.

"Remember, the tiger has a first-class sniffer," he said. "He can smell from miles away. Perfume, smokers, even bad BO will scare him off." We were guilty of these scent infractions and several more. That was why camera traps never caught the thylacine on film, he said. The cameras were lousy with foreign scent. When Col went out looking for the tiger, he anointed himself and his gear with eucalyptus or tea tree oil, a trick he learned from his father, who had been a trapper.

"You get an atomizer and you dilute it fifty to one with water," he said. "And you spray everything—your pack, your clothes. It fools the tiger."

Despite years of drenching himself in bush odors and searching the island's backcountry, Col had yet to see a thylacine in Tasmania. But he believed he had been in their presence. "I've smelled them in the bush and I can tell you they have a very rank odor." He had also heard them. "The tiger makes a very distinctive call like the fox terrier. *Yip, yip*—with an echo or callback. In the bush, they'll grunt like a pig." And several times Col had gotten the feeling he was being watched by a tiger. "This tiger's a curious animal," he said. "They'll keep out of sight, but you'll have the feeling they're there. You start to get a sixth sense in the bush."

While Col was explaining his thylacine strategy, Alexis was laying out his paintings of Tasmanian animals on the grass next to the picnic table. Col got up from the table and eyeballed them. He focused on one, a lone thylacine shown from the side, with its head turned to stare at the viewer.

"This tiger's had a good feed," said Col critically. "He's overweight."

"She's carrying pouch young," said Alexis a bit defensively.

"Could be," said Col. "Just a suggestion, make them thinner. They do taper down at the belly."

Col launched into a spontaneous lecture. "The thylacine had a six-foot-long body (some people say five feet, but I say six). It was two-and-a-half-feet high. It has short legs and a big woofy head and a long stiff straight tail." We noticed that Col was shifting back and forth between the past and present tense.

"It's like a greyhound dog, very narrow in the loins but with a big deep chest which speaks of an animal that has big endurance. And stripes of course. And big jaws that can open very wide to crush and suffocate. The female tiger, which used to be called a slut or a bitch, is a third smaller. She has a backward-opening pouch, which she kept her young in. The male had a flap of skin over his private organs—it was protection, not a pouch. The male's head is much woofier. Female is daintier. But just like you get some blokes that are more feminine, it's the same with tigers."

Just then, a warm breeze kicked up and the paintings started to flutter off. Alexis scrambled to pick them up before they dropped into the nearby stream.

Col suggested we all go for a drive. "Got room in the bus?" he asked. "I'll take you near the Florentine and Tiger mountain ranges. It's where the last tigers were caught in the wild. It's the real Never-Never."

As we headed up into the mountains, the sun was startlingly bright, shimmering off the eucalyptus leaves and revealing range after range: the Sawbacks, the Sentinels, the Tiger Range. The landscape was so folded it might have concealed anything. "In some of these valleys there are phenomenal amounts of wildlife," Col said. He pointed at a rocky cliff. "I've been up there and I can tell you . . . they *could* live up there."

We told Col about our visit to Pyengana and asked if he was familiar with that sighting. He, too, had gone up to check it out. "Yes, it was true that one was a hoax," he said. "But did you at least see the big fat alcoholic pig?"

Col shared that he had recently suffered a setback of his own. He frequently fielded calls from people hoping to launch expeditions in search of the tiger—and one he had received recently had sounded like a tiger hunter's dream. An American (whom we shall refer to as "C." here) called Col up, claiming to represent a well-financed worldwide conservation group called Save the Species. "He rang me up and told me he was going to invest millions of dollars in a hunt for the tiger. He wanted *me* to lead the hunt," said Col.

C.'s crew was going to bring in powered hang gliders to conduct aerial searches over vast sections of trackless wilderness. The gliders were going to be equipped with heat-seeking devices invented by the U.S. military that could pinpoint animals through the dense foliage. If anything was seen, they would parachute down and track the nocturnal thylacines with night-vision goggles. "Let's face it," Col said. "You Yanks have got some good gadgets. He'd ring me up and talk for an hour at a time. They were also going to hire local helicopters."

C. had shown up in Tasmania just months before for some pre-expedition scouting. "The bloke was an overweight sort of guy. I took him for a walk on an asphalt path and he fell flat on his face and broke his nose. Here's a guy who reckoned that he went into the South American desert and lived with the natives. He said he was a Vietnam vet."

Bit by bit, other elements of C.'s story didn't add up. For example, the supposedly wealthy American was driving an '84 Mazda. And C. let it slip that he lived with a roommate and had to go to the library to check his e-mail. "I thought, this guy's a fraud. He's not a rich man." He sighed. "You get all sorts bashing your ear over this tiger."

"Yeah, cryptozoologists have adopted the tiger, too," we said.

This reminded Col of another hoax. "That's stunning about your Bigfoot," he said. Not long before we had left the United States, the man who had originally inspired the search for Bigfoot was revealed posthumously to be an inveterate practical joker who in 1958 had made Bigfoot tracks using carved wooden feet.

Australia was not short on its own crypto-animals. The Yowie was Australia's answer to Bigfoot, a giant hominid covered in thick hairy fur. The people who looked for it were called Yowie hunters, and there were even Yowie candies. The Bunyip was a celebrated cryptid seen on the Australian mainland. In the book *Cryptozoology A to Z*, it is listed as a large hairy creature with the head of a horse that lives in rivers and lakes. But we had personally heard the Bunyip described as a ten-foot-high beast that combined every Australian marsupial and had huge fangs.

Col was adamant that the thylacine should be removed from the pantheon of cryptozoological animals. "Bigfoot, the Loch Ness Monster, Yowies, and Bunyips have never been proven. The thylacine existed. They slot the tiger in with the cryptids because it's a mystery and presumed to be extinct. Strictly speaking, cryptozoology looks for things that are *unknown*, whereas the tiger is *known* to have existed."

Alexis and Col discussed a cryptozoologist who went to the Congo to look for a dinosaur called Mokele-mbembe and ended up being imprisoned by rebel soldiers. "Is it worth risking your life looking for some fanciful animal?" Col asked. "Dinosaurs in the Congo? Come on!"

Then again, Col admitted to risking his own life when he ventured alone into the bush. "I get out into areas that nobody else goes into. I'm getting old. If I fall down, I'm devil meat. And they *will* eat you. An old bushie who worked in forestry told me that he lost one of his workmen and didn't know where he had gone. Then the police came to him and said we would like you to identify him. All they had was a wristwatch and the soles of his shoes. They eat from the anus up, you know."

"It starts out fun but then goes terribly wrong," said Alexis.

As we drove up the narrow mountain road, a lake came into view that presented a misty, mysterious scene. The white spars of thousands of dead trees rose from underneath the water. It was a drowned forest.

"This is Lake Gordon," Col told us. "It used to be forested hills and valleys with small rivers, but it was dammed in the late 1960s." The Hydro-Electric Commission of Tasmania had constructed a 460-foot-high concrete dam across the Gordon River, flooding 105 square miles of Tasmanian wilderness just north of Lake Pedder.

"It's haunting," Alexis said. "An ancient forest submerged like a lost city."

Col said dry weather in recent years had dropped the level of the lake 130 feet and unveiled the ghost forest. Red-stained rocky banks were also being exposed, and the original contours of the land were reemerging from the lake like a buried corpse. "They didn't count on having so many dry years," said Col. "Before they logged and built this road, this area used to have more rain. When they took the trees out, it seemed to do something."

Next, we passed columns of white, green, and blue wooden boxes stacked up by the roadside. "You might want to close your windows," Col suggested. For a moment, we were reluctant—it was so hot and the breeze was so pleasant. Then we heard the telltale *bzzzzzzzzzzzzz*. Bees—perhaps indignant, perhaps just curious—had begun flying up to the Pajero.

"Whenever you see the hives, you know there's a leatherwood forest," said Col.

Alongside the road, among the eucalyptuses and myrtles, we saw thickly foliated trees with long oblong leaves, blanketed in white blossoms. These trees were leatherwoods, a rain forest species that grows only in Tasmania and is very slow growing. Leatherwoods don't produce nectar-rich flowers until they are more than seventy years old, and they are most productive between the ages of 175 and 210. By feeding on their blossoms, bees in fourteen thousand hives around Tasmania make more than one million pounds of honey a year—and it is one of the rarest and strangest honeys in the world. We had bought some leatherwood honey back in Mole Creek and found it had an unexpectedly intense quality. Not cloyingly sweet like most honeys, it had a distinct floral aroma and a smoky flavor that lingered on the palate.

"There's rogue beekeepers who come out and milk the honey in the night and the poor old beekeeper comes back and there's nothing left," said Col. Worse was when honey rustlers stole the entire hive.

We turned off from Gordon River Road, which was paved, onto Clear Hill Road, which was covered only with loose gravel. It cut north through a pass in the mountains. Col turned his head from left to right, scanning the surrounding bush. "Many thylacines have been seen walking across this road, I can tell you," he said as we rattled along.

The road crossed a bridge, where two small rivers cascaded down a rocky hillside and converged into a single stream. "It's the Adam and Eve rivers, going down to the Garden River," Col said. The rapid rushing waters frothed against red and black rocks. On the crumbling stream banks, gnarled tea trees and wattles bloomed pink and white.

As we passed the provocatively named rivers, our minds drifted into the mid-twenty-first century. Scientists were ready to release the first pair of cloned Tasmanian tigers. It had been a long road of trial, error, devil moms, and thylacine diapers. But the tigers had been reborn, complete with stripes and wicket-shaped grins. And there were Don Colgan and Karen Firestone from the Australian Museum. Through gene therapy, they had extended their life spans just long enough to witness the fruits of their labors. The confluence of the Adam and Eve rivers seemed like a fitting place to unveil the first mated pair. The tigers would walk into the wild in the same place they had seemingly walked out of it, and we would watch the newly minted thylacines stroll off together into the sunset . . .

We asked Col if cloned tigers would ever be an acceptable substitute for wild-bred thylacines.

Col nearly shook with exasperation. The cloning project drove him mad. Even if scientists were successful, he thought cloning was all wrong. "It's going to be a clinical tiger. It will be sickly and diseased, not one you can stick in the bush. It will be an imposter without natural instincts."

People should be *looking* for tigers not *making* them, Col said. He had met with the director of the Australian Museum, the man who had started the thylacine DNA project, and told him, "When I find a tiger, I'll let you know. Then you can stop the cloning."

He asked us to turn off the gravel road onto a small dirt track. It was blocked by a gate with a "No Entry" sign. Col produced a key, unlocked the gate, and instructed us to drive up a road, littered with huge rocks and tree branches, slicing through thick green forest. We felt like we were about to take a meeting with a rebel leader.

After jostling over deep ruts, we reached two abandoned shacks made from graying wooden slats and corrugated metal. They stood alongside the Adam River. "This is Adamsfield," Col said. "What's left of it." In the 1920s, these shacks marked the edge of a mining boomtown, where prospectors mined for a black gold called osmiridium, a rare alloy used for making the nibs of fountains pens and jewelry, and even in the creation of a poisonous gas. It commanded £30 per ounce. Osmiridium was discovered in the area in 1909, mining began in 1925, and by 1926, two thousand people were living in Adamsfield.

Thylacines lived in the area, too. "The last six tigers in the Hobart zoo were found within thirty miles from here," said Col, gesturing at the nearby hills. "Elias Churchill caught one and put it in a sideshow. I got to Elias in '69, and he said he was in on the last capture near here. It was in the Florentine valley and weighed fifty-five pounds."

Alexis bent down to pick up some soil to use for pigment, and Col told him to be careful. The area was booby-trapped with abandoned mine shafts. Some of the shafts had been used as temporary holding pens for captured thylacines. "They would throw down a live wallaby to feed them," Col said. Eventually the thylacines would be transported to Hobart on the back of a pack mule.

Col believed thylacines were still living in the Adamsfield region. He had caught wind of a story that a thylacine had been killed nearby—but that the perpetrators had hidden the body so they wouldn't be prosecuted for killing a rare animal. "In 1990 there were some men hunting wallaby. A thylacine reared up and they shot it. They got rid of it somewhere. The legend is it's in a cave around here, but I can't find the cave."

We stood on the banks of the Adam River. Eucalyptus and scrubby shrubs were reflected in the water like a mirror. Col wanted to show us what was left of the town on the other side of the Adam. Presumably, there had once been a bridge.

"Don't drive on the mud side or we'll get stuck," Col said as we coaxed the Pajero over flat river rocks and created a spray worthy of the SUV commercials we so despised back in the United States.

After crossing the Adam, we drove for a mile on a rough track until it became impassable. Col then led us on foot through thick vegetation to a lane covered in moss and tree ferns.

"This was Main Street," he said. Underneath drooping fern fronds, we found a wooden sign with Adamsfield written on it. Next to the sign was a small collection of antique trash—a cooking pot, a bucket with its bottom rusted out, a rubber boot, and brown glass bottles. Adamsfield, which had once contained three general stores, a pub, a school, a hospital, and a community hall, had burned in a series of bush fires and its remains were being swallowed up by the rain forest. We took a stroll down Main Street, squeezing between tree ferns and the trunks of stringy-barked eucalyptus saplings.

We walked silently until Col found an animal trail and turned off. He motioned for us to go ahead of him, and parted some woody shrubs for us to take a look. Through the green brush, we could see a sunken plain surrounded by low wooded hills. It looked like a vast natural amphitheater. "It's a very rare find when you get something like this," Col said in a low voice. "This is all natural. It's never been cleared. We're thirty miles from the nearest town."

In the foreground, the green and tan grasses of a marsupial lawn had been nibbled down by wallabies and wombats. On the horizon, rugged mountains of bare rock gleamed white in the sunshine. "There's the Tiger Range," said Col. "They hide up there during the day and come down to hunt at night. They'll creep along through these grasses and pounce on a wallaby."

We had gotten so used to the pattern of the animals in Tasmania, invisible during the day and abundant at night, that the thought of a thylacine emerging from the wooded hills to dispatch a wallaby seemed entirely plausible. The wild landscape, the ghost town, and the hot breath of the leatherwood-scented wind were working their magic.

We closed our eyes and mouthed, "We *do* believe in thylacines. We *do* believe in thylacines." When we opened them, we half expected to see a Tasmanian tiger standing in front of us. But the natural amphitheater remained empty.

30. REMAINS

We spent the next couple of nights in the Tyenna valley slowly trolling the roads for wildlife, looking for eye shine caught in the headlights. Maybe a thylacine would wander by. There were plenty of pademelons and wallabies hopping about. Once we caught sight of a small chubby owl sitting in the middle of the blacktop. We checked our bird guide. It was called a boobook.

On the third night, we headed back to Hobart, and as we were traveling down an unlit back road, three white cats crossed right in front of us. We could have struck a blow for the island's ecology and run them over, but driving instincts (or perhaps our inner cat ladies) kicked in. We screeched on the brakes and stopped in time. The trio prowled off into a paddock. Their fur glowed with a spectral light in our high-beams.

"Damn," said Alexis. "We can't catch a break. Even the ghosts we see are placentals."

Placentals. The word reminded us that we would soon be leaving upside-down pouch world. And we hadn't seen a thylacine, the king of the marsupial beasts. We hadn't even been fooled by a skinny dog.

We were feeling a little deflated. "Do you think we came in the wrong season?" we asked Alexis.

"I think we came in the wrong century."

We experienced a moment of irrationality. Why hadn't we come in the 1800s? The early European settlers in Tasmania had not appreciated the thylacine. They had called it a hyena.

We wondered what would have happened if the Tasmanian aboriginals had ventured north and colonized Eurasia instead of the other way around. They could have sailed on ships made out of giant trees and flown under the flag of the thylacine, or Ghost Corinna. They might have found the animals north of Wallace's Line as bewildering as Europeans had found the wildlife of Australia and named the Bengal tiger "pouchless corinna" and the timber wolf "stripeless pouchless animal with the corinna head."

"What do you think they would have called the beaver?" we asked.

"How about the wombat that swims with the fishes."

As we were crossing the Tasman Bridge into Hobart's city center, we retrieved a message on our cell phone from Chris Vroom. We had not seen him since we parted company in the Milkshakes, though he had updated us periodically. Since then, Chris had gone scuba diving in the Tasman Sea, flown in a seaplane down the remote Gordon River, and crossed paths with three venomous tiger snakes on a hiking trail. But this last dispatch was different. He had chanced on an exhibition about the tiger in Strahan, a tourist hub on Tasmania's west coast. "I found something unbelievable," he said. "There was a rug made out of the skins of eight thylacines." The reception was crackling but we heard the emotion in his voice. Chris, who had been so cheerful, now sounded depressed. "The pelts were so beautiful and strange. Seeing them stitched together like that, as if they were going to upholster a couch . . . it's just so sad about the tiger . . . I get it now."

The next morning Alexis packed some of his supplies into a box to mail back to New York. "You never know what the Department of Homeland Security's attitude is going to be toward devil scat," he said. We noticed he had addressed the package to Dorothy's brownstone in Greenwich Village.

"How much of that scat are you sending?"

"Just a few pieces. I got rid of most of it."

What did that mean? We went into the bathroom of the motel where we were staying and saw that he had dumped most of the Baggie-ful of chunky wombat scats down the toilet. It was horribly clogged.

"You have to do it one at a time," we screamed, frantically trying to stop the overflow. We spent the next ten minutes with a coat hanger helping to guide the scats to their final destination.

This was going to be our last day in Tasmania. And our last stop was the old Beaumaris Zoo, the spot where the last known Tasmanian tiger had perished in 1936—the one that Col said had been captured in the area around Adamsfield. Alexis wanted to get some material from the zoo to use as pigment for a portrait of the tiger. The zoo had closed decades earlier, but some of its ruins still stood in the Queens Domain, an old section of Hobart originally reserved for the use of the island's colonial governor and that was now public parkland.

Just off the Tasman Highway on the Domain Road, we found the abandoned zoo. It was tightly locked and surrounded by a chain-link fence topped with barbed wire. But it hadn't been forgotten. A section of fence had been cut out and flat, metal animal sculptures inserted. One of them was a sad-eyed, cartoony-looking thylacine depicted behind bars. A sign below read "Ghosts of Fur and Feathers."

To get a closer look, we squeezed through a hole in the fence. The zoo had been built into a cliffside overlooking the Derwent River and was on knobby, rough terrain. We walked past what had once been the polar bears' moat. It was drained and deserted. Otherwise, all that remained were a few stone walls on the bare, brown ground.

At one time Hobart's zoo had held thylacine mothers and their pups, monkeys, lions, peacocks, wallabies, elephants, and wombats. We imagined the *yip, yip* of the thylacine harmonizing with the roars of lions and blares of elephants.

As we walked through the meager ruins, Alexis became agitated. He offered a running commentary as if he were channeling the emotions of the long-dead animals. "It's so hilly and uneven. There's no flat ground to get comfortable. It feels like you could never get your footing . . . It has a vibe of neglect. It's horrible."

The enclosure that held the zoo's last Tasmanian tiger had been located on the hillside behind the polar bear moat. But it had long since been razed. Not even the foundation was left. So there wasn't much to see, just dead grass. It was here that the films of the last Tasmanian tiger were taken by the naturalist David Fleay. He had filmed the last thylacine pacing in its pen, jumping up for food, and opening its powerful jaws nearly to the ears.

According to Col, this last thylacine was a twelve-year-old male that had come to the zoo as a pup in 1924 after being captured with its mother and two siblings in the Florentine valley. But the provenance of the tiger was a matter of some debate. Other researchers suggested it was a younger female tiger, captured in the Florentine by Elias Churchill in 1933. The zoo's records were unclear.

Male or female, old or young, the last days of this last tiger were not pleasant. Like most of the world, Tasmania was in the middle of the Great Depression, and the zoo had fallen into disrepair. The zoo's longtime caretaker had died and his daughter, Alison Reid, who lived next to the grounds and had taken over her father's duties, had just been fired. The city council had taken away her keys to the enclosures. The new keepers who had taken her place often left the animals in the open at night, not giving them access to shelter. On the night the last thylacine died, it was terribly cold and Alison could hear the animals crying out. The thylacine made a coughing bark—but there was nothing she could do. The last thylacine passed away on the night of September 7, 1936. The same year the thylacine was officially declared a protected species, but it was never caught again. September 7 is now commemorated as Threatened Species Day in Australia.

"That is beyond pathetic," said Alexis as he squatted to scoop soil from beneath an uprooted tree trunk. "I usually don't get upset over the loss of an individual animal. To me the tragedy is when the entire species is gone. But that's so heartbreaking. The thylacine is considered a treasure now, and this individual was completely squandered."

Alexis meant the tiger's life. But its body was squandered, too. The last thylacine's pelt and bones were not saved by any museum. They were cast away at the rubbish tip and allowed to disintegrate. The zoo itself closed the following year.

We thought about what David Pemberton had told us at the Tasmanian Museum. The Tasmanian wilderness began on the island's five-thousand-foot-high mountains and ended offshore where sperm whales attacked giant squid on the continental shelf. It was all interconnected. The rocks, soil, and nutrients that flowed through the island's rivers were bits and pieces of Tasmania. Included in the outpouring were fragments of thylacines, too, their bones eroded over the eons, flowing across the landscape, seeping into poppy-filled paddocks, and pouring into the ocean.

Alexis had the right idea painting the thylacine with soil, leaves, bark, and seaweed. These organic materials held traces of the tiger, making their way through the island's circulatory system. Tigers were in Tasmania's trees. In the water we drank from the Styx. Even in the wombat and devil scat we had carried with us for weeks.

Perhaps the Tasmanian tiger was a blood feeder after all. It had taken a bite and left something behind that coursed through the aortic vessel, bored into the kidneys and got into the brain, infecting us with thylacine visions.

"I can't get the image of the forest flooded by Lake Gordon out of my head," said Alexis as he picked up his Baggie of soil. "I've had dreams of swimming through the giant trees. I'll have to turn that into a painting when I get home."

We had dreams, too. Of stripes in the grass and shadows darting through the bush. The tiger and Tasmania were obsessions we would never shake.

acknowledgments

All three of us would like to thank: Judy Sternlight for her boundless enthusiasm and brilliant editing; Peter McGuiguan for being the stealthiest (and friendliest) carnivore in town; Mary Bahr for believing in tigers; everyone at Villard/Random House including Bruce Tracy, Libby McGuire, Carole Schneider, Simon Sullivan, Robbin Schiff, Tom Perry, and Vincent La Scala; copy editor Fred Chase; Joanne Cassullo at the Dorothea L. Leonhardt Fund for her friendship and generous support of this project; Darrin Lunde and Steve Quinn for taking us behind the scenes at the American Museum of Natural History; and Jay Gorney, Sheri Pasquarella, and Kristen Becker at the Gorney Bravin + Lee Gallery New York and Kimi Weart for their kind attention to the artwork.

This book would not have been possible without the warmth, hospitality, and patience of the people of Tasmania and the Australian mainland. Thanks to: Geoff King for turning the world's most beautiful coastal real estate into a nature preserve; Todd Walsh for revealing the secret world of the *tayatea;* Les Bursill for taking time out during a difficult period in his life to show us the tiger's past; Michele McGinity and Brand Tasmania for vital, much-appreciated support; Nick Mooney for invaluable advice; Maria Lurighi for a place to stay in Hobart; and Senator Bob Brown, our favorite politician on either side of Wallace's Line.

We would also like to express our gratitude to: James Malley; Col Bailey; Trudy Richards; Don Colgan, Karen Firestone, and Sandy Ingleby of the Australian Museum; Tony Marshall of the State Library of Tasmania; Jim Nelson, Danny Soccol, Alison Green, John Simmons, and the members of the Launceston Field Naturalists Club; Androo Kelly, Darlene Mansell, and Chris Coupland at the Trowunna Wildlife Park; Suzi Pipes of the Wilderness Society; Chris Parker, Ken Wright, John McConnell, Terry Reid, and Brooke Cohn at the Tasmanian Parks & Wildlife Service; Warren and Betty Murphy in Arthur River; Richard Gerathy at the Cascade Brewery; Peter Althaus of Domaine A; Menna Jones and Kevin Bonham at the University of Tasmania; and David Pemberton, Leslie Kirby, and Peter West of Tasmanian Museum and Art Gallery.

All of our friends and family at home and in Australia, including: Kay Clayton; Siabon and Shawn Seet; Sarah Reilly; Jennifer Soo; Peter Rathborne; Pamela Gregory; Nellie Castan; Ned Rockman; Sandy Rockman; Sara and Ashley Simon; Tazzy diZerega; Huma Baba; Diana diZerega Wall and Murray Wall; Gabrielle Wall; Raphael Wall; Varuni Kulasekera; David Quammen; Jack Schwartz at the *Times;* Ricardo Hinkle, Richard Sandman, John Denaro, Julie Rose; Mari Muki; Judy Sklar; Robaire Warren; Karen Bender; Matthew Testa; Frank, Paul, Mary, Gabrielle, and Stella Mittelbach; Mark Fresh; Jocko Weyland; Mark Binke; Anabel Ressner; Carole, Gregory, Ivy, and Lilianna Crewdson; Natasha and Liam; Ellen Levy; and Chris Vroom and Dorothy Spears.

notes

1. a peculiar animal

PP. 8–9, L. 36 and LL. 1–7. *forty-second black-and-white film of the Tasmanian tiger:* This clip is available at www.naturalworlds.org/thylacine/. C. Campbell, "The Thylacine Museum."

2. rock art

P. 21, LL. 5–12. *The day was fine . . . Anxious for the slaughter:* Hugh Anderson, " 'Paddy' The Sydney Street Poet," *Labour History,* vol. 82 (May 2002), p. 137. The poem "Hacking Shark Tragedy" was written by Sydney poet Patrick Francis Collins in 1927 and distributed as a broadside.

5. crossing the strait

P. 51, LL. 4–11. *The first day that we landed:* Philip Butterss and Elizabeth Webby (eds.), *The Penguin Book of Australian Ballads* (Ringwood, Australia: Penguin Books Australia, 1993), pp. 17–18. This version of the nineteenth-century ballad "Van Dieman's Land" was taken from "a broadside in the National Library" in Canberra, Australia. "Van Dieman's land" was an early alternative spelling of "Van Diemen's Land."

6. DAY OF THE DEAD

P. 56, LL. 5–11. *One of the few sad things:* "Help! There Is Livestock on the Road," *Cradle Mountain & Lakes District Visitor Gazette,* vol. 1, edition 1 (2002), p. 10.

P. 61, LL. 30–32. *"the Tasmanian devil":* Barbara Triggs, *Tracks, Scats and Other Traces: A Field Guide to Australian Mammals* (South Melbourne, Australia: Oxford University Press, 1996), p. 52.

P. 63, LL. 5–7. *"For many people who visit":* Triggs, *Tracks,* p. v. This quote is from the book's foreword by Hugh Tyndale-Biscoe.

7. THE ROAD TO TIGERVILLE

P. 74, LL. 8–24. *The recent sighting:* Nick Mooney, "Tasmanian Tiger Sighting Casts Marsupial in New Light," *Australian Natural History,* vol. 21, no. 5 (Winter 1984), pp. 177–180. Used by permission of Nick Mooney. In 2004, Nick Mooney reflected on the intensive search for the thylacine following Hans Naarding's reported sighting in 1982:

In retrospect, the search was as thorough as the available technology and resources allowed, especially considering we chose to be discreet. Carnivores make extensive use of the area's many vehicle tracks which were muddy for months at a time, legitimizing the focus on such sites.

But an almost inescapable problem in finding footprints was the abundance of Tasmanian devils. This "omnipresent" species uses tracks and roads and is attracted to all manner of carnivore lures, following scent trails and quickly devouring carcasses. In these circumstances, the odd thylacine print or scat could easily be overlooked, distorted, or obliterated by devil (and wallaby) "noise." (Nowadays we would make extensive use of DNA scat analysis and the much better automatic digital cameras.)

Devils are still abundant in the area but this might not last for long. An epidemic is devastating devil numbers and is likely to eventually turn up in the Northwest. This Devil Facial Tumor Disease might make conditions ideal for the recovery of any remaining thylacines, both drastically reducing competition for food and dens and likely predation on thylacine pups. (I'm sure devils had a hand in making thylacines "functionally" if not bio-logically extinct: as thylacines got rare, devils became more common, and what was incidental predation of the odd pup may have become critical and unsustainable.) Ironically this disease may be the ultimate test of thylacines' extantion or extinction; a test I would much prefer never happened. Devils are every bit (if not more) the fantastic animal thylacines were, and the thought of losing them too fills me with dread.

An adjunct is that in wilderness areas we are using automatic digital cameras to assess devil populations—who knows what we might turn up.

The inland Arthur River area has changed dramatically in the past twenty years. Most of the complex eucalypt forests there in 1982 have been or are being felled and replaced by plantations, and the swamp forests are being cleared for agriculture. The consequent new roads and increased traffic have not produced anything of the quality of Hans's report, in fact almost nothing. The area was never ideal thylacine habitat, so it is possible the changes in the last twenty years were enough to tip the scales. However, there still remains much potential prey and I find it hard to believe thylacines could not persist in this landscape. I suspect, at best I was right and thylacines are not resident in the area. Or worse, I was wrong and they are simply not there—or worse still, not anywhere.

It is seventy-one years since there has been indisputable evidence of living wild thylacines and sixty-eight since any at all. There have been many searches, some unknown to the public and of excellent quality in what we think are the "best" areas. Sadly, all have come to nothing.

We are now battling a few foxes in Tasmania, a species that the devils' demise might allow to dominate the vertebrate landscape here forever. However, even a well-known species such as the red fox, if very rare, is extremely difficult to find by searching; it seems the rarer an animal the more luck plays in the finding. To me this somewhat humbling experience makes the thylacine question a little worth revisiting. If nothing else, it demonstrates how homo-centric we have become in our assumptions that "if it's there, of course we can find it." Let's hope there is still time for us to get lucky.

9. HOPPING

P. 95, LL. 24–25. *"The wombat is a Joy":* William Michael Rossetti, *Dante Gabriel Rossetti: His Family-Letters with a Memoir, Volume II* (New York: AMS Press, 1970), p. 220. Originally published in 1895, this collection of more than three hundred letters is reproduced electronically in "The Complete Writings and Pictures of Dante Gabriel Rossetti: A Hypermedia Research Archive" at www.iath.virginia.edu/rossetti/. This online archive is published by the Institute for Advanced Technology in the Humanities at the University of Virginia.

P. 95, LL. 31–34. *I never reared a young Wombat:* Dante Gabriel Rossetti, pen and ink drawing in the collection of the British Museum, November 6, 1869. The drawing/poem combination is reproduced electronically in "The Complete Writings and Pictures of Dante Gabriel Rossetti" at www.iath.virginia.edu/rossetti/.

11. SUICIDE HEN

P. 115, LL. 8–15. *From Smithton to Marrawah:* Bernard Cronin, "The Way to Marrawah," *Bulletin,* March 15, 1917.

13. A TIGER HUNTER

PP. 142–43, LL. 32–34 and LL. 1–18. REPORT BY JAMES MALLEY: "The Report of the Search for the Thylacine that was conducted by Jeremy Griffith, James Malley, and Robert Brown" dated December 17, 1972, p. 16. [Unpublished.] Used by permission of James Malley.

15. LISTENING FOR TIGERS

P. 155, LL. 11–16. *Indeed, in neither its broad outline:* Michael Sharland, *Tasmanian Wild Life* (Parkville, Australia: Melbourne University Press, 1962), p. 22.

P. 155, LL. 30–32. *"mainly nocturnal":* Dave Watts, *Tasmanian Mammals: A Field Guide* (Kettering, Tasmania: Peregrine Press, 2002), p. 32.

P. 156, LL. 34–35. *"making a curious yapping":* Sharland, *Tasmanian Wild Life,* p. 10.

P. 158, LL. 23–25. *"is probably extinct":* Triggs, *Tracks,* p. 49.

16. 1-300-fox-out

P. 165, LL. 2–3. *"kookaburra sits"*: Marion Sinclair, "Kookaburra" song (Larrikin Music Publishing, 1936).

17. the red fog

P. 182, LL. 12–15. J. E. Kinnear, "Eradicating the Fox in Tasmania: A Review of the Fox Free Tasmania Program" (March 2003).

22. mythical creatures

PP. 222–23, LL. 1–38 and LL. 1–20. *Palana, the little star:* Jackson Cotton, *Touch the Morning: Tasmanian Native Legends* (Hobart, Tasmania: O.B.M., 1979), pp. 17–18. Used with permission from Jane Cooper.

P. 225, LL. 6–11. *Tasmanian aboriginal legend of the platypus:* Cotton, *Touch the Morning,* pp. 45–46.

24. blood and slops

P. 237, LL. 18–24. *An exceptionally large proportion:* Steven J. Smith, "The Tasmanian Tiger—1980: A report on an investigation of the current status of thylacine *Thylacinus cynocephalus*" (National Parks and Wildlife Service, Tasmania, May 1981), p. 97.

P. 238, LL. 10–13. *Sideling Aboretum:* public sign posted by Forestry Tasmania.

P. 241, LL. 23–27. *What I viewed for two minutes:* James Woodford, "New Bush Sighting Puts Tiger Hunter Back in Business," *Sydney Morning Herald,* January 30, 1995.

25. beaches and beasts

P. 249, LL. 3–15. *A vast pulpy mass:* Herman Melville, *Moby-Dick or, The Whale* (New York: Modern Library, 2000), pp. 401–402.

P. 249, LL. 16–19. *The first known sighting:* Richard Ellis, *The Search for the Giant Squid: The Biology and Mythology of the World's Most Elusive Sea Creature* (New York: Penguin Books, 1999), p. 257.

P. 252, LL. 10–14. *Last known thylacine died:* Tasmanian Museum exhibit film.

PP. 255–56, LL. 32–36 and LL. 1–16. *It was our business to squeeze:* Melville, *Moby-Dick,* pp. 600–601.

26. IN THE NAME OF GEORGE PRIDEAUX HARRIS

P. 259, LL. 21–26. *Another day I ascended:* Charles Darwin, *The Voyage of the Beagle: Journal of Researches into the Natural History and Geology of the Countries Visited During the Voyage of H.M.S.* Beagle *Round the World* (New York: Modern Library, 2001), p. 400.

P. 260, LL. 4–8. *In some of the dampest ravines:* Charles Darwin, *The Voyage of the Beagle,* pp. 400–401.

P. 262, LL. 20–25. *We know kangaroos:* Barbara Hamilton-Arnold (ed.), *Letters and Papers of G.P. Harris, 1803–1812: Deputy Surveyor-General of New South Wales at Sullivan Bay, Port Phillip and Hobart Town, Van Diemen's Land* (Sorento, Australia: Arden Press, 1994), p. 59. The letters of G. P. Harris are held in the Manuscript Collection of the British Library, London (Mss Add 41556 & 45157).

P. 263, LL. 3–4. *the most beautiful:* Hamilton-Arnold, *Letters and Papers of G.P. Harris,* p. 61.

LL. 14–15. *This land is cursed:* This quote is commonly attributed to Dirk [Dirck] Hartog, a Dutch explorer and the first European to land in Australia.

LL. 20–24. *"Black Swans":* Hamilton-Arnold, *Letters and Papers of G.P. Harris,* p. 61.

LL. 28–35. *The hills and sides:* Hamilton-Arnold, *Letters and Papers of G.P. Harris,* p. 66.

P. 264, LL. 9–14. *My dearest mother:* Hamilton-Arnold, *Letters and Papers of G.P. Harris,* p. 72.

P. 265, LL. 16–22. *I take the liberty:* Hamilton-Arnold, *Letters and Papers of G.P. Harris,* p. 89.

LL. 31–34. *"That from which this description":* Hamilton-Arnold, *Letters and Papers of G.P. Harris,* p. 90.

P. 266, LL. 12–17. *The history of this new:* Hamilton-Arnold, *Letters and Papers of G.P. Harris,* pp. 90–92.

LL. 20–26. *These animals:* Hamilton-Arnold, *Letters and Papers of G.P. Harris,* pp. 92–93.

27. SENATOR THYLACINE

P. 276, LL. 29–32. *The Native Tigers:* Eric Guiler and Philippe Godard, *Tasmanian Tiger, A Lesson to Be Learnt* (Perth, Western Australia: Abrol-

hos Publishing, 1998), p. 123. A photograph of the original 1885 petition is reproduced in *Tasmanian Tiger.*

P. 277, LL. 25–30. *is extremely rare:* T. Thomson Flynn, "The Mammalian
Fauna of Tasmania," *Tasmania Handbook* (British Association for the
Advancement of Science, Australian Meeting, 1914), p. 53.

L. 31. *"tall hunk of scholarship":* Errol Flynn, *My Wicked, Wicked Ways*
(Cutchogue, New York: Buccaneer Books, 1978), p. 19.

P. 278, LL. 34–36. *The river through the valley:* Bob Brown, *The Valley of the
Giants* (Hobart, Tasmania: Bob Brown, 2001), p. 26.

28. fLailinɡ in the styx

P. 283, LL. 8–10. *Look up!:* public sign posted by Forestry Tasmania.

LL. 26–33. *A single 70 meter:* public sign posted by Forestry Tasmania.

P. 284, LL. 13–14. *"You're the one that I want":* lyrics from *Grease* soundtrack,
words by John Farrar.

29. cryptid

P. 297, LL. 16–17. *a large hairy creature:* Loren Coleman and Jerome Clark,
*Cryptozoology A to Z: The Encyclopedia of Loch Monsters, Sasquatch,
Chupacabras, and Other Authentic Mysteries of Nature* (New York: Fire-
side, 1999), p. 50.

SUGGESTED READING AND VIEWING

NONFICTION

Bailey, Col. *Tiger Tales: Stories of the Tasmanian Tiger*. Sydney, Australia: HarperCollins, 2001.

Flannery, Timothy Fridtjof. *The Future Eaters: An Ecological History of the Australasian Lands and People*. New York: George Braziller, 1995.

Guiler, Eric, and Philippe Godard. *Tasmanian Tiger, A Lesson to Be Learnt*. Perth, Western Australia: Abrolhos Publishing, 1998.

Hamilton-Arnold, Barbara (ed.). *Letters and Papers of G.P. Harris, 1803–1812: Deputy Surveyor-General of New South Wales at Sullivan Bay, Port Phillip and Hobart Town, Van Diemen's Land*. Sorento, Australia: Arden Press, 1994.

Hay, Ashley. *Gum*. Potts Point, Australia: Duffy & Snellgrove, 2002.

Hughes, Robert. *The Fatal Shore: The Epic of Australia's Founding*. New York: Vintage Books, 1986.

Launceston Field Naturalists Club. *A Guide to Flowers and Plants of Tasmania*. Sydney: Reed New Holland, 2000.

Low, Tim. *The New Nature: Winners and Losers in Wild Australia*. Camberwell, Australia: Viking, 2002.

———. *Feral Future: The Untold Story of Australia's Exotic Invaders*. University of Chicago Press, 2002.

Owen, David. *Tasmanian Tiger: The Tragic Tale of How the World Lost Its Most Mysterious Predator*. Baltimore: Johns Hopkins University Press, 2003.

Paddle, Robert. *The Last Tasmanian Tiger: The History and Extinction of the Thylacine*. Cambridge, United Kingdom: Cambridge University Press, 2000.

Quammen, David. *The Song of the Dodo: Island Biogeography in an Age of Extinctions*. New York: Scribner, 1996.

Triggs, Barbara. *Tracks, Scats and Other Traces: A Field Guide to Australian Mammals*. South Melbourne, Australia: Oxford University Press, 1996.

Watts, Dave. *Field Guide to Tasmanian Birds*. Sydney: New Holland Publishers, 1999.

———. *Tasmanian Mammals: A Field Guide*. Kettering, Tasmania: Peregrine Press, 2002.

Weidensaul, Scott. *The Ghost with Trembling Wings: Science, Wishful Thinking, and the Search for Lost Species*. New York: North Point Press, 2002.

Woodford, James. *The Secret Life of Wombats*. Melbourne: Text Publishing, 2001.

fiction

Flanagan, Richard. *Death of a River Guide*. New York: Grove Press, 1994.

———. *Gould's Book of Fish: A Novel in Twelve Fish*. New York: Grove Press, 2001.

Kneale, Matthew. *English Passengers*. New York: Anchor Books, 2000.

Leigh, Julia. *The Hunter*. Ringwood, Australia: Penguin, 1999.

video

The End of Extinction: Cloning the Tasmanian Tiger. Discovery Communications, 2002.

Howling III: The Marsupials, written and directed by Philippe Mora. Bancannia Pictures, 1987. [Comic horror flick featuring were-thylacines.]

website

Campbell, C. "The Thylacine Museum." www.naturalworlds.org/thylacine/.

MARGARET MITTELBACH and MICHAEL CREWDSON (right) regularly join forces for *The New York Times* and other publications, revealing nature in the strangest of places. Their previous book, *Wild New York,* uncovered the unsung natural wonders of the city that never sleeps. They live in Brooklyn, New York, and give frequent talks and lectures on nature.

ALEXIS ROCKMAN's artwork examines the history of how nature is portrayed and is in the collections of the Whitney Museum of American Art, the Guggenheim Museum, the Museum of Contemporary Art in Los Angeles, the Boston Museum of Fine Arts, and London's Saatchi Collection. He and his work have been featured in *The New Yorker, Vanity Fair, The New York Times, Travel + Leisure, Discover,* and *Natural History.* He has also contributed artwork to several books including *Future Evolution,* by Peter Ward, a prediction of the future of the global ecosystem. He lives and works in New York and has traveled around the world experiencing the wild firsthand.